3/23

Who's Afraid of the Unmoved Mover?

To my friend John,

You encouraged me in my pursuit
of truth and helped me to be
able to find God in all things.
May God's face shine brightly on
you!

Ike

Who's Afraid of the Unmoved Mover?

Postmodernism and Natural Theology

ANDREW I. SHEPARDSON

Foreword by J. P. Moreland

PICKWICK *Publications* · Eugene, Oregon

WHO'S AFRAID OF THE UNMOVED MOVER?
Postmodernism and Natural Theology

Pickwick Publications
An Imprint of Wipf and Stock Publishers
199 W. 8th Ave., Suite 3
Eugene, OR 97401

www.wipfandstock.com

PAPERBACK ISBN: 978-1-5326-5677-4
HARDCOVER ISBN: 978-1-5326-5678-1
EBOOK ISBN: 978-1-5326-5679-8

Cataloguing-in-Publication data:

Names: Shepardson, Andrew I., author. | Moreland, James Porter, 1948–, foreword writer

Title: Whose afraid of the unmoved mover? : postmodernism and natural theology / Andrew I. Shepardson, with a foreword by J. P. Moreland.

Description: Eugene, OR: Pickwick Publications, 2019 | Includes bibliographical references.

Identifiers: ISBN 978-1-5326-5677-4 (paperback) | ISBN 978-1-5326-5678-1 (hardcover) | ISBN 978-1-5326-5679-8 (ebook)

Subjects: LCSH: Faith and reason | Postmodernism—Religious aspects | God—Proof | Philosophical theology | Christian philosophy | Religion and science

Classification: BT55 S32 2019 (paperback) | BT55 (ebook)

Manufactured in the U.S.A.   01/09/19

To my bride, Kelsey Walsh Shepardson

Contents

Foreword

IN A FEW MONTHS (late November, 2018) I will have been a Jesus-follower for fifty years, one half of a century. Two years after my conversion, I joined the staff of Campus Crusade for Christ (now called *Cru*), and have been in vocational Christian work for forty-eight years. One of the things that attracted me to Christianity was that it is based on reason and evidence. It is the only religion that values knowledge, rationality, and persuasion/argumentation.

As I grew as a young believer, a whole new world of thought was opened up to me—biblical study, learning to think theologically and in light of a Christian worldview, and the role of apologetics in strengthening believers and persuading unbelievers to come to Christ. But very few other Christians I knew were interested in reason (loving God with the mind) and, more specifically, apologetics. The sad truth is that throughout my fifty years of being a Christian, things are basically the same. While there is an encouraging and growing interest in apologetics, still, the average local church has little place for apologetic training among its priorities, and the average believer does little with apologetics in his/her own growth and ministry.

I define apologetics as a ministry of caring for people by helping them enter the Kingdom or grow in the Kingdom by providing evidence for the truth of Christianity and responding to objections raised against it. But how does apologetics relate to the actual practice of evangelism and discipleship. To answer that, we need to get before us the notion of a plausibility structure.

A person's plausibility structure is the set of ideas the person either is or is not willing to entertain as possibly true. For example, no one would come to a lecture defending a flat earth because this idea is just not part of our plausibility structure. We cannot even entertain the idea. Moreover, a person's plausibility structure is a function of the beliefs he or she already has. Applied to evangelism, J. Gresham Machen got it right when he said:

> God usually exerts that power in connection with certain prior conditions of the human mind, and it should be ours to create, so far as we can, with the help of God, those favorable conditions for the reception of the gospel. False ideas are the greatest obstacles to the reception of the gospel. We may preach with all the fervor of a reformer and yet succeed only in winning a straggler here and there, if we permit the whole collective thought of the nation or of the world to be controlled by ideas which, by the resistless force of logic, prevent Christianity from being regarded as anything more than a harmless delusion.[1]

The simple truth is that ideas have consequences. If a culture reaches the point where Christian claims are not even part of its plausibility structure, fewer and fewer people will be able to entertain the possibility that they might be true. Whatever stragglers do come to faith in such a context would do so on the basis of felt needs alone, and the genuineness of such conversions would be questionable to say the least. And fewer believers will grow in the confidence that their faith is based on solid fact and evidence.

And this is where apologetics comes in. And the relevance to evangelism and discipleship of apologetics, reason, argumentation, evidence and the like seem virtually self-evident and commonsensical. But there has been a growing leaven in the church that, however well-intentioned are its advocates, this leaven is poisoning the church. In various ways, this leaven can correctly be called *postmodernism*. Postmodernists as a group are against the use of natural theology (e.g., arguments for God's existence from the natural world) and historical apologetics (appealing to historical reasoning and facts to show the historical reliability of the scriptures, the New Testament documents, and the bodily resurrection of Jesus). There has been a tremendous need for careful, focused works that analyze postmodernism and provide an intelligent and biblical response to it. That is until now. Andrew Shepardson's *Who's Afraid of the Unmoved Mover?* is for a time such as this. In it, Shepardson skillfully delineates and dissects the claims of postmodernism and shows this ideology to be a gravedigger of the church. And he shows a way forward. I highly recommend this book and hope it will be read by all those who care for the truth and for staying on the right track in our evangelism and discipleship.

---

1. J. Gresham Machen, *What is Christianity?* (Grand Rapids: Eerdmans, 1951), 162.

J. P. Moreland, Distinguished Professor of Philosophy, Talbot School of Theology, Biola University

Acknowledgments

I OWE A SUBSTANTIAL debt of thanks to the many teachers and professors who encouraged my academic pursuits over the years. I appreciate especially Jerry Rouse, Linda Iovino, John Kane, Fr. James Guyer, S. J., Thomas Leininger, Daniel Clayton, Rev. David Holman, Rev. Alan Eastland, Rev. Peter Henderson, and Elodie Emig.

Donald Wiebe has been a constant champion for my work and has loyally challenged and encouraged me to be a better thinker and a clearer writer. Douglas Groothuis has provided excellent counsel and encouragement on my academic work, and his mentorship and friendship has graciously extended far beyond my studies, as well.

Special gratitude is owed to my parents, who have instilled in me a love for God and for learning. Their faith in me has been unflinching, and their encouragement has been abundant.

My precious wife, Kelsey Walsh Shepardson, has been the greatest supporter of my dreams, and in addition to editing my written work, has lovingly helped me to become a better man.

1

Elucidation of the Problem and Definitions

INTRODUCTION

In terms of Christian theology, natural theology is understood as that branch of human inquiry which seeks to discover knowledge about the existence and nature of God apart from sources of revealed theology (i.e. the Bible, the person and work of Jesus Christ, the Holy Spirit, and various forms of prophecy). Knowledge of this kind is based on the validity or suggestive power of arguments made from observations of the natural world, human experience, and necessary truths. Various argument forms are employed including deduction, induction, and inferences to the best explanation. Closely related to natural theology is the practice of positive apologetics, where the arguments of natural theology and other aspects of Christian theology are defended rationally, with the claim, either explicit or implicit, that the doctrines and practices of Christianity correspond to reality, are internally consistent, and are existentially viable.[1]

The Evangelical philosophers James K. A. Smith, Myron B. Penner, and Carl A. Raschke claim that most forms of natural theology are dependent on modern conceptions of reason, truth, and language. Marshalling

1. Many Christians employ apologetics as an internal discipleship strategy to increase confidence and to assuage doubts of those in the Christian community; however, positive apologetics also forms a part of some evangelistic strategies aimed toward those not in the community of faith. The latter, and not the former, is within the scope of this work.

1

postmodernism's critiques of foundationalist epistemology, the correspondence theory of truth, and referential semiotics, these authors argue that Evangelicals should reject natural theology. Appeals to common ground in nature to demonstrate or infer the existence of God will fail because these appeals are beholden to modernity's outmoded grounds for knowledge. Moreover, because of their dependence on modernism, natural theology and apologetics are often hindrances to authentic Christian faith. According to these authors, notions like objectivity, neutrality, and rationality are various forms of idolatry, and any philosophical dependence on knowledge informed by these values will be a kind of idolatry.

I ask this key question: *Do these postmodern Evangelical philosophers provide sound objections to natural theology?* I will explicate the objections to natural theology made by Carl A. Raschke, James K. A. Smith, and Myron B. Penner and show that their objections fail by employing primarily analytic philosophical strategies and on occasion, biblical and systematic theology regarding the issues of truth, rationality, general revelation, and evangelism.

Postmodern Evangelical voices have been ascendant in theology and philosophy in the last fifteen years, and these three authors represent the more academic stream in the convergence of postmodern philosophy with Evangelical theology. Each of the authors shares the conviction that postmodernism and Evangelicalism share a number of important values. Though the initial plausibility of this conviction may be low for many Evangelicals, the authors provide a stunning cultural critique of Evangelicalism. The problem is that the cultural critique carries with it an epistemology that is fundamentally at odds with Evangelical assumptions regarding God-talk, evangelism, and the nature of religious truth because the epistemology denies that propositions about God are either true or false and undercuts a key evangelistic strategy: the use of natural theology for apologetics. I will support the intuition that our speech about God can relate to reality in meaningful and objective ways, buttressing the notion that religious truth, while having deep existential components, is not of a different kind than other truths about the universe.

The implications are important, though, especially for Evangelical theologies of mission and general revelation. As David Bebbington has argued, a key characteristic of Evangelicalism is *conversionism*, and if natural theology is biblically supported and culturally preferable, then it could be a valuable tool for Christian evangelists, preachers, teachers, and scholars. In the past generation, the scholarship of people like Francis Schaeffer and Josh McDowell has gained notoriety in using natural theology and apologetics in evangelistic endeavors. If the validity of the enterprise can be sustained in a world characterized by a postmodern *zeitgeist*, then Evangelical colleges and seminaries should provide training in philosophy and theology in general, and in natural theology and apologetics in particular.

PRESUPPOSITIONS

The thesis that the postmodern Evangelical rejection of natural theology fails involves some key assumptions, and my key assumptions are highly plausible for Evangelical theologians:

1. Propositions about the existence and nature of God are either true or false in relation to actual states of affairs in reality.[2]

2. Some features of Western logic, including some syllogistic argument forms and the laws of identity, non-contradiction, and the excluded middle, are reliable avenues toward adjudicating the truth or falsity of various truth claims. These are the benchmarks for a reasonable epistemology.

METHOD

In this work, detailed attention will be given to the works of Carl A. Raschke, James K. A. Smith, and Myron B. Penner. Carl A. Raschke provides a postmodern reinterpretation of a number of Evangelical and Reformation values including *sola fide*, *sola scriptura*, and the priesthood of all believers, applying these reinterpretations to a number of cultural developments in Evangelicalism, including natural theology and apologetics. Smith appropriates Derrida's axiom that "there is nothing outside the text," and Lyotard's principle that postmodernism is "incredulity toward metanarratives," in addition to his agreement with the Reformed objection to natural theology. In his *The End of Apologetics*, Penner provides the most focused and lengthy critique of natural theology considered in this thesis. He spells out in this work (and others) his rejection of objective, universal, and neutral

---

2. When I use the term *reality*, I refer to both empirical and metaphysical reality. Throughout, I will defend a correspondence theory of truth.

reason that he claims is at the heart of Evangelical apologetics, and he offers a number of cultural critiques.

To date, few have attempted to address these authors' key objections to natural theology, and because the authors' work is copious and increasingly influential, a critique of their critique will help to reestablish natural theology as a relevant part of Evangelical philosophy of religion, systematics, and missiology for a new generation of scholars. While analytic thinkers like Douglas Groothuis, Richard B. Davis, W. Paul Franks, William Lane Craig, J. P. Moreland, and D. A. Carson have criticized the postmodern sympathies of some fellow Evangelicals, a detailed analysis of and response to postmodern attitudes toward the project of natural theology is yet to emerge. This work is original in that sense.

Below I will provide stipulative definitions of some key terms (Evangelical, postmodern, general revelation, natural theology, and apologetics). The second chapter will present vital background material which frames the intra-Evangelical debate about natural theology. Beginning with the Dutch Reformed tradition of Abraham Kuyper and the Princeton tradition exemplified by B. B. Warfield, and then discussing other key figures like Barth, Brunner, C. S. Lewis, Cornelius Van Til, Carl F. H. Henry, and William Lane Craig, that chapter will trace the development of Evangelical apologetics from the late nineteenth through the early twenty-first centuries to demonstrate how the terms of the current debate are set by older issues in Reformed theology and the practice of evangelism. The chapter will then summarize key works in postmodern philosophy and theology upon which Smith, Penner, and Raschke rely including those by Jacques Derrida, Jean-François Lyotard, Michel Foucault, Paul Ricoeur, Merold Westphal, and John D. Caputo.

The third and fourth chapters will set out in systematic form the key objections provided by Raschke, Smith, and Penner. The method for considering the authors' various criticisms of natural theology and apologetics will be (1) to explicate their criticisms with reference to any specific employment of key postmodern philosophical voices, (2) to identify their key presuppositions, and (3) to situate their arguments in the works in which they appear and in their larger projects. After providing careful analysis of their criticisms (4), I will rebut their arguments by showing that they lack internal coherence, involve questionable presuppositions, and/or fail to account for key issues in Evangelical Christian theology (biblical and systematic) (5). The success of the rebuttal can be measured by showing the weaknesses of the postmodern philosophical and theological arguments and by showing how natural theology can take its rightful place in evangelism and systematics.[3]

The final chapter will offer a proposal for natural theology and apologetics after the failure of the postmodern Evangelical critique. Even though Evangelicals should find unconvincing the postmodern philosophical and theological arguments that attend the general rejection of natural theology, there is a broader postmodern *zeitgeist* in which Evangelicals live and minister that can affect the perceived pertinence of natural theology. Evangelical natural theology can thrive in a cultural situation where people diminish the importance of objective truth (except with respect to the sciences), doubt humanity's ability to use reason in the search for knowledge, and have difficulty applying concepts of truth and rationality to religious commitments.

DEFINITIONS

Evangelical

Evangelical Christians form a significant subset of the populations of the United States and Canada.[4] Though perhaps best known for their advocacy of political candidates or causes (81% of white Evangelicals supported Donald Trump in the 2016 election[5]), what is most pertinent about this diverse collection of Christians for this present work is their commitment to certain theological ideas and the modes in which certain values

---

3. I employ the term "rebuttal" because it is more modest than refutation. See Walton, "Objections, Rebuttals and Refutations," 3–4. "A rebuttal requires two things. First, it requires a prior argument that it is directed against. Second, the rebuttal itself is an argument that is directed against this prior argument. Third [*sic*], it is directed against the prior argument in order to show that it is open to doubt or not acceptable . . . A refutation is a species of rebuttal that shows that the argument it is aimed at is untenable." I attempt to argue that the postmodern arguments are not acceptable philosophically or theologically. Some of my arguments will, indeed, do much more than this, showing that various postmodern positions are necessarily false, but the "rebuttal" is the benchmark of success for this book. The reason I honor this distinction is that many of my arguments will focus on logical deficiencies, and postmodern philosophy looks at logical analysis with an attitude of suspicion and irony.

4. Evangelicals have a serious presence in Europe, as well, but they are growing rapidly in numbers in the two-thirds world. See Jenkins, *The Next Christendom*.

5. Worthen, "A Match Made in Heaven," line 47.

inform their theological commitments.[6] Stated stipulatively, Evangelicals are those Protestant Christians who have a theological commitment to the Bible and to a high Christology and who apply to these commitments the qualities (coined by David Bebbington) of conversionism, activism, biblicism, and crucicentrism.[7] While neither a denomination nor a monolithic social movement, "Evangelicals take the Bible seriously and believe in Jesus Christ as Savior and Lord."[8] Surely, different Evangelical groups (indeed, individual Evangelicals themselves) would add to this minimalistic theological definition, yet they are united in commitment to these two theological emphases. Certainly, there are many Christian denominations and movements that share these theological commitments, yet Evangelicals are distinctive in the values or qualities they hold and that inform their theological commitments. Bebbington best identifies the qualities that inform the Evangelical commitment to the Bible and Christ. "There are four qualities that have been the special marks of Evangelical religion: *conversionism*, the belief that lives need to be changed; *activism*, the expression of the gospel in effort; *biblicism*, a particular regard for the Bible; and what may be called *crucicentrism*, a stress on the sacrifice of Christ on the cross."[9] For Evangelicals, Christians should make a personal decision to convert to become followers of Jesus Christ, and they should encourage others to do the same. In the process of conversion, one becomes born again and is empowered to live a good life for God. Christians should advocate for just causes and righteous living in their own lives and churches and in the world around them. Christians should read the Bible, and their views on everything should be influenced by the Bible's authoritative words. The death and resurrection are central to the Christian life, securing forgiveness for the Christian in this world, and everlasting life in the world that is to come.

Various philosophers and theologians throughout this work are identified as Evangelical. Certain Evangelical accounts of natural theology are identified in chapter 2, and while it could be anachronistic to refer to writers like Abraham Kuyper and B. B. Warfield as Evangelicals (and simply inaccurate to refer to Karl Barth and Emil Brunner thusly), these works

6. Many have offered excellent definitions of Evangelicals primarily rooted in a shared history. See Marsden, "Introduction;" Noll, *The Rise of Evangelicalism*; Noll, "What is 'Evangelical'?"; and Worthen, *Apostles of Reason*.

7. See Bebbington, *Evangelicalism in Modern Britain*, 2–3.

8. National Association of Evangelicals, "What is an Evangelical?" lines 1–2.

9. Bebbington, *Evangelicalism in Modern Britain*, 2–3.

are included under the heading "Evangelical" Natural Theology because they hold vital import for the intra-Evangelical debate about natural theology considered in this work. It is possible that the primary postmodern authors whose works are considered here (James K. A. Smith, Myron B. Penner, and Carl A. Raschke) may balk at being referred to as Evangelicals. However, I have applied the term to them as their books are often released through Evangelical publishers (primarily Baker Books of Grand Rapids, Michigan) and because they passionately exemplify the commitments to the Bible's centrality and to a high Christology. They also reflect well the four key qualities identified by Bebbington. My hope is that my inclusion of them in the Evangelical tradition that I cherish is a compliment and not a disappointment to them.

Postmodern

For the purposes of this paper, postmodernism will be treated as a philosophical style or school (even though it may encompass many incongruent voices), one that has had profound influence on Christian theology, particularly among the key authors considered here. In many ways, postmodernism is more a feeling or *zeitgeist* embodied in things like the student riots of 1968 and the sexual revolution or in the more contemporary sensibility that old ways of thinking about truth and morality are outmoded.[10] Tracing its roots to French philosophy of language and post-structuralism, postmodernism generally exemplifies the following characteristics. First, postmodernism involves the claim that there is no determinate meaning in human language. This entails a denial of the propositional view of truth, the notion that the proposition (or that which a declarative statement asserts) is a truth-bearer. Instead (and expressed in Jacques Derrida's famous declaration: "*There is nothing outside the text*"[11]), a text's meaning arises in communities of interpretation and can be drawn from many contexts, even those about which an original speaker or writer are unaware.[12] Second, postmodernism is a denial of human objectivity with respect to knowl-

---

10. Smith, *Who's Afraid of Postmodernism?* 19. Smith argues, "Trying to pinpoint the advent of the postmodern condition by linking it to a historical epoch, particular event, or even a particular cultural sphere . . . seems counterproductive, given the widespread disagreement about such historical claims."

11. Derrida, *Of Grammatology*, 158.

12. See Derrida, "Afterword," 146.

edge and truth. Appropriating some insights from the later Wittgenstein, postmodernism claims that "meaning and knowledge are ineluctably *social* and communal."[13] Reason and science are valuable tools, but they cannot provide objective knowledge about reality. Instead, they are simply discourses, of which there are many, and any attempt to be a totalizing discourse (a metanarrative) will be met with incredulity by the postmodern person (Jean-François Lyotard says that postmodernism is "incredulity toward metanarratives"[14]). Third, postmodernism involves the sense that people ought to be humble about their interpretations of texts and of the world and especially with respect to their claims about truth, knowledge, morality, and meaning. Each person's finitude and cultural context prohibit them from seeing things as they are; therefore, each ought to welcome new perspectives and withhold judgments about truth and morality from alternative perspectives and lifestyles.

I use the adjective *postmodern*, and its ideological companion *postmodernism*, throughout the paper to refer to various philosophers and theologians (and their work) as a heuristic tool to encompass their general affinity toward the three characteristics identified in the preceding paragraph. While most would use the term to describe their own work (Smith, Raschke, and Penner all accept the terms), my application of the terms to them or to their work is simply an attempt to use the terms to show meaningful connections between the many ideas that are considered in this thesis and not to ungenerously associate them with ideas with which they may disagree.

General Revelation, Natural Theology, and Apologetics

Many works on natural theology and apologetics are unconcerned with a taxonomic analysis of the terms general revelation, natural theology, and apologetics. However, I stipulate in this work particular ways in which these terms should be understood. Evangelical theology is animated by the conviction that God speaks and reveals truth about God's self to humanity. The first four volumes of Carl F. H. Henry's *God, Revelation, and Authority* carry the subtitle "God who speaks and shows." God has "reveal[ed] himself in sovereign freedom" and only because God has spoken and shown

13. Smith, *Who's Afraid of Relativism?* 60. See also Raschke, *The Next Reformation,* 17–18.

14. Lyotard, *The Postmodern Condition,* xxiv.

God's self can humanity have knowledge of God.[15] The Bible itself, along with the persons and works of Jesus Christ and the Holy Spirit, is part of a class of God's self-revelation known as special revelation. However, God has also revealed God's self in the natural world, as well, and this is known as general revelation. John Stott argues that general revelation has four key characteristics. (1) It is made known to everyone. (2) It is disclosed in the natural world. (3) It is continually communicated through the natural world. (4) "It is 'creational,' revealing God's glory through creation, as opposed to 'salvific,' revealing God's grace in Christ."[16] Paul states, "For since the creation of the world God's invisible qualities—his eternal power and divine nature—have been clearly seen, being understood from what has been made, so that people are without excuse" (Rom 1:20, NIV). There is a natural understanding of who God is and what God expects from people that everyone has access to in nature and in their own minds. As Evangelical theologian Wayne Grudem argues, "People can obtain a knowledge *that God exists*, and a knowledge of *some of his attributes*, simply from observation of themselves and the world around them."[17] General revelation also gives humanity knowledge of the moral law (see Rom 2:14–15) because God has revealed moral truths to the human conscience. This revelation is not exhaustive, nor is it salvific. God's revelation in Jesus Christ is required for one to receive God's salvation, and the Scriptures are necessary to know about God's actions in providing the gift of salvation. General revelation simply begins to show to humanity the existence of God and of the moral law.

As people rationally reflect on general revelation, they engage in natural theology. "Natural theology is an attempt to discover arguments" that confirm the existence of God without appealing to special revelation.[18] Natural theology is more explicitly philosophical than general revelation. While general revelation is God's self-revelation, natural theology is humanity's philosophical reflection on general revelation. Natural theology is "that branch of theology that seeks to provide warrant for belief in God's existence apart from the resources of authoritative, propositional revelation"

15. Henry, *God, Revelation, and Authority*, 2:30. Throughout, I will use the term *knowledge* to refer to justified, true belief.

16. Stott, *The Message of Romans*, 73; quoted in Groothuis, *Christian Apologetics*, 173.

17. Grudem, *Systematic Theology*, 121. Emphasis in the original.

18. Nash, *Faith and Reason*, 93.

(i.e. the Bible).[19] Natural theology is not explicitly Christian, though, and the tradition of natural theology includes philosophers of all stripes such as Plato, Aristotle, Thomas Aquinas, al-Kindi, Spinoza, Descartes, and many others. C. S. Lewis provides a famous popular example of natural theology (in the moral argument for the existence of God) when he argues from "The Law of Nature," expressed in the observation that "men have differed as to whether you should have one wife or four. But they have always agreed that you must not simply have any woman you liked."[20] He argues that if there is a moral law, then there is a Moral Lawgiver.[21] He employs reasoning to draw a conclusion about the phenomenon of "The Law of Nature." Natural theology can employ deductive arguments, inductive reasoning, and inferences to the best explanation. Natural theology develops many kinds of arguments for God including, but not limited to, ontological arguments, design arguments, and cosmological arguments.

Apologetics is the Christian ministry of defending the Christian religion as true, rational, and relevant. Derived from the Greek word *apologia*, meaning to give a defense as in a court case, this task is modeled or commanded throughout the New Testament, but most memorably in 1 Peter 3:15: "But in your hearts revere Christ as Lord. Always be prepared to give an answer to everyone who asks you to give the reason for the hope that you have. But do this with gentleness and respect" (NIV).[22] Apologetics may be divided into two modes: negative and positive. Negative apologetics seeks to provide "answers to challenges to religious faith," challenges like the problem of evil or the alleged impossibility of miracles.[23] This mode of apologetics also seeks to expose the internal tensions and contradictions in non-Christian perspectives, helping others to see "the tension between the real world and the logic of [their] presuppositions."[24] Positive apologetics is the task of providing support for Christian faith. It seeks "to make the case for God from natural theology—ontological, cosmological, design, moral and religious-experience arguments for God."[25] Positive apologetics goes

19. Craig and Moreland, "Introduction," iv.

20. Lewis, *Mere Christianity*, 6.

21. His argument is much more beautiful and complex than this brief word. See chapter 2 for a full explication.

22. See Groothuis, *Christian Apologetics*, 23–24.

23. Nash, *Faith and Reason*, 14–15.

24. Schaeffer, *The God Who is There*, 160.

25. Groothuis, *Christian Apologetics*, 21.

beyond natural theology, though, in pointing to other confirmations of the truth of the Christian religion such as the historicity of the Bible or the resurrection of Jesus Christ. Apologetics plays an important role in confirming the Christian worldview for those who already confess Christian faith and in supporting the preaching and teaching of the Christian gospel to those who are outside of the household of Christian faith.

The authors in question in this thesis (James K. A. Smith, Myron B. Penner, and Carl A. Raschke) reject both natural theology and positive apologetics. It is unclear to what extent each would reject negative apologetics (though they would certainly rebuke any reference in negative apologetics to a universal conception of reason), but it is beyond my scope to explore their attitudes to negative apologetics. It is also beyond my scope to consider their potential attitudes toward historical confirmations of biblical faith such as the reliability of the Bible or the historicity of the resurrection. That said, the task is to explain how these authors reject natural theology and how their rejection of natural theology fails. Prior to this task, though, it is necessary to illuminate the background for the intra-Evangelical debate regarding natural theology and the postmodern philosophical and theological milieu against which Smith's, Penner's, and Raschke's work may be better understood.

2

"Evangelical" Natural Theology and Postmodern Philosophy and Theology

THIS CHAPTER PRESENTS THE background material for the intra-Evangelical debate about natural theology. Beginning with the Dutch Reformed tradition of Abraham Kuyper and the Princeton tradition exemplified by B. B. Warfield, and then discussing other key figures like Karl Barth, Emil Brunner, C. S. Lewis, Cornelius Van Til, Carl F. H. Henry, and William Lane Craig, this chapter will trace the development of Evangelical natural theology from the late nineteenth through the early twenty-first centuries to demonstrate how the terms of the current debate are set by older issues in Reformed theology and in theologies of evangelism. The chapter will then summarize key works in postmodern philosophy and theology upon which Smith, Penner, and Raschke rely including those by Jacques Derrida, Jean-François Lyotard, Michel Foucault, Paul Ricoeur, Merold Westphal, and John D. Caputo.

"EVANGELICAL" NATURAL THEOLOGIES

Abraham Kuyper

Situating the life of Abraham Kuyper (1837–1920) neatly in the present discussion about *Evangelical* natural theology would surely be unfair to the complexity of the Dutch polymath's particular place in the history of theology. He served as Prime Minister of the Netherlands from 1901–1905 and founded the Free University of Amsterdam, and his influence in North American (and, of course, Dutch) Evangelicalism has been profound through the lives and ministries of people like Herman Dooyeweerd, Francis A. Schaeffer, and Carl F. H. Henry. His influence persists among philosophers like Nicholas Wolterstorff and Alvin Plantinga and among Neo-Calvinist streams of Evangelicalism, represented by pastors and theologians like John Piper, John Ortberg, and Albert Mohler.[1] Further problematizing Kuyper's inclusion in this study is his complicated relationship with the subject of natural theology. Kuyper, at times, appears sympathetic to a natural theology project, such as when he proposes the hypothesis that "God has not unintentionally left behind Him traces of His works and revelations of his thoughts in monuments and documents."[2] At other times, his words are meant to persuade those who would use natural theology to support Christian belief to stand fast against modernism instead of cowering to and mimicking modernity's modes of argumentation. "Apologists have invariably begun by abandoning the assailed breastwork, in order to entrench themselves cowardly in a ravelin behind it."[3] Indeed, Kuyper's position is nuanced with respect to natural theology and apologetics, yet in his cultural and theological objections, his support for a natural theology that both precedes and is completed by special revelation is rooted in Calvinist notions of new birth (or, as Kuyper calls it, *palingenesis*), common grace, and the *sensus divinitatus*.

Kuyper's objections to natural theology are best viewed with an eye to his particular intellectual and theological context. Kuyper sees that both Schleiermacher and Hegel, though with differing emphases, embraced a natural theology of the inner human consciousness that ended up undermining orthodox Reformation theology altogether. In their work,

> Natural theology includes two elements: first, ectypal knowledge of God as founded in the human consciousness, and secondly, the pistic capacity of man to grasp this ectypal knowledge with his inner consciousness. Hegel made the ectypal knowledge of God to appear in the foreground of human consciousness; Schleiermacher,

---

1. Of course, other Reformed movements such as the Christian Reformed Church continue to see themselves as part of Kuyper's legacy.

2. Kuyper, *Encyclopedia of Sacred Theology*, 217.

3. Kuyper, *Lectures on Calvinism*, 11.

> on the other hand started out from the pistic capacity increated in the inner nature of man.[4]

The revelation of God is a matter of a subjective state of consciousness or a latent capacity rather than the conviction that God has revealed God's self in nature. The problem with this kind of natural theology is that it denies the "abnormal" sense in which Christian revelation is given to humankind.[5] Unable to attribute the unique place that Christianity has among the "highest and the lowest" religions to the supernatural revelation of God in Christ, Schleiermacher and Hegel "glided off into Pantheism."[6] The failure of this anthropocentric natural theology is that, in placing the data of religious knowledge in the internal human experience, all religions become simple manifestations of Hegel's impersonal *Geist* or Schleiermacher's naturalistic psychology.

The failure to remain faithful to orthodox dogma and practice is key to Kuyper's concerns with natural theology. Still seeming to have in mind what he sees as the failures of Schleiermacher and Hegel, Kuyper argues against the subjective foundation of natural theology whereby "dogma after dogma tumbled," and one was taught not to trust the Scriptures to reveal facts about God and the world.[7] What is needed is not apologetic argumentation, but a lived faith that shows its validity through action. This lived faith is rooted in the new birth, or *palingenesis*, whereby the transformation of the individual establishes Christian theology and practice with a true foundation. While the natural theology of the day was edging close to pantheism, Kuyper was also concerned that apologetics was giving too much ground to naturalism, Kuyper's name for Darwinian accounts of the human being.[8] Naturalism denies Christian belief and causes the apologist to become anxious and bitter. Christian belief cannot be maintained when it is reified into the result of an evolutionary process or if the locus of revelation is in the inner human consciousness.[9] This places the apologist in the untenable position of making concession after concession, such as admitting that natural theology properly leads to pagan religions as well as to

4. Kuyper, *Encyclopedia of Sacred Theology*, 310–11.

5. Kuyper refers to the "abnormal" to speak of the ways in which Christianity is antithetical to all other Life-systems.

6. Ibid., 312.

7. Kuyper, "Use and Abuse of Apologetics," 376.

8. Kuyper, *Encyclopedia of Sacred Theology*, 167.

9. Kuyper, "Use and Abuse of Apologetics," 375–78. See also, *Encyclopedia*, 161.

Christianity, to the peril of his or her soul. Moreover, natural theology leads to idolatry, for in placing the foundation of religion in the human person, the development of religion from Animism to Christianity is a legitimate process, for the religious devotee is in touch with "the vitality of the seed of religion," regardless of his or her particular stage of development.[10]

This undermines the deep antithesis that Kuyper recognizes between true Christian theology and all other theologies. His notion of antithesis is rooted in his conviction that in Calvinism, one finds an independent "all-embracing life-system" of belief and action that is fundamentally distinct from "Paganism, Islamism, Romanism, and Modernism."[11] Grounded in the starting-point concept of the sovereignty of God, Calvinism offers a unique conception of relations to God, humanity, and the world that is irreconcilable with any other life-system.[12] This suggests that common ground between Calvinism and other life-systems may be illusory. *Palingenesis* is the key here. The new birth is a radical change that grants the Christian a new and "abnormal" consciousness, one fundamentally different from the unregenerate consciousness.[13] This means that there are two different consciousnesses at play in humanity, that of the regenerate person and that of the unregenerate person, and these form unique starting points for all human inquiry. Therefore, "it is an impossibility that both should agree, and . . . every endeavor to make them agree must be doomed to failure."[14] This places the prospects for any natural theology that may be commended in jeopardy, for if there is no agreement between starting-points, then it is unclear how one could find in nature common ground to demonstrate or infer God's existence or attributes.

Though it seems as if Kuyper's view on natural theology and apologetics is overwhelmingly negative, he leaves room for a natural theology

10. Kuyper, *Encyclopedia of Sacred Theology*, 305.

11. Kuyper, *Lectures on Calvinism*, 32. See also, Kuyper, *Encyclopedia of Sacred Theology*, 300–303.

12. Ibid., 19.

13. This antithesis is not necessarily that, through regeneration, the person is altered metaphysically. Rather, the Christian is under a new covenant. See Edgar and Oliphint, "Abraham Kuyper," 335. "As made in God's image, all people are either covenant keepers in Jesus or covenant breakers in Adam. So, when we speak of an absolute antithesis, we are speaking covenantally, not metaphysically."

14. Kuyper, *Lectures on Calvinism*, 138. The consciousness requires an altering force in order to perceive spiritual things. With the idealism of Fichte in mind, Kuyper writes, "We do not become aware of right, for instance, as a poetic product of our own spirit, but as a power which dominates us," in *Encyclopedia of Sacred Theology*, 100.

that both precedes and is completed by special revelation. The Calvinist life-system, Kuyper's term for worldview, emphasizes the "general cosmological principle of the sovereignty of God" and makes "objective" claims regarding the nature of reality under God.[15] Even though *palingenesis* marks an absolute point of differentiation for any field of inquiry (including the search for God), there is common grace apart from salvific grace which "relaxes the curse . . . arrests its process of corruption, and thus allows the untrammeled development of our life in which to glorify [God] as Creator."[16] This certainly leaves open the door for some kind knowledge of God discovered apart from salvific grace. Common grace unites all human inquiry by showing the Calvinist that knowledge of God is possible in "*all his works*" (that is, God's works).[17] This enabled the Greeks and Romans to have insight in philosophy and the arts despite the fact that they lacked the heritage of the revelation of God in the people of Israel and in the Church. It even enables the ability of humanity to recognize the presence of God apart from salvific grace in the revelation of God in Christ. With Calvin, Kuyper posits the existence in each person of a *semin religionis* and a *sensus divinitatus*. Though limited to a mere seed of religion and a sense of the Divine, humans may have a deeper existential and cognitive connection to the presence of God apart from *palingenesis*. Rather than trying to deny natural theology, Kuyper wants to ensure that natural theology cannot serve the greater *religionswissenschaft* project wherein Christianity appears on a similar positive continuum alongside "the Moloch ritual."[18] Great discontinuity (antithesis) must be asserted between Christianity and all other religions. This contextual element, similar in scope to the objections to the work of Schleiermacher and Hegel mentioned above, is key for Kuyper's natural theology.

> The Christian Religion and Paganism do not stand related to each other as the higher or lower forms of development of the same thing; but the Christian religion is the highest form of development natural theology was capable of along the positive line; while all paganism is a development of that selfsame natural theology in

---

15. Kuyper, *Lectures on Calvinism*, 22.

16. Ibid., 30.

17. Ibid., 125. Emphasis in the original.

18. Kuyper, *Encyclopedia of Sacred Theology*, 300.

the negative direction. Christendom and Paganism stand to each other as the *plus* and *minus* forms of the same series.[19]

If this antithesis can be maintained, then natural theology becomes an essential part of God's revelation. Drawing upon the important ways in which Romans 1:19 and 2:14 inform the issue biblically, Kuyper claims that Christian theology even requires natural theology as a precondition. Common grace requires natural theology of this kind, for it is the only way that sin might be restrained and the sinner be "without excuse."[20]

Natural theology forms a foundation upon which special revelation is, then, possible. This, however, does not mean that natural theology can adequately be received by the unregenerate person prior to *palingenesis*. To the contrary, humanity's utter sinfulness has made knowledge of God apart from special revelation an absurdity to those who are not regenerate. According to Kuyper, any effort to place natural theology as a prologue to special revelation will end with the destruction of special revelation as a secondary and irrelevant sequel to reason and mysticism.[21] This means that apologetics cannot serve as a preparation for special revelation. "You cannot depend upon natural theology as it works in fallen man . . . [but] only when an *accidens* enables you to recover this defective ideal for yourself, and natural theology receives this *accidens* only in special revelation."[22] New birth is thus essential. The natural theology is still necessary, though, for the *semin religionis* and the *sensus divinitatus*, as the vehicles for "the natural knowledge of God" are required for understanding and experience.[23] Apologetics, then, remains only at the level of antithesis, where the whole Christian life-system denies the coherence of non-Christian life-systems. This nuanced picture does not neatly match the vision for natural theology that will be presented in this work, and indeed, Kuyper's view of natural

---

19. Ibid., 302. This quote may appear contradictory. If Christianity and Paganism are not higher and lower forms of the same thing, then how are they on the same line, one side being positive and one side being negative? It seems like Kuyper is asserting Paganism as a kind of anti-religion, the fruit of a natural theology apart from *palingenesis*.

20. Ibid. "Natural theology is with us no schema, but the knowledge of God itself, which still remains in the sinner and is still within his reach, entirely in harmony with the sense of Rom. i. 19 *sq.* and Rom. ii. 14 *sq.*"

21. Ibid., 609–10.

22. Ibid., 307.

23. Ibid. See also McGlasson, *Church Doctrine*, 25–26. McGlasson commends this interpretation, arguing that Kuyper claims that revealed theology requires natural theology as a precondition.

theology was problematic for some of his contemporaries, including the Princeton theologian B. B. Warfield.

B. B. Warfield

Benjamin B. Warfield (1851–1921), who served as Charles Hodge Professor of Polemic and Didactic Theology at Princeton Seminary, offers both a criticism of the limited role given to apologetics in Kuyper's theology and a vision for a more robust natural theology. Because knowledge about God is possible through revelation, and this knowledge is available in nature, Scripture, and experience, apologetics serves a central role in becoming a Christian in Warfield's view. Warfield is concerned that Kuyper's view, which weakens apologetics to a "subdivision of a subdivision," makes Christianity the "great assumption."[24] First, Warfield claims that Kuyper's assertion of a *sensus divinitatus*, implanted by God to impel each person to seek to discover knowledge about God, is something that requires apologetics.

> We must, it seems, vindicate the existence of a *sensus divinitatus* in man capable of producing a natural theology independently of special revelation in deed and word; and as well the reality of a supernatural preparation of the heart of man to receive it; before we can proceed to the study of theology at all, as Dr. Kuyper has outlined it.[25]

One must develop an apologetic for the existence of the *sensus divinitatus* prior to the study of theological sciences. Second, Warfield rejects the notion that sin so injures the human ability to know God as to make natural theology apart from *palingenesis* (rebirth) impossible. He agrees with Kuyper that there are two kinds of people, those who have been reborn and those who have not been reborn, yet the faculties of intellection (including those that are used to know God) exist in both, albeit in a more complete way in the regenerate person. This amounts to a difference in degree, not in kind.[26] Finally, Warfield rejects the notion that the gift of faith given by the Holy Spirit does not come to the individual without intellectual grounding. Rather, faith is an ability to respond to the grounds of Christian belief that already exist. Not only can apologetic arguments "silence gainsayers," but

24. Warfield, "Introduction to Beattie's *Apologetics*," 2:95–96.

25. Ibid., 2:97.

26. Ibid., 2:100–101. See also Warfield, "A Review of *De Zekerheid*," 2:117.

they can also "provide conviction" that is then prevailed upon by the Holy Spirit in the granting of faith.[27]

Key to Warfield's legitimation of natural theology is the idea that knowledge of God is possible for finite and sinful humanity. Knowledge of God is employed in the science of theology. Warfield uses the term *science* in an encyclopedic manner, implying that Christian theology is a branch of human inquiry that discovers and codifies truth about God similar to how astronomy discovers and codifies truth about the heavens. Yet for anything to be considered a science, "Three things are presupposed: (1) the reality of its subject-matter; (2) the capacity of the human mind to apprehend, receive into itself, and rationalize this subject-matter; and (3) some medium of communication by which the subject-matter is brought before the mind and presented for its apprehension."[28] Theological studies must assume that knowledge of God is possible. If we are to have knowledge of God in the Christian Scriptures, then we must assume that there is knowledge of God in the world. If there is knowledge of God in the world, then we must assume that humanity is capable of knowing this God.[29] Inherent in each notion is a more general assumption about humanity and knowledge of God. Behind all of this abstraction is a key affirmation presupposed by theological science: "That God is, and that He has relation to His creatures."[30] Because God is personal, God may relate to human persons, which is exactly what one must presuppose to study the revelation of God in the Scriptures. More specifically for Christian theology, this revelation of God in the world and in the Scriptures is evidence upon which one may ground one's faith with certainty.[31] Because knowledge is possible, "arguments adduced for the support of the foundations of the Christian religion" may be objectively valid.[32] This is why Warfield quotes M. E. Arnaud approvingly, "It does not suffice to submit our heart and will to the Gospel: we must submit also our mind and our reason."[33] Humans may have objective knowledge of God

27. Warfield, "A Review of *De Zekerheid*," 2:115.

28. Benjamin B. Warfield, "The Idea of Systematic Theology," 246.

29. Warfield, "Introduction to Beattie's *Apologetics*," 2:98.

30. Warfield, "The Idea of Systematic Theology," 247.

31. Warfield, "A Review of *De Zekerheid*," 2:112, 2:122.

32. Warfield, "Introduction to Beattie's *Apologetics*," 2:103. He continues by saying, "It is not even true that the minds of sinful men are inaccessible to the 'evidences,' though, in the sense of the proverb, 'convinced against their will,' they may 'remain of the same opinion still.'"

33. Arnaud, *Manual de Dogmatique*, ix; quoted in Warfield, "The Idea of Systematic

and may employ reason for the attainment of this knowledge. With this confidence, Warfield argues that "the task of apologetical theology" is to discover if God exists and is knowable to humanity, and "what sources of information concerning him are accessible."[34] All of this is tempered by a key distinction for Warfield, however. Though revelation of God in the natural world is possible via experience and reason, knowledge of Christ is superior because in it God reveals God's self personally, definitively, and for the sake of the salvation of God's people.[35]

What Warfield refers to as "apologetical theology" (or simply "apologetics") plays a foundational role with respect to systematic theology. God has revealed God's self "in divers manners" through nature, the human mind, conscience, history, and special revelation.[36] Systematics cannot benefit from these revelations of God, however, without apologetical theology first establishing systematic theology's "necessary presuppositions without which no theology is possible—the existence and essential nature of God, the religious nature of man which enables him to receive a revelation from God, the possibility of a revelation and its actual realization in the Scriptures."[37] This level of inquiry provides the content of a natural theology, which, though not as robust as Scriptural revelation, is vital to the establishment of the theological disciplines.[38] When supplemented by the Scriptures, the content of theology may blossom into a fuller account of God and the world, yet apologetical theology plays the key role in making this possible. Apologetical inquiry must be "the first among the five essential theological disciplines," and once it has done its work, the other disciplines may work together to produce systematics.[39]

Theology," 269.

34. Warfield, Brown, and Smith, "Task and Method," 192.

35. Warfield, "The Idea of Systematic Theology," 251.

36. Ibid., 250. Warfield identifies special revelation as God's "grace, our experience under the tutelage of the Holy Ghost—or whether it be through the open visions of His prophets, the divinely-breathed pages of His written Word, the divine life of the Word Himself."

37. Ibid., 254.

38. Ibid., 253.

39. Warfield, "Introduction to Beattie's *Apologetics*," 2:98. For Warfield, these other disciplines are Exegetical, Historical, Systematic, and Practical. He notes that Kuyper renamed these disciplines as Bibliological, Ecclesiological, Dogmatological, and Diaconological.

The work of apologetical theology, further, serves as preparatory work in those that are to receive Christian faith. Whether through traditional natural theology, establishing the historicity of the Scriptures, or through answering gainsayers, apologetical theology is a "persuasive science," helping the individual to consider and assent to Christian truth claims.[40] Christianity can be proved to be true by apologetics. Warfield claims that the content of the Scriptures, especially Christianity's historical claims, can be authenticated.[41] (This is no less a work of the Holy Spirit than any other revelation of God.) Because apologetics is a work of the Holy Spirit, it is able to prepare the soul for a confession of faith, convincing the individual of the truth of Christianity prior to any volitional commitment.[42] Though faith itself is a gift from God, not an attainment of human cognition or volition, faith is a conviction that has grounds in evidence, evidence provided by apologetics. "The Holy Spirit does not work a blind, an ungrounded faith in the heart . . . rooted in nothing and clinging without reason to its object . . . but just a new ability of the heart to respond to the grounds of faith, sufficient in themselves."[43] Belief in Christianity is rational, known to be so because of the work of apologetical theology. This entails that reason and apologetics have a key role in the Christian mission of "Christianizing the world."[44] When Christians practice evangelism and discipleship, instruction in apologetics is necessary to provide reasoned grounds for faith for those who are outside the household of the Christian religion.

The Debate Between Emil Brunner and Karl Barth

In 1934, a debate appeared between the neo-orthodox theologians Emil Brunner and Karl Barth, one which would give further texture to historical disputes regarding natural theology. Translated into English and published in 1946, *Natural Theology: Comprising "Nature and Grace" by Professor Dr. Emil Brunner and the reply "No!" by Dr. Karl Barth* addresses the key issues of the *imago dei*, revelation, and the nature of grace. While its historical character is fascinating, this debate is noteworthy as it is representative of some of the debates that exist today among Evangelicals with respect to the

40. Warfield, "Christian Evidences," 2:126.

41. Warfield, "Introduction to Beattie's *Apologetics*," 2:98.

42. Warfield, "A Review of *De Zekerheid*," 2:113–14.

43. Warfield, "Introduction to Beattie's *Apologetics*," 2:98–99.

44. Ibid., 2:99.

validity and scope of natural theology. This section will discuss this debate as representative of their positions with some reference given to their other works.

Emil Brunner (1889–1966) was a professor of systematic and practical theology at the University of Zürich and was a one-time cobelligerent with Barth against the theological liberalism of the nineteenth and early twentieth centuries. In his contribution, which appears first in the volume, he claims that his particular doctrine of natural theology, especially with respect to his views on the *imago dei*, revelation, and the nature of grace, corresponds best to the views of the Reformers, particularly to that of John Calvin. First, he argues that the *imago dei* is not utterly destroyed in humanity through the fall. While the material image of God is completely lost in humanity, the functional image remains.[45] The original way in which God creates humanity is in the divine image. This entails that humanity is good and is able to perform good works. However, sin destroys this ability in humanity. "Man is a sinner through and through and there is nothing in him which is not defiled by sin."[46] This references a material ability of humanity that is lost, rendering humanity unable to do anything that could merit salvation or favor from God. However, humanity remains human. Still distinct from the rest of creation (including non-human animals), humans have both the powers of speech and of moral responsibility, and these are not lost in the fall. This is the formal image of God which humanity retains, and it is the point of contact for hearing the Word of God, a term which Brunner broadly uses to refer to God's special revelation. If humanity lacked the ability to be addressed by God, then human moral responsibility would be nonexistent. "Only a being that can be addressed is capable of sin. But in sinning, while being responsible, it somehow or other knows of its sin. This knowledge of sin is a necessary presupposition of the understanding of the divine message of grace."[47] So the formal image

---

45. Brunner, "Nature and Grace," 23–24. "The formal sense of the concept is the human, *i.e.* that which distinguishes man from all the rest of creation . . . he is a subject, a rational creature . . . If the formal side of the *imago dei* is thus conceived, it does not in any way result in an encroachment upon the material concept of *justitia originalis*, nor in a lessening of the weight of the statement that this *justitia originalis* is completely lost . . . Materially the *imago* is completely lost, man is a sinner through and through, and there is nothing in him which is not defiled by sin."

46. Ibid., 24.

47. Ibid., 31.

of God makes possible knowledge of sin and makes one able to hear the message of grace.

Brunner argues that this position is consistent with Calvin. Calvin speaks of a loss of the *imago dei* that can only be repaired through the *regeneratio* brought by Christ and the Holy Spirit. However, this loss of the *imago dei* does not entail a complete break with the original nature of humanity as created in God's image; human nature as such remains. "The result of this is the fact that man still and indeed always can and must be spoken of as the image of God. On the other hand, the *imago* must be described as destroyed and spoilt."[48] Humanity apart from regeneration, thus, has a dual nature. There is a remnant of the image of God that is retained, and Calvin says that this remnant amounts to "the entire human, rational nature, the immortal soul, the capacity for culture, the conscience, responsibility, the relation with God."[49] This remnant is what distinguishes humanity from other animals and allows humanity to know God in nature, albeit in a non-salvific manner. Furthermore, the image of God is presupposed in Calvin's ethics, Brunner argues. Human life ought to be respected because humans are made in the image of God, and the Christian is urged to respect the life of other humans because they bear the image of God. Brunner claims that this common nature, the repaired image of God in the Christian and the remnant of the image of God in the one who has not received regeneration, actually forms a point of contact for the Church's proclamation. Because humans retain the "capacity for words and responsibility," those who have not received regeneration can understand the message of the Church, even if they can only respond to the message through the enablement granted by the Holy Spirit.[50]

Prior to this point of contact in Brunner's theology is the revelation of God, most importantly in the Word of God, but also in nature. For Brunner, the *theologia naturalis* is the "Christian theological thinking which tries to account for the phenomena of natural life."[51] God's revelation in nature serves a secondary role to God's redemptive revelation that is received through faith. This means that, taxonomically, natural theology belongs to either God's "ordinances of creation" or "ordinances of preserva-

48. Ibid., 40.

49. Ibid.

50. Ibid., 56. My capitalization of the "Church" simply follows Brunner's standard of general reference to those to whom the message of Jesus Christ has been entrusted.

51. Ibid., 30.

tion" as a function of God's preserving grace.[52] Natural theology consists of God's revelation in nature, the human conscience, natural ordinances like marriage, and in the issue of objective moral responsibility. God makes an imprint upon everything that God creates, one that humanity may receive as God's "self-communication."[53] Sin is proof of natural theology because sin can only be considered an offense against the will of God if that will may be known by the sinner. "Without knowledge of God, there can be no sin."[54] Again, Brunner argues that natural theology is affirmed by Calvin, "All that Calvin says concerning the ethics of matrimony and of the State is derived from his *theologia naturalis*."[55] These institutions function as a response to natural law revealed by God and received by humanity apart from regenerating grace.

It is no small detail that Brunner sees natural theology as an outworking of God's preserving grace over the world which has fallen into sin. First, God's revelation exists in everything that God has made, which entails that God is revealed to prelapsarian humanity in nature as well as in God's word. Of course, this is not controversial. What is at stake in Brunner's doctrine of natural theology is whether God's revelation extends to fallen humanity. Brunner's answer to this has been a resounding "Yes!" though this affirmation is rooted in God's grace. Brunner posits the notion of a preserving grace, which "does not abolish sin but abolishes the worst consequences of sin."[56] God preserves humanity through natural provision and through ordinances like the State. "He gives life, health, strength, etc.—in short the whole sphere of natural life and its goods."[57] This is affirmed by Calvin in how he sees marriage and the State as ordained by God to counter the worst effects of sin. Brunner argues that, for Calvin, God's grace functions in the ordinance of the State in a preserving grace and in the ordinance of the Church as a redemptive grace.[58] Though this grace is much more complete in the message and the existence of the Church, even those outside the Church may experience a limited portion of God's preserving grace. Since grace comes from God, it is rightly understood through natural theology.

52. Ibid.
53. Ibid., 25.
54. Ibid., 32.
55. Ibid., 44.
56. Ibid., 28.
57. Ibid.
58. Ibid., 45.

Perhaps the most famous line in this debate between Emil Brunner and Karl Barth (1886–1968) is Barth's firm "Nein!" against any suggestion that natural theology rightly belongs to the Reformation or the Evangelical[59] Church. While Barth's rejection of natural theology is documented elsewhere,[60] his historical context, critique of Brunner, theological concerns, and doctrine of revelation as grace are all perhaps best represented in his essay responding to Brunner's "Nature and Grace." First, Barth's rejection of natural theology is historical. He is concerned that the doctrines of the Evangelical Church had been compromised throughout the eighteenth and nineteenth centuries through historical criticism and theological liberalism.[61] In particular, he sees natural theology as a tool in the belt of the German Christians to make the Christian religion become subservient to contemporary scientific and philosophical arguments regarding the superiority of the Aryan race and of the German culture.[62] He wants to ensure that the spirit of the Reformation is protected from Catholic natural theology, as well. "What Calvin wrote in those first chapters of the *Institutes* has to be written again and this time in such a way that no Przywara and no Althaus can find in it material for their fatal ends."[63]

Second, Barth is concerned that Brunner violates some deep elements of Reformation theology. In claiming that humanity can know God apart from the Word of God and by means of the formal *imago dei*, Brunner violates the standards of *sola scriptura* and *sola gratia*. In claiming that a point of contact exists in the formal image of God, Brunner has actually rejected *sola fide*, as well.[64] Barth thinks that Galatians 2:20 ("I live, yet not I, but Christ liveth in me.") and 1 Corinthians 2:10 ("But God hath revealed

---

59. This term denotes the German Lutheran Church for both Barth and Brunner, not primarily the Evangelical churches considered in this work.

60. "What is true human knowledge of divine revelation?—on the assumption that revelation itself creates of itself the necessary point of contact in man. But if this relationship is set aside, if the contradiction of human reason is made the subject of enquiry and its overcoming the goal, the sphere of the Church is abandoned and 'another task' is indeed substituted for the task of dogmatics . . . [Dogmatics] will refrain from attempted self-vindication." See Barth, *Church Dogmatics*, 29.

61. For example, he writes that Schleiermacher had embraced a "secularised Thomism" that became "part of the armoury of modernist Protestantism." See Barth, "No!," 101.

62. See Barr, *Biblical Faith and Natural Theology*, 7–14.

63. Barth, "No!," 104. He is referring to the Jesuit Erich Przywara's doctrine of the *analogia entis* and of Paul Althaus' theological alliance with National Socialism.

64. Ibid., 90.

them unto us by his Spirit."), which Brunner has taken as support for his own position, in context show not that there is a formal *imago dei* which is a point of contact for revelation, but that the capacity for revelation is provided through the miracle of repair that God works to make one "a new man, a new creature."[65] Brunner has misrepresented Calvin, whose theology affirms that

> God and his law, the mystery of election, the incarnation and re-demption, the Holy Spirit as divine subject, Baptism and the Lord's Supper are divine signs, justification and sanctification as divine acts, are everything. Through the gift of revelation and faith man as a rational creature is together with his world *included* in these.[66]

Humanity cannot attain to any of these elements of Reformation theology through any human effort or inquiry. These are received as gifts and explored through theology. Barth further argues that Brunner's position contradicts his earlier views that the only ability that humanity retains with respect to revelation is that humanity is in despair.[67] Moreover, Brunner contradicts himself in "Nature and Grace," by affirming both the "sovereign, freely electing grace of God" and humanity's "capacity for revelation."[68] Barth thinks that these two notions are mutually exclusive, and Brunner's failure to see this simple fact is fatal.

Third, natural theology poses a real danger for the Church. Barth defines natural theology as:

> Every (positive or negative) *foundation of a system* which claims to be theological, *i.e.* to interpret divine revelation, whose *subject*, however, differs fundamentally from the revelation in Jesus Christ and whose *method* therefore differs equally from the exposition of Holy Scripture.[69]

This brings into focus Barth's chief concern: that natural theology is an abandonment of Christian theology for reflection on a revelatory tradition which lacks a Christian subject and Christian methods of inquiry. Natural theology is not a field of study for the student of true theology; rather one only observes natural theology as an "abyss into which it is inadvisable to

65. Ibid., 94. See also 117–21.

66. Ibid., 104. Emphasis in the original.

67. Ibid., 115.

68. Ibid., 79.

69. Ibid., 74–75. Emphasis in the original.

step if one does not want to fall."[70] The abyss is simply that of idolatry. The only capacity that humanity retains after the fall is to "know and worship the gods of his own heart."[71] Because the *imago dei* has been destroyed and because humanity can do no good work apart from God's grace, seeking the revelation of God in anything other than the Word of God will result in the worship of other gods. Barth does not deny that Calvin leaves open the possibility of knowledge of God available to those who have not received regeneration. However, he claims that sin is the key doctrine for reflection on the actualization of this possibility. "One might call it an objective possibility, created by God, but not a subjective possibility, open to man. Between what is possible in principle and what is possible in fact inexorably lies the fall."[72] The human situation is so precarious because of sin, that only a radical *reparatio* through grace can make knowledge of God in creation again a live possibility. Because the revelation and knowledge of God are *sola gratia*, natural theology is a denial of grace, an affront to this central Reformation slogan. For this reason, theology's task remains singular.

C. S. Lewis

The next figure whose work has helped to shape the development of Evangelical natural theology in the twentieth and twenty-first centuries is someone whose background greatly differs from that of the Calvinist theologians heretofore considered. The Cambridge and Oxford author, literary scholar, and popular apologist C. S. Lewis (1898–1963) exerts considerable influence on Evangelicals in the field to this day. Lewis' natural theology is primarily characterized by an apologetic method which integrates reason, experience, and imagination.[73] While the imaginative elements of Lewis' fiction writings will not be considered in this section, two of Lewis' key nonfiction works, *The Abolition of Man* and *Mere Christianity*, commend a natural theology that proves God's existence from human reasoning about and experience of the Moral Law and infers God's existence through an argument from transcendent desire.[74]

70. Ibid., 75.

71. Ibid., 107.

72. Ibid., 106.

73. See McGrath, "Reason, Experience, and Imagination," 129–46.

74. For a treatment of myth as an apologetic in Lewis' writings, see McGrath, "A Gleam of Divine Truth," 55–81, esp. 59–69.

C.S. Lewis' book *The Abolition of Man* is an argument for natural law and against the philosophical rejection of objective moral values. He takes, as an occasion for this discussion, a book from the upper grades in the English educational system which he calls *The Green Book*.[75] This book claims that even though values are stated in objective language, they are merely emotive constructions reflecting the state of the speaker. Lewis argues against this assertion by bringing in an argument against the subjectivity of *The Green Book* and an argument for natural law. Lewis identifies the borrowed capital on which an anti-objectivist ethical system exists, and he shows that humanity would cease to exist as we know it through the removal of objective ethics.

Gaius and Titius (Lewis' names for the authors of *The Green Book*) assert that statements which include a predicate of value do not reflect a real axiological injunction; rather, they only reflect the sentiments of the speaker. This kind of assertion is a type of moral subjectivism. The example given by Gaius and Titius is of a Coleridge story where two people are looking at a waterfall. One person says that the waterfall is "pretty," and the other person says that it is "sublime."[76] Coleridge rejects the first suggestion, claiming that the waterfall is sublime. Gaius and Titius interpret this statement by stating that Coleridge is really just having sublime feelings. *The Green Book* states more generally, "We appear to be saying something very important about something; and actually we are only saying something about our own feelings."[77] This is the extent of the development of the subjectivist arguments in *The Green Book* that Lewis presents. Lewis, however, draws out a number of logical implications from this argument.

First, Lewis points out that if value statements only reflect the sentiments of the speaker, then all value statements are unimportant.[78] The reasoning behind this is clear: if an axiological statement only reflects an individual's feelings, then that statement has no relation to ultimate reality. If there is no relation to ultimate reality, then an individual has no reason for obeying the injunction. Second, Lewis notes that in a subjectivist system, people lose their evaluative moral compass.[79] In fact, Gaius and Titius

---

75. Lewis was likely referring to King and Ketley, *The Control of Language*.

76. Lewis, *The Abolition of Man*, 2.

77. Ibid., 3.

78. Ibid., 4.

79. Ibid., 25.

have cut out a part of the human soul.[80] There is no objective foundation that a person's moral sensibilities can connect with, rendering people soulless. Third, this reinterpretation of values that *The Green Book* exemplifies is an attempt by humans to control nature, including their own natures, but nature ironically conquers humankind via subjectivism.[81] People are left to rely only on their instincts, thereby rendering humanity a hodgepodge of subhuman instinct and baseless sentimentality. This is what Lewis calls "the abolition of man."[82]

Lewis goes beyond simply drawing out the logical implications of the argument of *The Green Book*; he develops an argument against subjective axiology and, by extension, for natural law. As stated above, the reinterpretation of objective ethical injunctions by Gaius and Titius renders humankind in a less than human state. Through trying to master Nature, people have been mastered by Nature, subject to their instincts and sentiments for value judgments. Lewis even points out that people become like animals through this deconstruction.[83] Lewis argues for this natural result because he wants innovators like Gaius and Titius to see that while few are willing to give up human distinctiveness, that is the necessary result. This emphasis on scientific thinking that leads people toward subjectivism is the focus for another Lewis critique. Lewis points out that it is impossible that scientific thinking could ever result in a basis for ethical values. This is because science is indicative rather than imperative or prescriptive.[84] People cannot expect to reject objective axiology, yet discover a scientific system that provides veridical ethical guidelines because science cannot provide the "ought," but only the "is." Furthermore, Gaius and Titius assert that people can rely on instincts for real ethics, but Lewis points out that instincts cannot be trusted, especially because instincts are often in disagreement.[85]

Instead, Lewis employs a word as a tag for the objective axiological foundation, the *Tao*, based on the vast sum of philosophies and religions that have offered humankind objective moral language.[86] He calls it "the doctrine of objective value, the belief that certain attitudes are really true,

---

80. Ibid., 9.
81. Ibid., 64.
82. Ibid.
83. Ibid., 24.
84. Ibid., 37.
85. Ibid., 36.
86. Ibid., 18

and others really false, to the kind of thing the universe is and the kind of things we are."[87] Lewis supports this idea by showing that it has been widely-held throughout trans-national human history. He argues that when the innovators step outside of the *Tao*, they are stepping into a moral "void," without any foundation for evaluative ability.[88] The *Tao* provides a "common human law of action which can over-arch rulers and ruled alike."[89] It is because the *Tao* is by nature objective that one can count on its authority in all areas of human existence.

In *Mere Christianity*, Lewis attempts to argue for the existence of God from objective moral value by a deductive argument.[90] (These are moral injunctions that Lewis identifies in *The Abolition of Man*, and they point to general ethical principles that exist among all peoples at all times.) Lewis assumes the success of the inductive argument in *The Abolition of Man*, yet rehearses some of its contentions in *Mere Christianity*:

> Men have differed as regards what people you ought to be unselfish to—whether it was only your own family, or your fellow countrymen, or every one. But they have always agreed that you ought not to put yourself first. Selfishness has never been admired. Men have differed as to whether you should have one wife or four. But they have always agreed that you must not simply have any woman you liked.[91]

Moral principles like these make up what Lewis calls "The Law of Nature."[92] Knowledge of this law haunts humanity in that its existence and implications are existentially and cognitively unshakeable. Of course, people do not abide by this law, which distinguishes it in kind from other laws like gravitation. These laws describe what things like stones and trees do, but the Law of Nature or the Law of Human Nature describes what humans ought to do, yet fail to do. Humans rightly understand the failure to do what one ought to do as wrong behavior.

At this point, Lewis addresses a possible objection to his argument thus far: the notion of behaving wrongly may only mean that one does not like

---

87. Ibid.

88. Ibid., 64.

89. Ibid., 73.

90. For more on different types of reasoning, see Minnemeier, "Abduction, Deduction and Induction," 239–51.

91. Lewis, *Mere Christianity*, 6.

92. Ibid., 16.

what another is doing. This objection fails, though, for humans react differently to various inconvenient or dissatisfying behaviors based on intent. "I am not angry . . . with a man who trips me up by accident; I am angry with a man who tries to trip me up even if he does not succeed."[93] One might say that some behavior is known as decent only because it benefits society. However, decent behavior is not always beneficial. Moreover, the appeal to the good of society fails, for "we may ask, 'Why should I care what's good for society except when it happens to pay *me* personally?' and then you will have to say, 'Because you ought to be unselfish'—which simply brings us back to where we started."[94] That is, there is a Natural Law that demands unselfishness.[95] This law explains why humans make moral judgments; it is an inescapable idea that "press[es] on us" from "above" and "beyond."[96]

What can best account for this law that is above and beyond? Lewis claims that there are two main possibilities on the issue. The first is the materialist view that claims that the universe is the result solely of material forces and chance. The second is "the religious view" that claims that the universe is caused by a mind of some kind.[97] Science cannot settle the question because science only describes the universe; it does not explain why there is a universe or why it exists as it does.[98] To settle the question, humanity must look internally. Humans know that they are under this moral law; it is inescapable and perfectly congruent with interior experience, though in conflict with external behavior. The materialist view can only say that the universe, including human knowledge of Natural Law, is as it is for no reason.[99] Matter and chance do not direct moral behavior. The religious view, however, says that there is power outside the universe that is evident in one's internal understanding of the Natural Law. This power is

93. Ibid.

94. Ibid. He seems to have in mind the fallacy of tautology.

95. Ibid., 20.

96. Ibid.

97. Ibid., 22. On pages 26–27, Lewis posits a third view, the "Life-Force" philosophy, wherein this force directs evolutionary development and thus, human behavior. This amounts to a kind of catch-all for teleological evolution. He thinks that the Life-Force may be just like a mind, in which case it is properly addressed under the religious view. If not, then he claims that it is incoherent because only minds have purposes for things like laws and morality. For a likely representative of the Life-Force view, see Bergson, *Creative Evolution*.

98. Lewis, *Mere Christianity*, 23–24.

99. Ibid., 24.

known internally, demanding obedience to the Moral Law, and this power is active in humankind more broadly, trying to urge people to obey the Moral Law.[100] This power is rightly understood as a "Director" or "Guide," though it is not clear that the power is the God of the Christian faith.[101] Stated formally, Lewis argues:

1. If there is a universal Moral Law, there is a Moral Lawgiver.

2. If there is a Moral Lawgiver, it must be something beyond the universe.

3. There is a universal Moral Law.

4. Therefore, there is a Moral Lawgiver.

5. Therefore, the Moral Lawgiver is beyond the universe.

Though not explicitly codified as such by Lewis, this is a deductive conditional proof.[102] If the premises are true, then the conclusion obtains necessarily.[103] Though based on Natural Law present universally, Lewis' argument also partially relies on his account of interior knowledge, wherein the Moral Law is known through internal investigation. This is interesting because it has parallels to the tacit knowing that Michael Polanyi claims that people employ in scientific research.[104] However, Lewis' argument does not have to completely rely on internal knowledge because it benefits from the empirical data presented in *The Abolition of Man*. Lewis' rhetoric and argumentation are compelling, showing that the existence of a God or an intelligent, purposive power is the logical conclusion of our knowledge of the inescapable moral intuition in humanity.

100. Ibid., 25.

101. Ibid.

102. See Moreland and Craig, *Philosophical Foundations*, 42–43. Key to this interpretation is Lewis' statement: "Suppose someone asked me, when I see a man in blue uniform going down the street leaving little paper packets at each house . . . The only packet I'm allowed to open is Man. When I do, especially when I open that particular man called Myself, I find that I do not exist on my own, that I am under a law," in *Mere Christianity*, 24–25. He is claiming to have both his internal perspective in mind along with an objective view toward all humanity's internal experience of the law.

103. Alister McGrath disagrees with this interpretation, claiming that Lewis presents an inference to the best explanation, a kind of abductive argument. See McGrath, *The Intellectual World of C. S. Lewis*, 133–37. On abduction, see Pierce, *Collected Papers*, 5:189. See also Harmon, "The Inference to the Best Explanation," 88–95.

104. Polanyi, *Science, Faith and Society*, 14. See also note 90 in McGrath, *The Intellectual World of C. S. Lewis*, 127. Lewis and Polanyi may have been acquainted through the Oxford Socratic Club where they both spoke.

Reason and experience are key in Lewis' natural theology, yet imagination plays an important role, as well, particularly in his argument from desire. The argument famously states, "If I find in myself a desire which no experience in this world can satisfy, the most probable explanation is that I was made for another world."[105] Alister McGrath argues that the desire to which Lewis points is rooted in two things in western culture: a longing for the indefinable and unattainable and a sense that God alone is the initiator and goal of human longing.[106] Lewis argues that desires in nature always have a natural means of fulfillment. "Creatures are not born with desires unless satisfaction for those desires exists. A baby feels hunger: well, there is such a thing as food. A duckling wants to swim: well, there is such a thing as water. Men feel sexual desire: well, there is such a thing as sex."[107] In the case of the desire for something beyond this world, humans long for meaning or purpose beyond their lives. They seek religious meaning, rooting themselves in grand stories which assert a teleology for the universe in general and for their individual lives in particular. This desire has echoes in Christian theological reflection in the writings of Augustine of Hippo, Gregory of Nyssa, Anselm of Canterbury, Bernard of Clairvaux, Julian of Norwich, and Blaise Pascal among others.[108] Lewis says that this desire is for a world beyond this one or Heaven, "my true country" or "that other country."[109]

This argument is a kind of abductive argument.[110] Phenomenologically, we sense an internal desire for something greater than anything pro-

105. Lewis, *Mere Christianity*, 136–37.

106. McGrath, *The Intellectual World of C. S. Lewis*, 106.

107. Lewis, *Mere Christianity*, 136.

108. McGrath, *The Intellectual World of C. S. Lewis*, 107–8. Pascal states, "All men seek happiness. There are no exceptions . . . What else does this craving, and this helplessness, proclaim but that there was once in man a true happiness, of which all that now remains is the empty print and trace? This he tries in vain to fill with everything around him, seeking in things that are not there the help he cannot find in those that are, though none can help, since this infinite abyss can be filled only with an infinite and immutable object; in other words by God himself" (148/428), in Pascal, *Pensées*, 45.

109. Lewis, *Mere Christianity*, 137.

110. McGrath, *The Intellectual World of C. S. Lewis*, 119. This interpretation is not without its challenges. Peter Kreeft, for example, interprets the argument from desire in a more deductive fashion where the conclusion is guaranteed by the truth of the premises and the validity of the argument form. While I think that McGrath's rejection of this kind of argumentation in natural theology is wrongheaded, I share his interpretation of this particular argument in Lewis. See Kreeft, "Lewis's Argument from Desire," 250.

vided by our present existence can account for or provide. This desire is best explained by the positing of the existence of another reality altogether, one beyond this present world of which we are inhabitants. Formalized, the argument appears as follows,

> Observation: I find in myself a desire which no experience in this world can satisfy.
>
> Supposal: If I were made for another world, this is what I would expect.
>
> Conclusion: The most probable explanation of this observation is that I was made for another world.[111]

This is the way in which Lewis' method for natural theology is imaginative. One considers one's experience of longing for another world and imagines the kind of reality in which that longing or desire makes the most sense. The appeal is to one's internal states and seeks to envision the kind of reality that would make these states meaningful. Lewis, of course, does not argue for this kind of abductive method. Rather, he employs the abductive and deductive methods in *Mere Christianity* to convincingly show that Christianity is the true vision of reality that best fits with human experience. Along with the inductive case made for the *Tao* in *The Abolition of Man*, Lewis commends a natural theology that continues to exert influence on Evangelical natural theology to this day.

Cornelius Van Til

Also enduring in influence is the apologetical work of Cornelius Van Til (1895–1987), a Dutch Reformed philosopher and theologian who articulated a natural theology that took the revelation of God—primarily in Scripture, but in the natural world, as well—as the starting point for a presuppositional apologetic. Van Til argues that all worldviews and philosophies have differing presuppositions which make the methods of classical apologetics untenable. Even so, the existence of God and God's revelation makes sense of the world in a way that no other set of presuppositions can. In looking at the world through the Christian set of presuppositions, one can see the truth of Christianity's claims including the existence of Christianity's God. While his style of apologetics and approach to philosophy are

---

111. McGrath, *The Intellectual World of C. S. Lewis*, 121.

fascinating, this examination of Van Til will focus on his natural theology, particularly his views on method, epistemology, and natural revelation.

First, with respect to method, Van Til argues that a neutral treatment of facts is impossible for Christians and for non-Christians.[112] Neutrality implies that one has suspended judgment on the foundational issue of the existence of God, but this means that one is opposed to this key presupposition.[113] For the Christian, the existence of the God who is immanent to his creation is prior to all analysis and reflection, yet the non-Christian's supposed neutrality toward this key background belief is actually a form of warfare against the centrality of that belief and against the God who has been ignored. This is why Van Til's method is known as presuppositionalism. All people approach analysis with certain presuppositions (commitments, background beliefs, etc.) which color their interpretation of the world. This is particularly so for Christians because they assert the starting point of the Christian God and God's revelation in Scripture as their key presuppositions. "To argue by presupposition is to indicate what are the epistemological and metaphysical principles that underlie and control one's method. The Reformed apologist will frankly admit that his own methodology presupposes the truth of Christian theism."[114] Therefore, there can be no neutral point of contact for method with the non-Christian, and not just because the Christian has her own unique starting point. The non-Christian, as well, wants to "suppress the truth in unrighteousness," using reason to deny or doubt the existence of God.[115] No one has a presupposition-less method. There is no neutral non-Christian method, for all sinners have "an axe to grind."[116] The Christian has her commitments, and the non-Christian has hers.

An appeal to "reason" is not particularly helpful either, for reason is not a neutral methodological tool. When one admits that one has presuppositions in the background, reason is shown to be a child of its parent presuppositions. Reason will be circular in this regard. "The starting point,

112. Some may object to Van Til's designations here; however, my reproduction of these terms "Christian" and "non-Christian" simply serves to do justice to the fact that Van Til's presuppositionalism implies a difference in kind in the soteriological status and methodological outlook of those who have been made regenerate by grace through faith in Christ and those who are outside the household of Christian faith.

113. Van Til, *Survey of Christian Epistemology*, 19–20.

114. Van Til, *Defense of the Faith*, 99–100.

115. Ibid., 84.

116. Ibid.

the method, and the conclusion are always involved in one another."[117] For the Christian, then, reason is a child reared by Scripture. Because God expresses God's authority in God's revelation (in the natural world, but definitively in Scripture), the Christian subordinates her use of reason to the authoritative pronouncements of Scripture.[118] In this way, reason can achieve its proper function with respect to human inquiry and divine sovereignty. Reason alone will be impotent because its use will always be colored by the presuppositions of the one who employs it. Since reason is not a valid candidate for methodology, one must affirm that there can be no agreement on method between the Christian and the non-Christian.[119]

However, one may affirm that non-Christian methodologies are deficient. Heuristically, the Christian may take up the non-Christian methodology which makes the self the "final reference point" in the universe and show that it fails.[120] An example of how one might do this kind of negative apologetic is contained in the work of A. E. Taylor, who Van Til approvingly cites. He says that the non-Christian employs reason in her scientific investigations. She believes that nature behaves in a reasonable way, that is, in accordance with natural law.

> Science has been built up all along on the basis of this principle of the "uniformity of nature," and the principle is one which science itself has no means of demonstrating. No one could possibly prove its truth to an opponent who seriously disputed it. For all attempts to produce the "evidence" for the "uniformity of nature" themselves presuppose the very principle they are intended to prove.[121]

By engaging in this kind of tentative analysis according to non-Christian presuppositions, the apologist shows that a non-Christian method ends in destroying its own foundation. Van Til goes further than this to argue that Roman Catholic and Arminian apologetical methodologies are deficient. Scholastic apologetics, originating with Thomas Aquinas, legitimizes the notion that one may look at the existence of God with a measure of neutrality to the nature of the God revealed in Scripture. Van Til argues that this also legitimizes an attitude of doubt with respect to the existence of

---

117. Ibid., 100.

118. Ibid., 108.

119. For a helpful exposition of this theme in Van Til's writing, see Bahnsen, *Van Til's Apologetic*, 144–48.

120. Ibid., 98.

121. Taylor, *Does God Exist?* 2, quoted in Van Til, *Defense of the Faith*, 103.

God. This entails that the non-Christian who is in rebellion against God is not morally responsible for her lack of belief. "Ignorance is not basically culpable."[122] Arminians can actually come to some agreement on method with the non-Christian because their "faulty" theology implies that a starting point for analysis is beyond "the control and direction of the counsel of God."[123] Humanity's moral responsibility is diminished in Roman Catholic methodology, and God's sovereignty is impugned in Arminian theology.

Even so, the Reformed Christian is not left without any reasonable criteria for analysis, especially given her commitment to the existence of the sovereign God revealed in Scripture. The method that Van Til commends he calls *transcendental*. Combining elements of deduction and induction (though rejecting their traditional philosophical applications), "a truly transcendental argument takes any fact of experience which it wishes to investigate, and tries to determine what the presuppositions of such a fact must be, in order to make it what it is."[124] The truth and meaning of any field or topic of inquiry will only be understood if the God of Scripture is presupposed. God is a kind of best explanation in Van Til's method. In fact, God's existence is the grounding for any kind of explanation at all. Indeed, this entails reasoning in a "spiral," but attempting to reason without the presupposition of God is a vicious circle that destroys reasoning altogether.[125] In reasoning this way, "true human knowledge" is that which "corresponds to the knowledge which God has of himself and his world."[126] Humans may have knowledge imperfectly or finitely, but they can know things truly as knowledge corresponds to an infinite reference point. Moreover, because God's thoughts are internally coherent, humans can have a measure of coherence insofar as the items of knowledge which humans possess are firstly possessed by God.[127] In fact, among humans, only Christians can claim to have coherence because only they have the presuppositional foundation of God in mind when making knowledge claims.

Second, Van Til articulates a uniquely Christian epistemology based on God's knowledge as the locus of any true human knowledge. The concept of God entails that God knows all things, those things about God's

122. Van Til, *The Reformed Pastor*, 12.

123. Van Til, *Defense of the Faith*, 98.

124. Van Til, *Survey of Christian Epistemology*, 10.

125. Ibid., 12.

126. Ibid., 1.

127. Ibid., 2.

self and those things beyond God, "analytically and completely."[128] Because human beings are created by God, human knowledge will always be based in God's knowledge, and any true interpretation of the universe will always be "under God," albeit never comprehensive in scope.[129] This is the only way that human inquiry is ever successful in a pragmatic sense or accurate in an objective sense. God is the source and locus of knowledge, and epistemic success is measured with respect to God's knowledge. Therefore, only God can make sense of the various features of human inquiry.[130] Since God alone knows all things completely and analytically, any human knowledge of the truth is only analogical to God's knowledge.[131] An analogical system of truth entails that human minds are only like God's mind in a (far) lesser and finite sense. The difference in kind between human comprehension of the truth and that of God is definitive, yet humans do know the truth as it is revealed by God. Therefore, it makes sense to see human knowledge of the truth as analogical to God's knowledge of the truth.[132]

Common grace has a role to play in the possibility of knowledge apart from saving grace. Those who have not been regenerate in Christ may still grasp knowledge of the natural world since the natural world does not require "the knowledge of God about salvation."[133] The Christian and the non-Christian may have common ideas about the natural world because they both share "an ineradicable sense of deity."[134] This is not a natural theology upon which both may build a doctrine of God apart from revelation; rather, their shared understanding of God, even if suppressed in the non-Christian, provides them common ideas on which to build common interpretations without vast differences. The fact that humanity is made in the image of God makes this line of thought clearer. For Van Til, the *imago dei* entails that humans were created with true, though not comprehensive, knowledge.[135] Though humanity's fall into sinfulness obscures knowledge

---

128. Van Til, *Defense of the Faith*, 40.

129. Ibid., 43.

130. Ibid., 177.

131. Ibid., 160.

132. This, of course, was the subject of the controversy between Van Til and Gordon Clark. See Frame, *Cornelius Van Til*, chapter 8.

133. Van Til, *Common Grace and the Gospel*, 143.

134. Ibid. Apart from regeneration, one cannot have an epistemology, however, that leads to truth.

135. Van Til, *Defense of the Faith*, 14.

required for salvation, "sin did not destroy any of the powers that God gave man at the beginning."[136] Humanity can still come to know the truth even though the truth about God is suppressed through sinfulness. Still, common grace limits sin's destructive nature, allowing knowledge under God to be possible. "By virtue of their creation in God's image, by virtue of the ineradicable sense of deity within them and by virtue of God's restraining general grace, those who hate God, yet in a restricted sense know God, and do good."[137] Again, though, this is an act of common grace given by God, not of natural theology whereby human beings can come to know God apart from revelation.

This brings us finally to Van Til's understanding of natural theology, which he thinks makes God subject to knowledge independent of the revelation of God. This cannot be right since God is the foundation of all knowledge. Even so, the knowledge of God is available in the natural world, not through natural theology, but through natural revelation. "For Calvin, revelation is always and everywhere clear," and this comes through Scripture and the natural world.[138] Natural revelation does not lead to positing the existence of a god as the conclusion of a syllogism, though, for God's existence revealed in nature cannot be separated from God's character. (People do not have a general awareness of deity; they have knowledge of the God of Scripture through nature even if this knowledge is suppressed by sinful humanity.) Sin leads humanity to believe that the self is the "final reference point of all predication."[139] This means that even though the knowledge of God is obvious, the non-Christian's intellect will be different in kind from the intellect of the Christian. The personal suppression of the knowledge of God changes the intellect to reject Christian arguments for the existence of God.[140] No argument will be subjectively successful to the sinful person.[141] Even so, proofs for the existence of God may have "absolute probative force," connecting with the sinful person's sense of God and bearing witness to the person of God, the self, and the world.[142] Though

136. Ibid., 159.

137. Van Til, *Introduction to Systematic Theology*, 27.

138. Van Til, *The Reformed Pastor*, 12.

139. Van Til, *Defense of the Faith*, 92.

140. Van Til, *Survey of Christian Epistemology*, 187. See also Bahnsen, *Van Til's Apologetic*, 146.

141. Van Til, *Defense of the Faith*, 104–5.

142. Ibid., 177.

the demonstrations will not be received as true, the sinful person will be charged by them to recognize the truth that is suppressed through sinful rebellion.

Van Til's notion of natural theology has staying power among key figures in Evangelical natural theology in the twentieth and twenty-first centuries. Francis Schaeffer's modified presuppositionalism was greatly influenced by Van Til's teaching and writing.[143] John Frame is a modern defender of much of the kind of apologetics that Van Til advocates, and James K. A. Smith sees some key similarities between the notion that one cannot accept the truth of Christianity through classical proofs and Derrida's claim that there is nothing outside the text.[144]

Carl F. H. Henry

In his introductory volume to Carl's Henry's *God, Revelation, and Authority*, G. Wright Doyle notes that Henry (1913–2003), while a young professor at Gordon College and PhD student at Boston University, read Cornelius Van Til's class syllabi during the summers of the late 1940s.[145] Though his approach to natural theology and apologetics is more sympathetic toward reason as a tool for connecting the claims of Christianity with those outside the household of faith, Henry is, like Van Til, essentially presuppositionalist in his doctrine of revelation and truth.[146] He claims, "God in his revelation is the first principle of Christian theology, from which all the truths of revealed religion are derived."[147] While natural theology, in the sense of humanity initiating a search for God using its own cognitive tools, is denied, Henry argues that extensive propositional and rational revelation in nature is given by God to humanity. Throughout his magisterial six-volume *God, Revelation, and Authority*, Henry argues that divine revelation (both general and special as a unity) is comprehensible by human knowers even though humanity suffers extensive limitations due to their finitude and the effects of sin.

---

143. See Schaeffer, *The God Who is There*.

144. Smith, *Who's Afraid of Postmodernism?* 50.

145. Doyle, *Carl Henry*, 5.

146. He was also greatly influenced by Gordon Clark. Thanks to Douglas Groothuis for making this connection.

147. Henry, *God, Revelation, and Authority*, 1:215.

The first four volumes of *God, Revelation, and Authority* carry the subtitle "God who speaks and shows," and this is key for understanding Henry's understanding of divine revelation and human knowledge. Any knowledge that humans have of God is because God has "reveal[ed] himself in sovereign freedom."[148] Only because God has spoken and shown God's self can humanity have knowledge of God. This affirmation of God's initiation of revelation is also a denial of human reason or natural phenomena as sources of truth about God.

> Human reason is an instrument for knowing the truth of God, but it is not the originating source of divine truth. The Bible acknowledges only God and God alone as the giver and source of divine truth . . . While the universe mirrors God's revelation, it is ontologically *other* than God and therefore cannot be the source of divine revelation.[149]

Moreover, because God speaks and shows, the revelation of God is propositional. This applies to the revelation of God in the natural world, of course, but more pointedly to God's revelation through Scripture. Henry rejects the theological non-cognitivism of neo-orthodox theologians like Emil Brunner, and in countering the non-propositional conceptualism of Schubert Ogden, he states, "The distinctive and authoritative significance of biblical concepts stems from their revelational meaning-content in the context of intelligible sentences and propositional truths."[150]

This implies that God's revelation is universally comprehensible in principle to humanity, for humanity is unique among created beings "on the receiving end of a divine initiative whereby God's self and God's plans may be known.[151] Humanity's role is passive, however, in coming to know God. It is only because God "chooses" to reveal God's self that humanity may have knowledge of the divine.[152] A key aspect of this self-revelation of God is the person of Jesus Christ. Among many other things, Jesus, the incarnate second person of the Trinity, is the Logos, and as such, is the locus of the "intuitive view of reason" presupposed by all humanity when attempting to make meaningful statements of any kind including statements

148. Ibid., 2:30.
149. Ibid., 2:73.
150. Ibid., 3:302.
151. Ibid., 2:30.
152. Ibid., 5:54.

about divine revelation.[153] The law of non-contradiction in particular is singled out by Henry as a key tool in speaking meaningfully about God's revelation, for one must assume the validity of the law in order to deny it. This means that statements about God's self-disclosure may be assessed on logical terms that are in principle accessible to all humanity.

The forms of this revelation are key to the discussion of what comprises Henry's views on natural theology. God's revelation is a unity, fully the result of God's supernatural initiative. However, this revelation takes various forms.[154] Henry rejects talk about "natural theology" because the word *natural* suggests that some of God's revelation is essentially non-supernatural and because *natural theology* implies that humanity is able to "translate" God's revelation into something meaningful.[155] Natural theology "underestimates the epistemic predicament of finite man," and fails to account for humanity's fallenness.[156] Rather, Henry prefers to speak of God's revelation as both general and special. Special revelation consists primarily of the person of Jesus Christ and the Scriptures, and general revelation, of particular interest for this study, includes a basic awareness of God's existence and character and of one's moral responsibility to God.[157] Humanity may have different concepts of God, yet God's unique existence and character are known through general revelation. He cites Psalm 19; John 1:4, 9; Acts 14:17; 17:26–28; and Romans 1:18–20, 28–32; 2:14–16 as texts which affirm that truth about God has been revealed by God and unmistakably known by humanity, truth for which humanity is accountable to God.[158] This truth about God extends to God's acts in history, as well. "God reveals himself not only universally in the history of the cosmos and of the nations, but also redemptively within this external history in unique saving acts."[159] This revelation is both general and special, in history of the cosmos and in the history of God's redemption recorded in Scripture. While studying history is subject to the limitations of all empirical investigations, history as an

---

153. Ibid., 3:229.

154. Ibid., 2:73.

155. Ibid., 2:86.

156. Ibid., 2:122.

157. Doyle, *Carl Henry*, 56. See also Henry, *God, Revelation, and Authority*, 2:83, 130.

158. Henry, *God, Revelation, and Authority*, 2:83.

159. Ibid., 2:247.

element of God's revelation is still useful for apologetic purposes. Still, "the living God has revealed himself in ordinary 'secular' history."[160]

The key question, however, of humanity's ability to respond to this revelation remains. Humanity is sinful and suppresses the truth of God's revelation. Doyle summarizes Henry's position well when he indicates that God enables humanity to understand revelation because that communication is "given in words that his Logos makes possible and our creation in his image makes intelligible. He is able to transcend our finiteness as well as our fallenness" to reach us with the truth.[161] The human side of the reception of revelation begins with the fact that humanity is created in the image of God. While not possessing any attributes with "the prefatory *omni-* appropriate only to all of God's perfections," humanity does reflect key features of the personal and intellectual life ("in a qualified way") that God enjoys.[162] Humanity is rational, moral, self-transcendent, and able to exercise some kind of authentic will. "The divine image, a cohesive unit of interrelated components that interact with and condition each other, includes rational, moral and spiritual aspects of both a formal and material nature."[163] Because of this, humanity knows that the God revealed in nature and Scripture is the true God and that humanity is morally accountable before God. God's propositional revelation is therefore accessible to humanity because being made in the image of God includes a capacity to cognitize revelation in language.[164]

Even though humanity has fallen into sin, the formal and material image of God remains, yet humanity has indeed suffered a "catastrophic personality shock" in the fall.[165] Humanity has rebelled against God, and this rebellion has devastated every aspect of humanity's mental, spiritual, and physical life. Even so, this does not result in humanity's inability to know the contents of general revelation. God's existence is still known to humanity through the *imago*, and humanity's sense of moral responsibility remains. Humanity is still able to reason rightly, as well. "Calvin insists

---

160. Ibid.,

161. Doyle, *Carl Henry*, 61.

162. Henry, *God, Revelation, and Authority*, 2:134.

163. Ibid., 2:125.

164. Ibid., 3:346.

165. Ibid., 2:134. The formal image for Henry is something akin to similarity in attributes but without the omni- prefix. The material image is primarily humanity's "rational competence" and "ethical accountability," 2:136.

that man's universal sense of divinity embraces the knowledge that God exists."[166] Even something of the moral law is known, as well, through God's general revelation received by the unregenerate *imago* in humanity, extending to knowledge of the Ten Commandments.[167] The fall is still catastrophic, though. All actions and attitudes in unregenerate humanity are marred by sin. This includes philosophical speculation and other aspects of the intellectual life. Yet logic ("the laws of valid inference [and] the law of noncontradiction"[168]) is unaffected, and true propositions are still true though human application of these cognitive tools may be sinful.

This has important consequences for the traditional application of natural theology in the realm of evangelism and apologetics. Because of the fall, the regenerate person does not share any epistemological axioms in common with the unregenerate person. Christian theism is a comprehensive worldview for Henry, meaning that "Christian axioms and theorems derive from divine disclosure, and not from cosmological, anthropological or historical considerations based on empirical investigation" to which a non-Christian worldview may appeal.[169] However, the intact divine image in all humanity ensures that the regenerate person and the unregenerate person are still able to exercise a rational ability with respect to generic notions of divinity and morality. This means that non-Christian religious and philosophical positions may be truth-bearing, albeit in a limited sense, "The *imago*-content is reduced, distorted and even falsified as it is incorporated into conjectural philosophical and religious perspectives, yet it is never wholly eradicated."[170] Therefore, reaching out to the unbeliever in evangelistic apologetics may have some success. Though Henry's approach toward general revelation is essentially presuppositionalist ("God in his revelation is the first principle of Christian theology, from which all the truths of revealed religion are derived."[171]), he is willing to use some traditional tools of evidentialist apologetics like defending the "factual redemptive history" as recorded in the Bible to show that Christianity is a rational worldview.[172] While he does not think that the traditional Thomist proofs for God suc-

---

166. Ibid., 2:136.

167. Ibid., 2:137.

168. Ibid., 2:135–36.

169. Ibid., 1:396.

170. Ibid., 1:406.

171. Ibid., 1: 215.

172. Ibid., 2:321.

ceed, he leaves open the door to use reason as a tool in apologetics even in making an appeal for the existence of God. *God, Revelation, and Authority* is a massive and impressive work. Henry's influence extended to peers like Billy Graham, but persists today among Evangelical apologists like Douglas Groothuis and William Lane Craig.

William Lane Craig

Perhaps one of the most well-known evangelical apologists and philosophers of religion working today is the Biola University professor William Lane Craig (1949–). Craig champions a classical approach to apologetics whereby one seeks to show that Christianity is true by arguing for the existence of God and then for key features of Christian doctrine like the resurrection of Jesus Christ. His approach is unique from others considered in this study because he weds his natural theology with an Arminian soteriology so that the unbeliever may be convinced of the truth of Christian theism primarily through the authenticating power of the Holy Spirit, but also through reason. His distinction between how one knows that Christianity is true and how one may show Christianity to be true is a unique contribution to religious epistemology, and his version of the *kalām* cosmological argument is one of the most important arguments employed by Evangelicals doing natural theology today.

Craig's religious epistemology is a unique contribution to discussions of natural theology in that it distinguishes how one knows that Christianity is true (primarily through the work of the Holy Spirit, though reason may serve a supporting role) and how one may show that Christianity is true (through logic forms of argumentation, probabilistic reasoning, and appeals to common ground).[173] In explaining how one may know that Christianity is true, Craig makes a distinction between how knowledge is attainable for the believer and for the unbeliever. Craig argues that because the believer is indwelt by the Holy Spirit through regeneration, God's internal presence authenticates for the believer several truths. He appeals to Paul's use of the term "*plerophoria* (complete confidence, full assurance) to indicate that the believer has knowledge of the truth as a result of the Spirit's work (Col 2:2; 1 Thess 1:5; cr. Rom 4:21; 14:5; Col 4:12)."[174] This confidence or assurance of one's salvation entails other truths of which the believer has knowledge

173. Craig, *Reasonable Faith*, 43.

174. Ibid., 44.

by the Holy Spirit including God's forgiveness and reconciliation. "For the believer, God is not the conclusion of a syllogism; he is the living God of Abraham, Isaac, and Jacob dwelling within us."[175] Though the Holy Spirit's role is primary, the believer may appeal to arguments for God's existence and other evidence of the truth of Christianity as support. Natural theology can strengthen one's assurance by addressing one's questions and doubts, yet natural theology does not serve "properly [as] the basis of faith."[176]

The situation is somewhat similar for the unbeliever, for the unbeliever may only know that Christianity is true by the Holy Spirit's influence. Craig appeals to John 16:7–11, which he claims shows that the Holy Spirit "convicts the unbeliever of his own sin, of God's righteousness, and of his condemnation before God. The unbeliever so convicted can therefore be said to know such truths as 'God exists,' 'I am guilty before God,' and so forth."[177] In addition to this kind of conviction, the Holy Spirit also draws the unbeliever to God (John 6:44). Knowledge is then the result of a personal encounter with the Holy Spirit through the Spirit's authenticating agency in the unbeliever's inner life. Because the Holy Spirit's role is fundamental in knowing Christianity to be true, reason and argumentation play a subsidiary role in how an unbeliever may know Christianity to be true. He appreciates Martin Luther's distinction between the magisterial and the ministerial uses of reason. "The *magisterial* use of reason occurs when reason stands over and above the gospel like a magistrate and judges it on the basis of argument and evidence. The *ministerial* use of reason occurs when reason submits to and serves the gospel."[178] Natural theology and other evidence for the truth of Christianity can provide warrant for Christian belief, but the individual who knows Christianity to be true is warranted in her belief without natural theology and other evidence. The upside of having additional warrant beyond the Holy's Spirit's authentication is that with natural theology and other evidences, one may have "dual warrant of one's Christian beliefs."[179] This can increase one's confidence and willingness in making the decision to receive the gift of salvation or to bear witness to others regarding the truth of Christianity.

---

175. Ibid., 46.

176. Ibid.

177. Ibid.

178. Ibid., 47. Of course, Luther did not endorse natural theology.

179. Ibid., 48.

The other side of Craig's religious epistemology addresses how one may show Christianity to be true. Classical apologetics (argument and evidence) serves a key role. He considers William Alston's case of a Christian who encounters an adherent of another religion, both of whom claim to have had a self-authenticating experience.[180] In this case, God may use argument and evidence to "crack [the non-Christian's] false assurance of the truth of his faith and persuade him to place his faith in Christ."[181] This is still achieved by God's grace, but the vehicles are the argumentation and appeal to evidence. In this spirit, Craig defends the use of logical argumentation such as deduction, induction, and the more specific form of induction known as inference to the best explanation.[182] Though not unassailable, these forms of logical argumentation may serve to support the truth of Christianity's truth claims. In fact, Craig argues that the success of these forms of argumentation may still be ensured if they function not as pure demonstrations, but as probabilistic accounts of religious truth. "Certainty is an unrealistic and unattainable ideal . . . What we're looking for is a comparative criterion: the premises in a good argument will have greater plausibility than their respective denials."[183] How an unbeliever receives this kind of probabilistic argumentation may be person-dependent; however, this is simply an opportunity to examine one's argument alongside the unbeliever to either alter the argument or to persuade the unbeliever of the plausibility of the argument's premises. Good arguments, then, will include the appeal to facts to which all parties may reasonably agree such as the laws of logic or common experiences.[184] This does not challenge the primacy of the Holy Spirit in how one may come to know that Christianity is true, though, for "the Holy Spirit may use our arguments to draw people to himself."[185] Again, reason may support someone's knowledge that Christianity is true while the Holy Spirit's internal witness is the fundamental warrant for Christian belief.

Arguments based in natural theology form an important part of Craig's apologetic. Before examining his most well-known contribution to apologetics, the *kalām* cosmological argument, it is important to establish

---

180. See Alston, "Religious Diversity," 433–48.

181. Craig, *Reasonable Faith*, 52.

182. Ibid., 52–54.

183. Ibid., 55.

184. Ibid., 56–57.

185. Ibid., 57.

how arguments like *kalām* fit into Craig's natural theology. Natural theology is "the branch of theology that seeks to prove God's existence apart from the resources of authoritative divine revelation."[186] This includes cosmological arguments like Leibniz's cosmological argument or the *kalām* cosmological argument, teleological arguments like fine-tuning inferences or arguments from design, axiological arguments like various forms of the moral argument, and ontological arguments.[187] These arguments support Christians' belief that God exists and that God has revealed God's self in nature. Craig finds support for natural theology in didactic biblical passages like Romans 1:18–20, but also in the example of the apostles who "appealed to God's handiwork in nature as evidence of the existence of the Creator (Acts 14:17)" in evangelism to the Gentiles.[188]

Craig makes this kind of appeal to nature in his influential *kalām* cosmological argument, so called because some of its most talented early defenders were Arabic philosophers who lived between the ninth and twelfth centuries of the Common Era.[189] Cosmological arguments "seek to demonstrate a Sufficient Reason or a First Cause of the existence of the cosmos."[190] It is a simple appeal to natural truths, but Craig defends it with philosophical appeals to mathematics and logic and to empirical appeals to big bang cosmology. This is Craig's formulation:

1. Everything that begins to exist has a cause of its existence.

2. The universe began to exist.

3. Therefore the universe has a cause of its existence.[191]

The bulk of his argumentation is concerned with defending the plausibility of the second premise, for which he appeals to philosophical arguments and empirical confirmations.

The key issue regarding the second premise is the conceivability that the universe is of infinite age. Craig labors to show that this cannot be the case. First, he argues for the impossibility of the existence of an actual infinite, "a determinate whole actually possessing an infinite number of

---

186. Moreland and Craig, *Philosophical Foundations*, 464–5.

187. See Ibid., 463–500.

188. Craig, *Reasonable Faith*, 22.

189. See Craig, *The Kalām Cosmological Argument*. Part I illustrates how the argument was formulated by al-Kindi, Saadia, and al-Ghāzāli.

190. Moreland and Craig, *Philosophical Foundations*, 465.

191. Craig, *The Kalām Cosmological Argument*, 63.

members."[192] A possible defeater for Craig's denial is Cantorian set theory, a mathematical postulation that deals with actual infinites. However, Cantorian sets apply only to an abstract mathematical world, and statements about Cantorian sets "do not imply existence in the extra-mental world" of actual sets of infinite members.[193] Cantor enables us to speak meaningfully of abstract mathematical sets, but not of real-world infinite sets. Craig illustrates this by positing the existence of a library with an actually infinite collection of shelved books equally divided between red and black books. He says, "Would we believe someone who told us that the number of red books in the library is the same as the number of red books *plus* the number of black books?"[194] The red books are half of the actually infinite set, yet they still form an actually infinite set of their own, but this is absurd.[195] Second, Craig argues against the possibility of forming an actual infinite set by successive addition. This is so because if one were to attempt to form an actual infinite in this way, one could always add one more member to the set.[196] In addition, Zeno's paradoxes illustrate the absurdities of forming an actually infinite set, and Kant's first antimony shows that "the present event could never arise if the temporal series of past events were infinite."[197]

Craig further argues for his second premise through two empirical confirmations. First, he argues that the universe is expanding, which implies that if one extrapolates the current expansion of the universe into the past, the obvious conclusion is that "we come to a point in time at which *the entire known universe was contracted into an arbitrarily great density . . .* [and] one reaches a state of contraction of *infinite* density."[198] This is why scientists explain the beginning of the universe by appealing to a "big bang." This theory is supported by Hubble's confirmation of the redshift effect, which shows that the universe is expanding isotropically.[199] It is further confirmed by Penzias' and Wilson's discovery of microwave background radiation which permeates the universe isotropically, supporting "the conclusion

192. Ibid., 69.

193. Ibid., 70.

194. Ibid., 83.

195. He also appeals to the famous thought experiment of Hilbert's Hotel. See Gamow, *One, Two, Three*, 17.

196. Craig, *The Kalām Cosmological Argument*, 109.

197. Ibid. See also pages 175–205.

198. Ibid., 113.

199. Ibid., 111–12.

that this cosmic radiation is indeed the relic of an early era of the universe in which the universe was very hot and very dense."[200] The infinite density required by big bang cosmology further implies that the universe came into existence out of nothing since infinite density is, in effect, nothing.[201] The second empirical confirmation of the second premise is the argument from the second law of thermodynamics, which Craig states as "spontaneously proceeding processes in closed systems are always attended by an increase in entropy."[202] This means that the universe's processes will eventually run down, and all of its energy will be evenly distributed. If the universe were to be of infinite age, then it would have already achieved this kind of heat death. Since the universe has not achieved heat death, then the universe is not of infinite age, and it began to exist at some point in the finite past. The cause of the beginning must be uncaused since an infinite number of causes is impossible. The cause must be powerful and outside of space and time. The cause must be personal, as well, because the cause is free to cause the universe's coming into existence. God is the cause of the universe's beginning to exist. Craig claims that this argument is successful. Its premises are highly plausible, and the conclusion follows from the premises in a proper deductive form.

This kind of natural theology forms an important part of the texture of Evangelical natural theology today. What is suspect about this approach in many Evangelical rejections of natural theology is informed by a larger conversation about postmodern philosophy and theology, the subjects to which we now turn.

POSTMODERN PHILOSOPHY

The approach that James K. A. Smith, Carl A. Raschke, and Myron B. Penner generally take in their rejections of natural theology is greatly informed by their commitments to the insights of twentieth century postmodern critiques of propositional and representational theories of language and denials of epistemic neutrality and objectivity. Since their work draws primarily on the philosophies of Jacques Derrida, Jean-François Lyotard, and Michel Foucault, it is fitting to briefly outline their work, focusing on that which is key for Smith's, Raschke's, and Penner's critiques.

200. Ibid., 114–15.

201. Ibid., 116.

202. Ibid., 131.

Jacques Derrida

The Algerian-born French philosopher Jacques Derrida (1930–2004) initiated a strategy of deconstruction of literary and philosophical texts and attempted to criticize and undermine Western philosophical metaphysics and theories of truth and meaning. His primary contributions to our study on postmodern Evangelical rejections of natural theology are in his philosophy of language, which seeks to undermine representational theories of meaning and to highlight the undecidability of texts with respect to meaning, and his deconstruction of the concept of truth with respect to traditional Western accounts of knowledge. First, Derrida's philosophy of language engages and challenges a traditional, perhaps even a commonsense, version of how language relates to concepts. There is the original act of writing, which he calls "the trace" or the signifier, and there is the thought or concept existing in the writer's mind, which he calls "the (pure) trace" or the signified.[203] However, this pure trace does not actually exist; rather, its non-presence is a condition for meaningful discourse. He calls this non-presence *différance*, a deliberate misspelling of the French word. "There cannot be a science of the origin of presence itself, that is to say of a certain nonorigin."[204] There is no concept that is accurately represented in writing or in speech. In addition, philosophical concepts typically trade in the categories of all or nothing, yes and no. There is a certain antithesis or "oppositional logic" in the meaning of normal philosophical discourse.[205] However, *différance* is Derrida's attempt to deconstruct the concept of the concept, "changing the rules" so that the concept of the concept may be idealized. *Différance* allows the written concept to remain legible, and therefore iterable or repeatable, so that the writing itself is no longer "an (ontological) modification of presence" of the addressee.[206] Here is the point: the addressee is not present in the original event of writing.

Furthermore, there is no metaphysical or transcendental place in which the concept resides. Derrida famously declares, "*There is nothing outside the text.*"[207] The context that makes any text meaningful is lost to us

---

203. Derrida, *Of Grammatology*, 61. Both "signifier" and "signified" are of Saussurian provenance.

204. Ibid., 63.

205. Derrida, "Afterword," 117.

206. Derrida, "Signature Event Context," 315.

207. Derrida, *Of Grammatology*, 158. Emphasis in the original.

as soon as the original trace is produced. The natural presence of original context has disappeared. This is a natural limitation inherent in all speech and writing, one that denies the metaphysics of meaning primarily because the original presence of the concept exists in a contextual schema of which the thinker may not even be fully aware, and which is unavailable to the reader. Thus, Derrida continues,

> There has never been anything but writing; there have never been anything but supplements, substitutive significations which could only come forth in a chain of differential references, the "real" supervening, and being added only while taking on meaning from a trace and from an invocation of the supple-ment, etc. And thus to infinity.[208]

With the act of writing, or speaking, the original natural presence of the concept is lost to us, and the links between signifiers from the original text to any interpretation are contingent and fallible. Thus, the reception of a text is an act of deconstruction of meaning that never arrives at the pure trace.

This is why the issue of context is vital because context both limits and opens the horizons of meaning. All texts originate in a system of writing, the linguistic conventions for "a determined system" in which the writer attempts to signify a given project.[209] However, one's attempt to reconstruct that linguistic context is doomed by "the disappearance of natural presence," the moment and linguistic horizon in which the signifiers have taken shape.[210] Derrida's reflection on context entails insurmountable limits for sharing and reconstructing linguistic contexts. While the context of production is fixed in the reader's imagination, the contexts of destination or reception are always changing.[211] The trouble (or opportunity) that this creates for the reception of texts is that any given text may be cited or quoted—Derrida calls this iterability—marking a break from the initial context which gave shape to the mark. Each new citation or iteration means a new context in which the mark may find new meaning. This is not to be mourned; rather, it is simply a feature of every text. In fact, this feature of texts is something to be celebrated, for texts only find meaning in the

208. Ibid., 159.
209. Ibid.
210. Ibid.
211. See Derrida, "Afterword," 111–12.

new contexts in which their iterations find a home.[212] Even the concept of *communication* lacks a determinate content, for it involves any number of linguistic and non-linguistic domains which are determined by context.[213]

There is an element of this analysis that is frustrating for the reader, for iterability presents a definitive limit on one's ability to understand a transcendent meaning in any text. One may respond to this limit by attempting to seek consensus from a community to make determinations or interpretations of any given text that could converge on this transcendent meaning. However, this very act of intending to converge on consensus is "actively interpretive and can therefore open the way to all sorts of strategic ruses in order to have constructions pass as evidences or as constative observations."[214] As serious as this difficulty is for collaborative reading and interpretation, the community is still the best tool for any meaningful discourse on a text, for the community sets its own standard for debate and interpretation based on its own semantic, linguistic, cultural, or academic standards.[215] Only minimal consensus is necessary for any meaningful discussion.

Second, Derrida's focus on context and iterability leads to an important interpretive method based on his notion of *différance*. Derrida deconstructs the concept of the concept, and in doing so makes writing and reading and meaning possible. "*Différance* is not indeterminacy. It renders determinacy both possible and necessary . . . it never comes to a full stop anywhere."[216] This *différance* frustrates the logic of opposition. Then, the iterability of the writing or the speech act makes possible again the logic of opposition that gives rise to meaning, allowing one to push through the inaccessibility of intention to arrive at genuine interpretation and insight. This whole process is summed up in the term *deconstruction*. Western philosophy has typically privileged speech and oppositional logic, but deconstruction upends and critically legitimates speech and writing, logic and absurdity. Deconstruction is a method of "inhabiting those structures" of Western philosophy, "borrowing all the strategic and economic resources of subversion from the

212. See Derrida, "Signature Event Context," 320–21.

213. Ibid., 309.

214. Derrida, "Afterword," 146.

215. For example, Derrida writes "whatever the disagreements between Searle and myself may have been, for instance, no one doubted that I had understood at least the English grammar and vocabulary of his sentences," in ibid., 146. In this case, contemporary standards of English language set the limits for debates on interpretation.

216. Ibid., 149.

old structure."[217] The result is a "doubling commentary," a way of making texts intelligible while reducing the risks that traditional interpretive methods pose to them.[218] This allows consensus within an interpretive community to develop without doing violence to the text. This stabilizes the work of reading and hearing texts so that one's interpretation is not minimized by the prevailing power structures and politics of interpretation that arise in Western society. This stability also ensures that one's readings do not lapse into relativism or nihilism, for these do not seek consensus, but only destruction.[219]

The implications for Derrida's method are global; all of philosophy is subject to the analyses of deconstruction and *différance*.[220] This is also the case for philosophical theology in general and natural theology in particular. Deconstruction may be applied to items which are traditionally vital to natural theology: concepts such as truth, neutrality, faith, and knowledge and to the philosophical branches of logic and metaphysics. Regarding logic, Derrida legitimates binary or oppositional forms of logic. This is the logic of either/or (such as the law of noncontradiction [P is not non-P.] and the law of the excluded middle [Either P or non-P.]). Derrida claims that he does not oppose this logic. However, he wishes to supplement it with another discourse which "takes into account the conditions of this classical and binary logic, but it no longer depends entirely upon it."[221] This amounts to a kind of critical transcendence of traditional logic which supplements and supplants logic while remaining subject to its own deconstruction. Objectivity and neutrality, too, are subject to deconstruction. Derrida argues that scientific objectivity is valid "in a given situation," yet neutrality and objectivity are not possible in every context.[222] While it is common sense that the individual lacks absolute neutrality and objectivity, Derrida challenges whether one can be neutral or objective in any given context. The truth-seeker's optimism should be challenged (or at least, qualified) by deconstruction. Writing is not a "decoding of a meaning or truth," and

217. Derrida, *Of Grammatology*, 24.

218. Derrida, "Afterword," 146.

219. Derrida borrows *destruction* from Heidegger and reappropriates the concept as *deconstruction*.

220. Even deconstruction itself would be subject to its own critique. "The enterprise of deconstruction always in a certain way falls prey to its own work." See *Of Grammatology*, 24.

221. Derrida, "Afterword," 117.

222. Ibid., 136.

deconstruction overturns "the exchange of intentions and meanings" that can be evaluated in terms of accuracy and truthfulness.[223] This seems to cast doubt on writing's ability to convey truth, yet Derrida qualifies his account of truth by claiming that there are true and false interpretations of texts which are aided by "rules of competence, criteria of discussion and of consensus, good faith, lucidity, rigor, criticism, and pedagogy."[224] He claims that it is false that the deconstructionist argues that there is no such thing as truth. Instead, Derrida deconstructs truth away from the metaphysics of correspondence toward more pragmatic considerations that are gauged by consensus-building.

Even revelation, a concept vital to Evangelical conceptions of natural theology, is subject to a linguistic critique that shows that it is only properly understood in a complex nexus of social relations. With religion, "what is at stake is language . . . an idiom which is inseparable from the social nexus, the political, familial, ethnic, communitarian nexus, from the nation and from the people."[225] This language is untranslatable to those outside the community. Faith is not an objective assurance, but a pragmatic relationship. Moreover, the pledge of faith is a performative act, not a communication of one's assent to an idea. The language of religion (such as the names of God) is not something that is merely known and confessed, but something that is practiced.[226] This means that confessions of faith are not merely propositional; they are active and relational. Even more, belief in the existence of God is more than just agreement with the conclusion of a philosophical syllogism, for the God of revelation is not to the God of the philosophers. This means that ontotheology is an illegitimate project. "Ontotheology encrypts faith and destines it to the condition of a sort of Spanish Marrano who would have lost—in truth, dispersed, multiplied—everything up to and including the memory of his unique secret."[227] Any philosophical reasoning which arrives at a ground of being or Being will do violence to faith, reducing the divine to a proposition or a metaphysical speculation. Derrida's works are many, and his commentary is extensive on many issues, yet this summary has briefly encapsulated key themes

---

223. Derrida, "Signature Event Context," 329. Derrida seems to have in mind here something like truth as correspondence.

224. Derrida, "Afterword," 146.

225. Derrida, *Acts of Religion*, 44.

226. Ibid., 46.

227. Ibid., 100.

that remain important for the intersection of postmodern philosophy and Evangelical natural theology.

Jean-François Lyotard

A second key figure in postmodern philosophy is the French philosopher and sociologist Jean-François Lyotard. A contemporary of Derrida and Foucault, Lyotard's most important contribution to the Evangelical critique of natural theology comes in his influential *The Postmodern Condition: A Report on Knowledge*, an essay commissioned by the government of Quebec and submitted to the *Conseil des universités du Québec*. While it is unclear to what extent Lyotard stood by his evaluations and prescriptions in *The Postmodern Condition*, the work remains influential for its suspicion of metanarratives and its discussions on legitimation, narrativity, and pragmatism with respect to knowledge. While not attempting a comprehensive summary of this book, this review will focus on these themes.

Lyotard defines the term *postmodern* as "incredulity toward metanarratives."[228] A metanarrative (*grand reçit*) is any attempt to unify or totalize discourses or inquiries by appeal to human progress, the teleology of the Hegelian Spirit, or anything else. "The grand narrative has lost its credibility, regardless of what mode of unification it uses."[229] Science has been a primary way to attempt to unify narratives if only by privileging its own status as a master discourse at the expense of any other narratives, for "scientific knowledge requires that one language game, denotation, be retained and all others excluded."[230] This minimizes narratives for any number of other inquiries outside the sciences: ethics, etiologies, folk psychologies, origin stories, etc. because they do not operate according to the same game rules as science such as verification and falsification. Against this, Lyotard argues that science has lost its preeminence in postmodernity. It is no longer the locus of a single vision for truth and meaning. In fact, "postmodern science . . . is theorizing its own evolution as discontinuous, catastrophic, nonrectifiable, and paradoxical."[231] It is this skepticism or incredulity to grand narratives like a unified vision of reality as told by

228. Lyotard, *The Postmodern Condition*, xxiv.

229. Ibid., 37.

230. Ibid., 25. This discussion of language games is indebted to Wittgenstein, *Philosophical Investigations*.

231. Ibid., 60.

science that marks the postmodern off from the modern. People simply do not see the world in the manner in which a modernistic science would paint it. Rather, they see the world for its complexity and paradoxicality. Lyotard sees this same suspicion in art history, as well, as part of "the modern." Cezanne challenged the Impressionists. Picasso challenges Cezanne. Duchamp breaks with cubism. "All that has been received, if only yesterday . . . must be suspected."[232] The postmodern is really just a nascent form of the modern, a condition that brings rupture or struggle against prevailing rules and standards. This is why Lyotard refers to the postmodern as a condition; people are now doubtful of any attempt to unify or standardize discourses by reference to an overarching principle or idea.

The attempt to unify into a grand narrative is really an attempt at legitimation of one language game over others, to bring all games into a master discourse that effectively governs all of the rules. However, the grand narratives of the past held within themselves the seeds of their own delegitimation. Consider the "Hegelian speculative narrative," where knowledge is only attained when the subjects of inquiry legitimate themselves through a second-level discourse. According to this paradigm, "Positive science is not a form of knowledge. And speculation feeds on its suppression. The Hegelian speculative narrative thus harbors a certain skepticism toward positive learning, as Hegel himself admits."[233] In its place, some thinkers like Habermas have suggested the notion of consensus as a social form of legitimation. However, consensus is just another attempt to unify discourses, and this is precisely what a plurality of language games seems to undermine. When the rules are heterogeneous and the games are manifold, there can be no successful attempt to unify under the aegis of consensus. Moreover, the history of science shows that science thrives not on consensus, but on agonistics. "This double observation (the heterogeneity of the rules and the search for dissent) destroys a belief that still underlies Habermas's research."[234] Consensus is no longer required under the postmodern condition, nor is it possible. Lyotard suggests that paralogy is our only recourse. Many *pétits récits* are necessary to allow the work of science to advance pragmatically.[235] Many scientific methods and non-scientific narratives fuel innovation and research, leading to breakthroughs that move knowledge forward.

232. Ibid., 79.
233. Ibid., 38. Lyotard refers in his notes to the preface to the *Phenomenology of Spirit*.
234. Ibid., 66.
235. Ibid., 60.

For Lyotard, knowledge is a matter of the pragmatic. Knowledge is much more than the denotative statements that comprise the corpus of scientific knowledge. "It includes notions of 'know-how,' 'knowing how to live,' 'how to listen.'"[236] It goes beyond the criterion of correspondence to reality of a justified, true belief that can be propositioned in a denotative statement. It goes beyond the "criterion of truth, extending to the determination and application of criteria of efficiency."[237] More broadly, all language games are played according to their ability to perform. Language games, according to Lyotard, belong to the "domain of a general agonistics."[238] This does not mean that all games should be seen as oriented toward conflict, but oriented toward a feeling of success in the speaker. This thought—that language games are part of agonistics—underscores that the language games in which our knowledge claims are articulated are played to accomplish something that brings success to the speaker. This leaves the concept of truth as a dynamic equivalent of concepts like wealth and efficiency.[239] Knowing the truth is a matter of pragmatic benefit, not of the correspondence of one's thoughts or statements to the nature of reality. The pragmatic principle is key to legitimation, as well, for linguistic practices in a given game are what provide the only legitimation that the game requires. The participants play their game because the game works according to the domain of agonistics. The games are self-legitimizing. This is precisely how science has *worked*. Science provides a framework (a set of rules like the scientific method or methods, the criterion of falsifiability, etc.) that helps its participants (those who play the game, namely, scientists) to accomplish things in keeping with their feelings of success.

The problem of modernity, according to Lyotard, is that scientific knowledge has been privileged as representing the totality of knowledge. Even if scientific statements are not seen to exhaust all knowledge, then all other knowledge claims (and their respective games) are legitimized only with respect to what scientific consensus dictates. In contrast to this, Lyotard argues that narrative knowledge has always existed alongside scientific knowledge. Narrative knowledge is superior to scientific knowledge with respect to its relation to "ideas of internal equilibrium and conviviality."[240]

236. Ibid., 18.
237. Ibid.
238. Ibid., 10.
239. Ibid., 45.
240. Ibid., 7.

Narrative knowledge provides internal strength to communities. It conveys authority on its recipients simply by virtue of its reception. Moreover, narrative knowledge is useful in many different language games:

> Denotative statements concerning, for example, the state of the sky and the flora and fauna easily slip in; so do deontic statements prescribing what should be done with respect to these same referents, or with respect to kinship, the differences between the sexes, children, neighbors, foreigners, etc. Interrogative statements are implied, for example, in episodes involving challenges (respond to a question, choose one from a number of things).[241]

Narration works in many social and cultural settings, and it is vital for the scientist. Lyotard agrees with P. B. Medawar that "a scientist is before anything else a person who 'tells stories.'"[242] The scientific method or the criterion of consensus are defended in games that are telling a story about the efficiency of the scientific approach. Science's legitimation by narration should not be surprising since knowledge claims trade in stories that are not evaluated for their correspondence to reality, but for their ability to perform. It follows, then, that science should not look down on narrative forms of knowledge. The stories that science tells and that non-scientific knowledges tell are oriented toward different performative outcomes. We should not judge narrative knowledge based on scientific knowledge; rather, "all we can do is gaze in wonderment at the diversity of discursive species, just as we do at the diversity of plant or animal species."[243] Narration, then, is one enduring aspect of human behavior, one not to be subsumed into a larger story, but one that is inherently diverse and to be celebrated.

Michel Foucault

A celebratory tone is certainly missing from Michel Foucault's (1926–1984) cutting critique of modernity's obsession with knowledge and truth. A French sociologist, philosopher, and historian, Foucault's contribution to the current discussion of postmodern philosophy is a Nietzschean deconstruction of modernity's idols. He targets, in particular, the notion of disinterested or objective knowledge, arguing that what is called knowledge is

241. Ibid., 20.

242. Ibid., 60. Lyotard references Medawar, *Art of the Soluble*, 116.

243. Ibid., 26.

inherently tied to systems of domination. He argues that truth is the result not of diligent inquiry or scientific methods, but of politics. He also rejects metaphysics. Like those of Lyotard and Derrida, Foucault's contributions to postmodern philosophy comprise important insights for the postmodern Evangelical rejection of natural theology.[244]

Against the epistemic optimism which would view the items of inquiry as discoverable through diligent methodologies yielding unadulterated and disinterested truth that he perceives in Enlightenment accounts of knowledge, Foucault argues that the beliefs that are known as "knowledge" are intimately tied to power relationships and systems of control. In his famous history of prisons, *Discipline and Punish: The Birth of the Prison*, he claims that "there is no power relation without the correlative constitution of a field of knowledge, nor any knowledge that does not presuppose and constitute at the same time power relations."[245] He is saying that when you see exertions of power and control, these will be attended and exercised through knowledge claims. Conversely, knowledge claims are always made in a context of power relations. Falling short of identifying knowledge with power, Foucault argues that the link between the two is a matter of necessity. Knowledge never appears for knowledge's sake. "It is not the activity of the subject of knowledge that produces a corpus of knowledge, useful or resistant to power, but power-knowledge, the processes and struggles that traverse it and of which it is made up, that determines the forms and possible domains of knowledge."[246] Knowledge of reality is not a matter of receiving and recognizing objective states of affairs. Rather, power "produces reality; it produces domains of objects and rituals of truth."[247] This means that systems of domination and control are inexorably woven throughout all forms of inquiry. Key systems in *Discipline and Punish* for Foucault are the penal and judicial systems. These systems involve a tradition of how to use words like truth, evidence, proof, and guilt with the purpose of maintaining their attendant power systems (political, economic, religious or otherwise). All these terms "have an operational function," not a detached or objective one, within the larger system of influence and control.[248] Progress, the Enlightenment, civilization, and modernity have not freed humanity of its systems

244. See chapters 3 and 4 for how this is so.

245. Foucault, *Discipline and Punish*, 27.

246. Ibid., 28.

247. Ibid., 194.

248. Ibid., 36.

of penal and judicial domination cloaked in knowledge. To the contrary, "the truth-power relation remains at the heart of all mechanisms of punishment," even those found in modern liberal democracies.[249]

In a similar way, truth is not the result of detached and objective inquiry into states of affairs in reality. The targeted Enlightenment notion is that truth is something that someone may obtain by applying a clear and distinct method of reasoning to discover facts about the world. However, Foucault argues that "truth isn't the reward of free spirits, the child of protracted solitude, nor the privilege of those who have succeeded in liberating themselves."[250] Rather, Foucault advances a theory of the political pragmatics of truth. The truth is a matter of which discourses society allows. The methods, language, and arenas of inquiry are the boundary markers that form what is acceptable to a given society. In Western society, truth is a matter of "the form of the scientific discourse and the institutions which produce it," but it could have been otherwise.[251] Therefore, any inquiries that fall outside of this standard discourse are afforded a lesser status according to the society's politics of truth. Further, convincing others of the truth is really just an exercise of power. When one battles for the truth, one is not contending for propositions that are "discovered and accepted," but for the political and economic purposes that form our fashioning of what counts as truth.[252] Truth is not universal; it is political.[253] Foucault illustrates this in *Discipline and Punish* by arguing that torture and truth go hand-in-hand. The acts of investigation that lead to torture of prisoners are exercises of power that purportedly can produce the truth from a patient. In fact, the investigation by torture "define[s] the truth."[254]

Foucault's critique of knowledge extends further to issues of metaphysics, as well, applying a Nietzschean critique of essences, human nature, and the soul. With a congratulatory tone, Foucault argues that Nietzsche's genealogist is able to rise above the fictions that are imposed by the search for the origins of humanity's moral impulses. Essences are a chief target here. These eternal, primordial truths and essences of which moral truths are a

---

249. Ibid., 55.

250. Foucault, *Power/Knowledge*, 131.

251. Ibid.

252. Ibid., 132.

253. Foucault, "Nietzsche, Genealogy, History," 163.

254. Foucault, *Discipline and Punish*, 41.

part are really just "fabricated in a piecemeal from alien forms."[255] Human nature, often viewed as a particular type of eternal essence, is the result of a process of historical remembrance wherein people reimagine past humans as somehow similar to themselves. Against this optimism, Foucault argues (with Nietzsche) that "nothing in man—not even his body—is sufficiently stable to serve as the basis for self-recognition or for understanding other men."[256] One cannot even make human nature a thoroughly materialistic conception; rather, one must view the history of humanity as a history of fracture without appeal to metaphysics. The soul is posited as a unifying entity in the human self or among a people (Here he has in mind the German *volk*), but there is no unity to be found by appeal to metaphysics. Moreover, the concept of the soul is an element in power-knowledge relationships. As peoples are colonized, enslaved, punished in the penal system, or otherwise subjugated through the more insidious politics of control, the soul emerges as a form of imprisonment, an element of human nature used to constrain the individual in the face of a transcendent order. The soul is "born out of methods of punishments, supervision, and constraint."[257] Of course, the soul is a fictive substance, but it is made real through the constitution of the self under subjugation. Foucault's genealogy of this concept is in keeping with his key contribution of power-knowledge, and his analysis of knowledge, truth, and metaphysics are important for what has become the postmodern Evangelical rejection of natural theology.

POSTMODERN THEOLOGY

Many theologians may not accept the postmodern modifier attached to their theological inquiries, yet the influence of twentieth century French post-structuralism and postmodernism on disciplines outside of philosophy, especially on the field of theological studies, is profound. The theological works (particularly those that might more properly be called philosophical theology) of Paul Ricoeur, Merold Westphal, and John D. Caputo incorporate key insights from postmodern philosophy. Indeed, these authors along with Carl A. Raschke, James K. A. Smith, and Myron B. Penner find resonance between their own Christian confessions and

255. Foucault, "Nietzsche, Genealogy, History," 142.

256. Ibid., 153.

257. Foucault, *Discipline and Punish*, 29.

postmodernism. The following investigates these areas of resonance with respect to the works of Ricoeur, Westphal, and Caputo.

Paul Ricoeur

The work of the French philosopher and theologian Paul Ricoeur (1913–2005) does not neatly fit into a discussion of postmodern theology, notwithstanding the problems of applying the word *postmodern* to any field of inquiry in general or to theology in particular. In many ways, his work is strictly separated into distinct philosophical and theological expressions, as we will see. However, his philosophical insights exert considerable influence in philosophical theology, particularly among those postmodern theologians suspicious of natural theology and apologetics. This brief survey of Ricoeur's work will explore his intention to strictly separate philosophy and what he calls biblical faith and his complex discussions around the nature of truth, particularly religious truth. This section will conclude with a discussion on his understanding of attestation and alterity. Truth and certainty are more complex when one considers the phenomenon of believing as a self. For Ricoeur, the relationship between the self and the other problematizes how one might engage the other in a dialogue of persuasion.

First, Ricoeur's method assumes a strict separation between the fields of philosophy and theology, and though he does not maintain it absolutely, his insistence on separation situates his overall negative evaluation of traditional natural theology. In the published version of his Gifford lectures, *Oneself as Another*, he explains why he chose not to include two lectures from his original presentation on "naming God" and "'narratives of vocations' of prophets and disciples."[258] He states that he attempts to pursue an "autonomous, philosophical discourse."[259] He is concerned that any philosophical argumentation that he pursues in his book may be weakened by explicit reference to the sources of what he calls "biblical faith." He is also aware that his philosophical works could be summarily rejected as "crypto-theology," just as his biblical argumentation could be assaulted for serving only a "cryptophilosophical function."[260] While he famously attempts to keep the disciplines separated, a posthumously published book of unfinished works indicates that he thought that perhaps some interaction may

258. Ricoeur, *Oneself as Another*, 23.

259. Ibid., 24.

260. Ibid.

be possible. A Christian, a person whose orientation is around the person and work of Jesus, may employ one's philosophical abilities without threatening "the liberty of thought and the autonomy" to which philosophical inquiry is entitled.[261] Thus, in applying one's philosophical acumen, the Christian may engage in the public square of ideas. While perhaps not too much should be made of this fragmentary musing—the fragment is just a handful of sentences—its existence adds some minor qualification that Ricoeur provides for the separation of philosophy and theology in *Oneself as Another*. Much more importantly, the sources of Christian theology, properly interpreted, have no common ground on the doctrine of God with philosophical sources. The religious language of the Christian confession of faith is comprised of numerous discourses that arise in the various legal, wisdom, poetical, etc. genres of the Bible. The narrative discourse in the Bible, in particular, leads to a tradition of proclaiming "Jahweh to be the grand Actor of a history of deliverance. Without a doubt it is this point that forms the greatest contrast between the God of Israel and the God of Greek philosophy. The theology of traditions knows nothing of concepts of cause, foundation or essence."[262] Not only do the various genres of the Bible problematize a unity of discourses for Christian confession, there can be no unity between philosophical and theological discourses.

Second, the previous discussion of the problem of the unity of various discourses underscores a more general feature of religious language, for in various texts, religious language challenges the interpreter to receive the world of the text unfolded therein. This is not a discourse about the everyday world. In fact, religious language cannot be neatly fit into a discourse about truth where truth is a matter of correspondence. When one reads a religious text, one encounters "a proposed world, a world that I might inhabit and wherein I might project my ownmost possibilities."[263] This means that one investigates and discovers a unity between the world of biblical faith and the everyday world with its various discourses, especially the scientific discourse. Moreover, any attempt to articulate a unified vision of the truth fails against the critique of history and a charge of imperialism:

> On the one hand, we have a series of philosophies which contradict and destroy each other . . . On the other hand, we are seeking a truth whose sign, if not the criterion, would be an agreement of

261. Ricoeur, *Living Up to Death*, 70.

262. Ricoeur, "Philosophy and Religious Language," 77.

263. Ibid., 80.

minds. If all history engenders a degree of skepticism, every claim to truth fosters a degree of dogmatism. From this point of view, history would only be a history of errors and truth would be the suspension.[264]

The history of philosophy shows the impossibility of this kind of unity. Instead, one must let the biblical "world" stand independent of any other unifying discourse. It is not that religious texts are not understood to be true among those who receive them. Rather, the revelation of a text can only happen in a given world. In this case, Christian revelation "is a trait of the biblical world."[265] Since the revelation happens within the context of the discourse of the biblical, the Bible can only have the status of revelation (and therefore "truth") in that world. Therefore, in the context of the world and the faith that it engenders to its devotees, the events of the Bible "are the events of deliverance which open and disclose the utmost possibilities of my own freedom and thus become for me the Word of God."[266] It is not just for religious language that truth is thusly problematized. Ricoeur's complex concept of the selfhood as a result of the agonistic process of attestation entails a mingling of "being-true and being-false" in the conscience.[267] This is because of the suspicion that arises from the attestation of selfhood.

Third, the very notions of the attestation of self and alterity are important considerations in Ricoeur's contribution to this study. Attestation is a way of believing in something with respect to the self. It is "the alethic (or veritative) mode of the style appropriate to the conjunction of analysis and reflection, to the recognition of . . . the hermeneutics of the self."[268] One can have agonistic assurance of selfhood, but only as one *believes in* X, not as one *believes that* X. This means that the *being-true* of attestation is different from the *being-true* of Aristotelean logic.[269] As suggested above, *being-true* and *being-false* are not opposites in Ricoeur's hermeneutics of the self. This is because suspicion is intimately related to any sense of the self, such as when one asks the question "Who?" with respect to one's own selfhood or to that of the phenomenon of the other. This suspicion in the hermeneutics of the self applies more broadly to all of our deepest commitments just

264. Ricoeur, *History and Truth*, 42.

265. Ricoeur, "Philosophy and Religious Language," 81.

266. Ibid., 85.

267. Ricoeur, *Oneself as Another*, 341.

268. Ibid., 21.

269. Ibid., 302.

as it does to the seminal issue of selfhood. "Human being has no mastery over the inner, intimate certitude of existing as a self; this is something that comes upon us, like a gift, a grace, that is not at our disposal."[270] Further, the concept of alterity shows how traditional notions of certainty and suspicion are mixed in Ricoeur's philosophy. When one is confronted with the other, one is confronted with a number of questions that problematize any epistemologizing of the identity of the other. Otherness is a polysemic notion that denies the self from finding an "ultimate foundation" for one's experience of the other.[271] This makes knowledge as certainty impossible for both the self and the other. Indeed, when one considers the other, one is not dealing with an object of thought, but with a subject of thought.[272] Not only does this make the self and alterity complex, it frustrates other binaries of confidence and doubt, truth and falsity, and permanence and change, as we have already seen. Paul Ricoeur's hermeneutics of the self suggest that evangelism and apologetics may not be as simple as the communication of propositions to which one may give assent, a concept to which we will return later.

Merold Westphal

The postmodern rejection of natural theology is nothing new, nor is it odd to find this postmodern orientation toward philosophical theology coming from conservative Protestant theologians. Given the criteria used in this work to define Evangelicalism, Merold Westphal (b. 1940), could easily have been included among the three authors around whose work we will focus. Limits on the scope of a study are, of course, a good thing, yet Westphal's work is highly influential on Smith's, Raschke's, and Penner's work. His concerns about natural theology echo the criticisms of Hume, Kant, Kierkegaard, and Heidegger that have been appropriated by postmodern philosophers and theologians. Moreover, he wields a forceful critique against "the Enlightenment project," especially regarding intimations toward objectivity and legitimation for which the "project" may be ambitious.[273] Instead of a Christian theology tied to modernity, Westphal

270. Ricoeur, "Metaphysics to Moral Philosophy," 455.

271. Ricoeur, *Oneself as Another*, 21.

272. Ibid., 332.

273. Westphal himself uses the phrase "the Enlightenment project" as an equivalent for any form of philosophical modernity that values objectivity, universal reason, and

champions the ways in which postmodern philosophy is consonant with authentic Christian confession and discipleship.

Natural theology is a regular target in Westphal's philosophical theology, primarily because natural theology is indebted to forms of reasoning that are philosophically suspect and to a metaphysics that is alien to authentic Christian confession. He takes for granted the success of Hume's and Kant's critiques that natural theology "produc[es] a being who comes conspicuously short of the glory of God."[274] A consistent survey of natural phenomena suggests, at best, a being whose moral character and ability to act in the powerful ways asserted by Christian theology are highly suspect. Moreover, the kind of insight required for natural theology to have any traction requires that one have cognitive access to what Kant calls the "a priori," yet Kant's philosophy has made possible the discovery that "the a priori is radically conditioned by historical, sociological, and psychological factors."[275] Any inquiry about God's self-revelation in the natural world will always be held hostage to the categories with which each person receives the phenomena. The nature and person of God, then, is mysterious because it is unconditioned. In fact, upholding the mystery of God is central to Westphal's rejection of natural theology. He looks to Heidegger's critique of ontotheology for additional ammunition. Ontotheology is any attempt to make God a subject of philosophical discourse or to posit God as an explanatory entity with respect to ontology. Speaking of God this way robs the world of mystery, leads to a God who does not inspire awe or worship, and, more dangerously, "opens the way for the unfettered self-assertion of the will to power in the form of modernity, namely the quest of science and technology to have everything at human disposal."[276] After all, if philosophy can make God an object at its disposal, what limits are there to human progress? Christianity, despite the onto-theological leanings of some of its defenders, is decidedly against ontotheology. Its best minds have always affirmed mystery with respect to God, and God's existence does not necessarily "make everything clear."[277] Still, Christian theologians need to be wary of ontotheology, especially when it comes in the forms of proofs. This kind of appeal to "Reason" to posit the existence of God produces deities "cre-

---

representationalism.

274. Westphal, *Kierkegaard's Critique*, 4.

275. Ibid., 5.

276. Westphal, "Onto-theology, Metanarrative, Perspectivism," 145.

277. Ibid., 146.

ated in the image of the communities" that take up the project of ontotheology.[278] This means that various natural theologies produce various kinds of counterfeit gods that attempt to legitimize the identity or practices of the community, not the God of Abraham, Isaac, and Jacob who enters the world mysteriously and challenges our assumptions. "If 'God' appears in the process, it is an idol, created in our own image and reduced to the function of justifying 'us,' agreeing with us that our practices indeed constitute the kingdom."[279] This is precisely the sin for which humanity is indicted in Romans 1: "They exchanged the truth about God for a lie, and worshiped and served created things rather than the Creator—who is forever praised. Amen" (1:25, NIV).

There are other idols, as well, toward which humanity may offer its philosophical and theological sacrifices. Many of these attend the practice of natural theology, Westphal warns, because they are deeply tied to Enlightenment forms of discourse which make God an object of human inquiry. First, the kind of objectivity for which philosophical modernity strives (and toward which many forms of natural theology point) is not possible for us because of our situatedness in our own cultures, language games, and times in history. What postmodern philosophy has successfully identified is "that we are not God . . . Objective knowledge of reality—seeing reality through, as it were 'God's' eyes—is not possible."[280] Also because of our cultural and temporal situatedness, reason cannot be employed with universal authority. According to Westphal, this was a key insight of Kierkegaard. The established order determines what modes of discourse are acceptable as they propagate their belief systems. Religions are often guilty of "world-building," and Kierkegaard "recognizes (and this is crucial) the degree to which this process determines what is to count as Reason in any given context."[281] Reason is deeply situated in various communities of discourse, and this is not to be lamented. In fact, in agreement with Lyotard's critique of metanarratives, Westphal agrees that "all human thought occurs within some hermeneutical circle or other as some faith or other seeking

278. Westphal, *Kierkegaard's Critique*, 6.

279. Westphal, "Blind Spots," 34.

280. Ibid., 32. See also Westphal, *Kierkegaard's Critique*, 10: "The objectivity proper to science is improper in relation to religious subject matter." This is primarily because God appears, most notably to Job, not as one whom we may question, but as one who questions us.

281. Westphal, *Kierkegaard's Critique*, 23.

understanding."[282] The opposite of this admission is, of course, to seek some kind of legitimation for an apologetic language game that governs all other games. Yet a project of legitimation would be alien to authentic Christian witness. The Christian story is "kerygma, not apologetics. So far from legitimizing the knowledge of any epoch of human history, it appeals to faith in every epoch."[283] This entails that faith cannot properly abide with any kind of legitimizing or totalizing discourse. Faith will always conflict with a conception of reason that is not part of a uniquely Christian discourse. This is because the Christian story is its own language game.[284] Agreeing with Wittgenstein that a plurality of language games admits of no hegemony of any single discourse, Westphal argues that we should resist any attempt to legitimize or defend the Christian story according to Enlightenment notions of truth or rationality.

Beyond agreement with earlier philosophical critiques of natural theology and modernity, Westphal argues that postmodern philosophy and Christian faith have profound agreement with respect to human finitude, a Christian language game, and the nature of truth. One of the key insights of postmodern philosophy is that human perspectives never escape historical, cultural, and linguistic contexts through which phenomena are received and out of which analysis is produced. This is why Derrida, Lyotard, and Rorty are often referred to as perspectivists. While this is not an "anything goes" relativism, it is "the dual claim that our insights, whether they be factual or normative, are relative to the standpoint from which they are made, and that the standpoint we occupy . . . inevitably betrays that it is not an absolute standpoint."[285] This insight is in concord with a Christian conception of human finitude in God's created universe. Moreover, because of the fall, Christians occupy a cognitive space that sets up for failure any attempt to universalize faith claims for those who are not a part of the Christian community. This is why Kierkegaard was suspicious of apologetics; any attempt to legitimize Christian faith will only lead to a corrupted faith that attempts to substitute Reason as an all-encompassing power over the God of Abraham. "Reason has become treason against God."[286] Postmodernism criticizes the Enlightenment optimism that humanity may rise above its sit-

---

282. Westphal, "Of Stories and Languages," 239.

283. Westphal, "Onto-theology, Metanarrative, Perspectivism," 150.

284. For a similar perspective, see Lindbeck, *The Nature of Doctrine*, esp. 128–34.

285. Westphal, "Onto-theology, Metanarrative, Perspectivism," 152.

286. Westphal, *Kierkegaard's Critique*, 23.

uatedness to know the world as it is. This is similar to the role of the biblical prophet, according to Westphal, who claims that hope is not found outside the Promised Land in alliance with other gods or with the Egyptians. The message of the biblical prophet is "untimely," and it "den[ies] the continuing validity of the old institutions."[287] However, it opens the way for the gospel, which is an invitation to participate in a "radically new" language game.[288] This game is not a discourse in legitimation or a seeking after objective truth, but an encounter with a person. Postmodern philosophy argues that "truth" is a discourse-relative concept, and for Christians, "truth is not ultimately mastery of the world's form but the personal God on whom we are dependent for the whole of life, including its knowledge."[289] God is the personal center of truth, meaning, and knowledge for Christians, but not an explanatory entity. Instead, God breaks into the world through the cultural and historical particularities of the Christ-event. There is, therefore, deep concord between Christian faith and postmodernism in the messages of human finitude, biblical prophecy, and the revelation of God in Christ.

John D. Caputo

A final fascinating marriage of postmodern philosophy and Christian theological inquiry appears in the work of John D. Caputo (b. 1940). The breadth of his work is impressive, covering Augustine, Thomas Aquinas, Heidegger, Derrida, and others. Key to this discussion is Caputo's application of Derridean *différance* to theology, his critique of ontotheology, and the concord that he sees between the tradition of negative theology and the insights of postmodern philosophy. These contributions illustrate how postmodern theology has a tendency to reject metaphysics in general and natural theology in particular.

Caputo's appropriation of postmodern insights is evidenced primarily in his interest in deconstruction as a tool for theological analysis. Christian faith is not an impenetrable fortress of truth about God in Christ within which the believer may find cognitive or existential refuge; rather, it is a horizon of possibility as seekers struggle through the doubts and challenges of an historic faith about an unknowable God. To that end, Caputo applies the principle of *différance* against the Eucharistic hermeneutics of Jean-Luc

287. Ibid., 17.

288. Westphal, "Of Stories and Languages," 235.

289. Westphal, *Overcoming Onto-Theology*, 277.

Marion to argue that experience of Jesus in history by the earliest Christians (in particular, the writer of the Fourth Gospel) merely found a culturally "felicitous way of expressing their faith" by referring to Jesus as the *logos*.[290] What we do not have in the Bible are timeless ways of expressing truth about God. Rather, applying Derrida's insights to religious language shows that "there is a dangerous gap between the event and the text."[291] We do not have timeless, objective access to the historical experience of Jesus. This insight casts suspicion on speech about God, not just the biblical texts. One's historical and cultural situation provides a "community of discourse" that mediates all religious language.[292] Speech or writing about God is not immune to this central Derridean point, and though this is difficult for Christians to accept, admitting the mediation of all texts actually situates Christian texts more profitably in a thoroughly mediated world of experience through which meaning may arise. This is unsettling for Christians not because it merely admits of some mystery with respect to God-talk; it also opens the possibility for heterogeneous expressions of Christian faith beyond the political control of a single theological discourse. "*Différance* has not come to bring peace but the two-edged sword of undecidability."[293] Caputo applies this principle to a deconstruction of Thomas Aquinas, particularly Thomistic metaphysics. While Caputo argues that Aquinas is guilty of the violence of ontotheology, there is "a more essential tendency in Thomistic metaphysics by which that metaphysics tends of its own momentum to self-destruct and to pass into a more essential experience."[294] Thomas' own mystical experiences form the hermeneutical principle for deconstructing his own ontotheology. Deconstruction is able to "shake loose from a text its essential tendencies, tendencies which the text itself conceals."[295] This kind of application of deconstruction to theology is a major influence on thinkers like James K. A. Smith, who was a student of Caputo.

The deconstruction of Thomas Aquinas' writings reveals another key interest for Caputo: the project of dismantling the pretensions of ontotheology. Deconstruction, though it opens theology to new horizons, "*does* limit

---

290. Caputo, "How to Avoid," 144.

291. Ibid., 145.

292. Ibid., 148.

293. Caputo, *Prayers and Tears*, 14.

294. Caputo, *Heidegger and Aquinas*, 8.

295. Ibid., 247.

the *metaphysical* side of theology."[296] It protects theology from "telling a bad story about itself" through affirmations of God as Being and even from describing God as the God beyond being.[297] Theology is writing, inscribed in the trace, not describing God as God is, but only in a way that makes faith necessary. His rejection of metaphysics is extreme, even extending to any metaphysics that would result from a thorough apophatic theology. Even as negative theology rejects the "metaphysics of presence" of which ontotheology is guilty, it merely substitutes *Being* for *presence*.[298] Deconstruction opposes negative theology in this way, for it really just replaces representationalism with a kind of "pure" presence. God is more mysterious than this. Indeed, since speaking of God as "cause" is idolatrous, it would also be idolatrous to speak of God without scare quotes: "Dieu."[299] This is a more consistent negative theology, and it has the benefit of allowing Christian theology to be more open to meanings that cannot be controlled through ontotheology. In Caputo's critique of Marion's Eucharistic hermeneutics, he notes that in making the sacrament the principle of interpretation, Marion places the politics of control into the hands of the priests who handle the sacrament. In this way, ontotheology becomes "onto-theo-politics."[300] It silences dissent and controls the Christian message.

Nowhere is ontotheology more of a problem than in traditional proofs of natural theology which subject God to Hellenistic concepts. Speaking about God as "cause" simply replaces the God of the Christian story with an idol, "the idol of philosophical conceptuality."[301] God cannot be equated with Being, any more than God can be equated with *différance*, but that is not to say that we cannot speak meaningfully of the existence of God. Refusing ontotheology goes a step further and opens Christian theology up to a more consistent negative theology. The kind of negative theology that becomes possible will not attempt to avoid violence by crafting a more suitable hermeneutical principle or by presuming to capture God in a philosophical concept. Rather, it will accept that language always does violence. There is no accurate way to speak about God. "It is not a question of finding a pure nonviolent discourse, but of giving in to the violence of discourse, of let-

296. Caputo, *Prayers and Tears*, 5. Emphasis in the original.

297. Ibid., 6.

298. Ibid., 11.

299. Caputo, "How to Avoid," 133.

300. Ibid., 147.

301. Ibid., 132.

ting words fly up like sparks from hearth fires everywhere."[302] This negative theology allows for a more radical pluralism, not a controlling negative theology, an ontotheology that is really onto-theo-politics. It is comfortable with mystery and with the truth that God does not speak. "For God does not speak at all; he does not have a tongue or vocal chords or make use of writing instruments."[303] If God does not speak, then he cannot be captured by our words, but this enables theology to give in to the violence of God-talk, just in a less pretentious form. This negative theology is an affirmation of human blindness toward the mystery of God, for "faith is structurally inhabited by blindness."[304] It denies knowledge to make room for faith, or perhaps more in keeping with deconstruction, it "[den]ies *savoir* in order to make room for *viens, oui, oui*," an inclusive and open discourse about God.[305]

CONCLUSION

This survey of "Evangelical" natural theology and postmodern philosophy and theology has illustrated the conceptual issues that are at stake in the postmodern Evangelical rejection of natural theology. The loci for this debate are deeply rooted in various complex disputes in Christian theology and in philosophy of religion. It is left to investigate both how these issues are articulated by Carl A. Raschke, James K. A Smith, and Myron B. Penner and in what ways it may be possible to counter or rebut their charges against natural theology and apologetics.

302. Ibid., 150.

303. Ibid., 143.

304. Caputo, *Prayers and Tears*, 312.

305. Ibid., 314.

3

Postmodern Evangelical Rejections of Natural Theology (Part 1)

THIS CHAPTER AND THE following set out in systematic form Smith's, Penner's, and Raschke's key objections to natural theology. Smith's objections chiefly regard the nature of religious language, his interpretation of Lyotard, his Reformed theology, and his sympathy toward presuppositional apologetics. Myron B. Penner's concern is that apologetics necessarily entails a number of ethical problems for Christians including idolatry, rhetorical violence, and the denigration of persons. Raschke's critique of natural theology is couched in his unique interpretations of key Protestant and Evangelical ideas (i.e. *sola scriptura*, revivalist evangelism, etc.). Despite their varied emphases, their arguments actually overlap. While the next chapter will explore some key theological objections to natural theology, this chapter will address the critiques of universal reason and the correspondence theory of truth. Each section will attempt to carefully represent Raschke's, Penner's, and Smith's views, and it will include a critique of their critiques for the purpose defending of natural theology.

THE REJECTION OF UNIVERSAL REASON

A whole set of objections to natural theology and apologetics is associated with Evangelical apologetics' supposed allegiance to Enlightenment rationalism, a style of reasoning about God that "appeal[s] to free, autonomous, and sovereign rational agents."[1] Alongside the concern that reason turns its devotees into idolaters (see below), Penner, Raschke, and Smith argue that Enlightenment rationality fails to provide objective insights about the world. Human temporality, contingency, and fallibility show that this style of reasoning fails to bring about the universal, objective, and neutral knowledge to which it aspires. Even more, the postmodern context is divorced from the conditions that originally made Enlightenment rationality meaningful.

Myron B. Penner classifies the enemy of the postmodern Evangelical paradigm when he refers to the "objective-universal-neutral complex" or "OUNCE."[2] He claims that Evangelical apologists revere reason as an avenue for defending Christianity "with arguments and evidences that are objectively true, universally accessible, and free from bias or partisanship."[3] Reason is something that is possessed by human beings. Therefore, all humans have equal access to reason as a tool for adjudicating between truth and falsity, understood in terms of truth as correspondence. Each person is also able to be his/her own authority on truth, using reason in an independent and impartial manner. This is the modern epistemic paradigm to which Evangelical apologists are devoted. However, the context in which this kind of reasoning is compelling "is defined by secularity" and is based on the authority of scientific proof.[4] This is markedly different from the earliest Christian apologists who "saw theology not just as a rational principle that governs the cognitive content of our beliefs but as intimately connected to a wider way of living and being together that embodies the truth of the gospel."[5] Natural theology treats reason as if it can provide objective truth about the world without recognizing that its method of OUNCE is deeply rooted in a particular context that precludes it from operating with objective scope. "Human reason always operates within a specific theoretical, physical, and social environment, including a constitutive set of practices."[6] If Christians attempt to employ reason outside of their own contingent and communal context, reason will fail them. This is because Christian truth lives in Christian contexts, and reason can only be employed meaning-

1. Penner, *The End of Apologetics*, 6.
2. Ibid., 32.
3. Ibid.
4. Ibid., 46.
5. Ibid., 45.
6. Ibid., 71.

fully within those contexts. Other stories can be told in other contexts to counter the Christian story, and accordingly, OUNCE cannot provide intercontextual adjudication between stories. Therefore, defending Christianity is "impossible in modernity."[7] Penner argues that Kierkegaard best illuminates how this is so. For Kierkegaard, "Truth is subjectivity," and the struggle to believe the truth accordingly is marked by inwardness and passion that are more related to living authentically than they are to satisfying a modern concept of reason.[8] Truth is subject-forming, constituting the subject through an inward, passionate, and dialectical struggle. This is "a critique of modernity's emphasis on objective reason," and it opposes "modernity's objectivism and infallibilism."[9] Christian truth cannot be defended by modernity's conception of reason because Christianity undermines modernity's conception of reason. With Ricoeur, Penner argues that the kind of justification that one has for belief is not that which is provided through reason, but through an internal struggle that causes one "to believe in (rather than merely believe that)" something is true.[10] Christianity demands a commitment, not assent; therefore, any activity geared toward securing assent through universal reason will be useless.

Smith agrees with this critique of universal reason, and this is precisely why he thinks that the work of Jean-François Lyotard is helpful for Christians. Lyotard's famous claim is that postmodernism is "incredulity toward metanarratives."[11] This is not a doubtful attitude toward all big stories. After all, Christianity is a big story, a "meganarrative" told through the Bible.[12] Instead, Smith claims that metanarratives take part in a legitimizing activity that makes a specific appeal to a universal account of reason. "For Lyotard, metanarratives are a distinctly modern phenomenon: they are stories that not only tell a grand story . . . but also claim to be able to legitimate or prove the story's claim by an appeal to universal reason."[13] Lyotard's statement, then, is an attitude of suspicion toward all such stories. This is simply because the appeal to autonomous and universal reason as

---

7. Ibid., 76.

8. Kierkegaard, *Concluding Unscientific Postscript*, 189.

9. Penner, "Kierkegaard's Subjectivity Principle," 80.

10. Ibid. For Ricoeur's notion of truth as attestation, see Ricoeur, *Oneself as Another*, 21.

11. Lyotard, *The Postmodern Condition*, xxiv.

12. See Westphal, *Overcoming Onto-Theology*, xiii.

13. Smith, *Who's Afraid of Postmodernism?* 65.

the legitimizing criterion is an attempt to escape the particularity of one's own language game. "Universal reason" is simply one discourse of legitimation, one that belongs to modern science, but it cannot rise out of its own game-relative situation and be "the game above all games," which is exactly what it attempts to do.[14] "Universal reason" is a discourse that cannot universally legitimate itself. Evangelical apologetics takes part in this ruse when it attempts to use universal reason to legitimate the Christian faith. The appeal to universal reason means that "classical apologetics is quite distinctly modern in its understanding of knowledge and truth," constituting it as a metanarrative, one toward which those who recognize their postmodern situation are rightly incredulous.[15]

The postliberal theology of George Lindbeck is a key resource for Smith on this point. Postliberalism is a kind of nonfoundationalist theology that seeks to speak meaningfully about Christian truth without reference to (and even against) the pretensions of modern empiricist or rationalist versions of truth.[16] Postliberalism accepts the Wittgensteinian paradigm that humans are "contingent social creatures whose knowledge *depends* on the gifts of the communities of practice" to which they belong.[17] "There is no knowledge outside community."[18] Lindbeck, then, is critical of apologetics because apologetics attempts to make Christianity rational and accessible to those who are not a part of its community of meaning. Not only is this fruitless, it can actually weaken the proclamation of the gospel. This is because the Christian faith, like a foreign language, cannot be grasped by translation strategies. It can only be proclaimed and lived. "The grammar of religion . . . cannot be explicated or learned by analysis of experience, but only by practice."[19] One comes to believe Christianity is true not through apologetics, but through living in the community that gives Christianity meaning: the church. If the church focuses on apologetics, proclaiming the rationality of Christian belief, this will weaken its ability to proclaim the

---

14. Ibid., 67.

15. Ibid., 69. Smith asserts that presuppositional apologetics (such as those of Francis A. Schaeffer and Herman Dooyeweerd) may not fall prey to this incredulity.

16. See Thiel, *Nonfoundationalism*, esp. 45–52.

17. Smith, *Who's Afraid of Relativism?* 172.

18. Ibid.

19. Lindbeck, *The Nature of Doctrine*, 129; quoted in Smith, *Who's Afraid of Relativism?* 173.

gospel with their practices.[20] As Merold Westphal reminds us, the Christian discourse is "kerygma, not apologetics."[21]

Carl Raschke agrees with the basic thrust of the rejection of universal reason when he laments how "Christian evangelical philosophers" have appropriated modernity's scientific styles of rationality, "demonstrating how faith statements can be turned into cogently defensible 'propositions,' frequently appealing to the latest and most sophisticated innovations in the philosophy of language or the philosophy of science."[22] With Kierkegaard, he objects to this misuse of reason because faith is deeply personal, and reason presents the wrong starting point for the individual's existential struggle. To be a human being is to be inexorably temporal. One cannot rise above temporality to employ a universal notion of reason, especially with respect to an existence-defining commitment like Christianity. The central element of the Christian message reinforces this temporality in that God (the eternal) has become temporal in the God-man Jesus. "Mortal beings cannot steel themselves against the ravages of time. Yet the object of Christian faith, Kierkegaard assures us, is a singular event in human history in which the eternal conquered the temporal."[23] When the eternal comes to participate in the temporal, the temporal human being is confronted with an absurdity that cannot be reconciled with reason. For all of its pretensions, philosophy cannot produce a natural theology or a reasoned apologetic that can make the Incarnation reasonable. The only proper response is faith.[24]

This rejection of universal reason—being indebted to the Wittgensteinian paradigm, assured that rationality cannot legitimize itself, and asserting that the central aspect of the Christian message is absurd—is troublesome because it misunderstands the way in which reason is universal and how reason functions in apologetics. Three key issues arise in this discussion of universal reason. In what follows, I will defend some key features of universal reason that are expressed in Aristotelean logic, show that the dichotomy between Christian apologetics and the witness

20. This paradigm of proclamation instead of apologetics matches well with what Stanley Hauerwas has called "The Necessity of Witness." See Hauerwas, *With the Grain of the Universe*, chapter 8.

21. Westphal, "Ontotheology, Metanarratives, Perspectivism," 150.

22. Raschke, "Faith and Philosophy in Tension," 48.

23. Ibid., 52.

24. Raschke's understanding of the meaning of the word "faith" is key to his rejection of natural theology. This is something that will be addressed in chapter 4.

of the church is a false dichotomy, and clarify a key distinction between cogency and reasonableness. First, at a minimum, the basic laws of thought as expressed by the laws of identity, noncontradiction, and the excluded middle alongside argument forms like *modus ponens* and *modus tollens* (along with other basic argument forms) are necessarily true. (Meaningful human communication would not be possible without the veridicality of these laws of thought.) In the *Metaphysics* and in the *Posterior Analytics*, Aristotle codifies these basic laws. "We must assume beforehand that some things are true . . . for example, that everything can be either asserted or denied."[25] The law (or principle) of noncontradiction "exhibits the fact that no thinker can question the principle which lies at the basis of all thinking and is presupposed."[26] Noncontradiction is presupposed by and supports all formal logic, including syllogisms and other forms of deduction as exemplified in arguments for the existence of God like C. S. Lewis' moral argument and the *kalām* cosmological argument. Noncontradiction does not guarantee the truthfulness of these arguments, but only the validity of their attendant forms. The arguments must rest on the truthfulness (or probability) of their premises and the relation of the premises in proper argument forms.

This present study is not a primer on logic, but it is important to say one thing in defense of logic, even when talking about God. Should one deny the law of noncontradiction, one must assume its terms to make such a denial. Consider the claim, "the law of noncontradiction is false." Or perhaps it is more profitable to phrase the claim this way, "The law of noncontradiction is not universal in scope and is only a feature of the modern scientific language game." If noncontradiction is said to be not universal in validity or scope, then one may simply retort that the law is, therefore, *universal*. (One is under no constraint to accept the *terms* of a denial of noncontradiction if noncontradiction itself is denied.) A perhaps apocryphal story of the famous Princeton philosophy professor Saul Kripke illustrates noncontradiction's universal scope. Princeton faculty from various departments had gathered for a meeting, and a discussion ensued about how the law should be discarded due to its male-dominated and provincial nature. Kripke apparently replied, "Good, let's get rid of it. Then we can keep it too."[27] This law of thought is self-evident, and denying it is absurd.

25. Aristotle, "Posterior Analytics," 161.

26. Copleston, *A History of Philosophy*, 283.

27. DeWeese and Moreland, *Philosophy Made Slightly Less Difficult*, 13.

In fact, many postmodern arguments do not get off the ground without the validity of the law of noncontradition. For example, Smith correctly criticizes the Christian "bumper-sticker reading" of Lyotard which claims that if the Bible is a metanarrative and postmodernism is incredulity toward metanarratives, then Christians should not embrace Lyotard's version of postmodernism.[28] When Lyotard uses the term *metanarrative*, he is referring to any grand story which is legitimized by an appeal to universal reason (AUR). Since the Bible does not make its appeal to universal reason, then it is not a metanarrative toward which the postmodern person will be incredulous. Christians may entertain Lyotard's principle (LP) without worrying that it denigrates the Bible. Smith's argument hinges on the correct reading of Lyotard's principle: the principle refers to grand stories that are legitimized by appeal to universal reason (A); it does not refer to grand stories that are legitimized in other ways (non-A). A≠non-A. This correct reading, then, opens the way for Christians to entertain postmodernism. Here is Smith's argument:

(1) Either LP refers to all big stories (LP1), or to a particular class of big stories that are legitimized by AUR (LP2).

(2) LP does not refer to all big stories (not-LP1).

(3) Therefore, LP2.

(4) If LP2, then Christians may entertain LP (because Christianity is not legitimized by AUR).

(5) LP2 (from 3).

(6) Therefore, Christians may entertain LP.

This is a conjunction of a disjunctive syllogism and a *modus ponens*. If the premises are true (or probably true), then the conclusion follows necessarily (or is likely). I agree with Smith that Christians may entertain LP without worrying that their consideration of LP threatens the Christian narrative. God legitimizes the Christian narrative. However, Christians will find that if LP entails that they be incredulous toward universal reason (as it does), then they will reject LP on these grounds since LP (and Smith's defense of LP) requires noncontradiction and some basic universal argument forms simply to be comprehensible.

---

28. Smith, *Who's Afraid of Postmodernism?* 64, note 5.

Furthermore, the notion that there are no intercommunity criteria like logic to adjudicate between truth-claims should be rejected. Paul Griffiths calls this the "strict incommensurability thesis."[29] Empirically, the strict incommensurability thesis—the notion that religious truth claims cannot be intercontextually assessed, that there are no neutral adjudicatory criteria, no common methods of argument—is easily rebutted. Griffiths considers the nondualistic form of theism of the Vishishtadvaitavedanta Hinduism and Anglican Christianity. Some of the Sanskrit writings of this school of Hinduism, in particular those of its founder Ramanuja, have been translated into English. The arguments and "doctrine-expressing sentences" in these documents can be easily understood by Anglican Christians.[30] There are some profound similarities between Vishishtadvaitavedanta Hinduism and Anglican Christianity and some irreconcilable disagreements. What are held in common by the two religions are "certain basic logical principles and argument-forms . . . The principles extend at least to the principles of identity, noncontradiction, and excluded middle; the argument forms at least to material implication and contraposition."[31] Using these common criteria, one could potentially understand and evaluate the doctrinal claims from another religion. He clarifies that his denial of the incommensurability thesis does not mean that commensurability will be complete, for there may be elements of incommensurability such as the sources of doctrinal authority like tradition or scripture. Commensurability also does not entail that one religious community will affirm the content of the other's doctrine-expressing sentences. Rather, it is the adjudicatory criteria of logic and argument that are commensurable. All this is to say that logic is not part of the game of modern scientific discourse. Rather, some forms of logic and logical argumentation form a "game above the games," which can serve to provide the common ground necessary for interreligious apologetics.

Second, the notion that one comes to believe through the lived gospel embodied in the practices of the church and not through apologetics rests on a false dichotomy. Lindbeck and Smith argue that the Christian faith

---

29. Griffiths, *An Apology for Apologetics*, 27.

30. Ibid., 28. He defines the phrase "doctrine-expressing sentences" thusly: "By this I mean sentences in some natural language (whatever the language of the community happens to be), which are taken by the community either to make or to entail claims about the nature of things, or claims about the value of certain courses of action; these sentences must also be regarded by the community as of some significance for its religious life, and for the salvation of its members." See ibid., 9.

31. Ibid., 28–29.

is understood and lived through the church, so translation strategies like apologetics will hinder authentic community-oriented faith. One may concede easily enough that one's Christian faith is only existentially meaningful when that faith is exercised in the community of faith. However, it is not clear that this line of argumentation from Lindbeck and Smith entails that apologetics could play no role in how one knows Christianity to be true. The life of the community is compelling, but it cannot address the questions and doubts of someone outside the community of faith. For example, someone who has not engaged in the church's practices still may wonder if God exists. This same person may wonder if suffering in the world suggests that God does not exist. This same person may wonder if Christians have publicly accessible reasons for their belief in the Resurrection. Should apologetics be marshalled to address these questions, this would amount to perhaps an important step in this person being willing to consider the gospel and the life of faith embodied in the church. No Christian apologist believes that apologetics is a substitute for authentic faith lived in community, nor do apologists claim that assent to an argument makes one a Christian. B. B. Warfield assures us, "We are not absurdly arguing that Apologetics has in itself the power to make a man a Christian or to conquer the world to Christ. Only the Spirit of Life can communicate life to a dead soul, or can convict the world in respect of sin, and of righteousness, and of judgment."[32] William Lane Craig argues, "A person who knows that Christianity is true on the basis of the Spirit may also have a sound apologetic which reinforces or confirms for him the Spirit's witness, but it does not serve as the basis for belief."[33] J. P. Moreland contends, "Saint Paul tells us that the church—not the university, the media, or the public schools—is the pillar and support of the truth (1 Timothy 3:15)."[34] It is simply a false dichotomy to argue that one must choose between the kerygmatic faith lived in the church and apologetics. Apologetics defends the truth and rationality of Christian beliefs. The life of faith is a life of trust in God, where one enters into relationships with God and the church. Moreover, apologetic endeavors may be characterized by rich relationships, and the life of faith can lead the faithful to a vibrant intellectual life.[35] Tellingly, Lindbeck,

32. Warfield, "Introduction to Beattie's *Apologetics*," 2:99.

33. Craig, *Reasonable Faith*, 48.

34. Moreland, *Love Your God*, 219.

35. See ibid., chapter 10.

Smith, Penner, and Raschke offer no reason to believe that these things should be mutually exclusive.

Third, it is important to briefly consider reason's relationship to certainty and cogency. Carl Raschke bemoans "the common view, particularly among Christian evangelical philosophers, that apologetics amount to developing consistent formal procedures for demonstrating how faith statements can be turned into cogently defensible 'propositions.'"[36] Penner paints things similarly when he describes the "Enlightenment picture of reason," the primary objective of which "is to establish a set of infallible beliefs that can provide the epistemological foundations for an absolutely certain body of knowledge."[37] None of our authors explicitly stipulates how they are using terms like *cogency* and *certainty*; however, it is clear from these statements that the terms are used as modifiers for the epistemic values which reason supports. In Raschke's case, *cogently* modifies defensibility, where what are being defended are propositions which relate to Christian faith. In Penner's case, *certain* modifies knowledge, where knowledge is referring to whatever it is that Enlightenment rationality delivers. The problem with using words like *cogency* and *certainty* in these ways is that Evangelical apologists, employing analytic methods which produce stricter stipulations with respect to their terms, use these terms to refer to person-relative conditions of the acceptance of arguments and not the epistemic features (knowledge, propositions) of those arguments proper. William Lane Craig argues that good arguments do not usually include premises about which one would typically be certain.

> Certainty is an unrealistic and unattainable ideal. Were we to require that we have certainty of the truth of an argument's premises, the result for us would be skepticism. What we're looking for is a comparative criterion: the premises in a good argument will have greater plausibility than their respective denials.[38]

36. Raschke, "Faith and Philosophy in Tension," 48.

37. Penner, "Introduction," 22.

38. Craig, *Reasonable Faith*, 55. He goes on to argue that what counts as plausible may often be person-relative, as well. The result is that apologetic arguments are often only probably true. We should not be troubled by this, keeping in mind "(1) that we attain no more than probability with respect to almost everything we infer . . . without detriment to the depth of our conviction, and that even our non-inferred basic beliefs may not be held with any sort of absolute certainty . . . and (2) that even if we can only *show* Christianity to be probably true, nevertheless we can on the basis of the Spirit's witness *know* Christianity to be true with a deep assurance that far outstrips what the evidence in our particular situation might support." See ibid., 55–56.

This is because soundness belongs to arguments, and truth belongs to propositions, whereas cogency and certainty belong to persons. Garrett J. DeWeese and J. P. Moreland carefully clarify that cogent arguments are ones where the validity of the form and its soundness (where soundness obtains from true premises in a valid form) are accepted by the reader. "Cogency, then, is person-relative. Many factors—psychological, personal, volitional, prejudicial or theological (think of original sin or the work of the Holy Spirit)—enter into the mix when a person evaluates an argument."[39] In the same way, "certainty is a psychological predicate," where one has no doubts about a proposition's truthfulness.[40] Truth is a feature of propositions, while certainty is an individual's internal state. The fact that Evangelical apologists define their terms this way has two important implications for the postmodern Evangelical rejection of natural theology. (1) One ought not to conflate—as Penner, Raschke, and Smith do—Enlightenment rationality with the universal conception of reason employed by Evangelical apologists. Evangelical philosophers are often and hastily grouped with a particular style of rationalism that they are careful to avoid in their stipulative definitions of terms like truth and certainty. Straw men are notoriously easy to upend.[41] (2) Even though Evangelical apologists employ universal reason, they are often only seeking to demonstrate probable truths, and are thus not at odds with the virtue of humility or of the theological truths of human finitude and fallenness of which we are so often reminded by postmodern Evangelicals. There may be counterexamples of Evangelical philosophers who do not exhibit humility or adequately address human finitude and fallenness, but the fact remains that leading apologists employ universal reason in a particular way, the contours and limits of which ought to be more fairly considered by Raschke, Penner, and Smith. Reason can serve as an avenue toward knowing that Christianity is true, and it is to the subject of truth (along with propositionalism and foundationalism) that we now turn.

---

39. DeWeese and Moreland, *Philosophy Made Slightly Less Difficult*, 15.

40. Ibid., 16.

41. Even the notion of "Enlightenment rationalism" may be an overly generalized term, relating perhaps only to a misreading of Descartes. See Groothuis, "Postmodern Fallacies," 41; and Moreland, "Truth, Contemporary Philosophy, and the Postmodern Turn," 80–83.

TRUTH, PROPOSITIONALISM, AND FOUNDATIONALISM

If postmodern philosophy is about anything, it is about language. Especially with Jacques Derrida's fascinating concepts of *différance* and deconstruction, the postmodern turn has been primarily linguistic. Denying that objective meaning can be encoded in propositions and that those propositions could correspond to objective reality is a cornerstone of the work of Raschke, Smith, and Penner. Even to use the word *cornerstone* is ironic since postmodern philosophy is one species of non- or post-foundationalism. The rejection of foundationalism and objective truth, these authors would say, is a rejection of the myth in modernity that humans can attain to objective knowledge. Evangelical apologetics, they say, has accepted the misleading modernist paradigm that we can know objective truth. When one presents arguments for the existence of God, one is attempting to represent the world (and perhaps more scandalously, God) as it is. Yet this is impossible. Not only is this an epistemic mistake in that we cannot escape both our contingency and the limitations of the linguistic signs in which our communication is delivered and received; it is a metaphysical mistake regarding the nature of truth. Truth is not propositional; it is relational. Truth is not something to which one gives mental assent; it is a way of life, an existential and relational struggle. In this section, we will examine Raschke, Smith, and Penner on truth, propositionalism, and foundationalism and respond to the irony of their absolute denial of objective truth.

First, postmodernism is a denial that human persons and contingent human language structures can know and represent the world as it is. Postmodern philosophy is consonant with Christian theology because of its assertion that "we are not God."[42] This challenges foundationalist epistemology and the correspondence theory of truth, and it forms part of the rejection of Evangelical natural theology in that natural theology and apologetics are beholden to these outmoded notions of knowledge and truth. Consider again Craig's *kalām* cosmological argument:

1. Everything that begins to exist has a cause of its existence.

2. The universe began to exist.

3. Therefore the universe has a cause of its existence.[43]

---

42. Westphal, "Blind Spots," 32.

43. Craig, *The Kalām Cosmological Argument*, 63.

This argument aims to use language to communicate truths about the nature of reality. God is not the antecedent explanans; rather, God is the consequent explanandum. That is, one claims to know a truth more foundational than God's existence (in this case, the premises 1 and 2), and that truth is how we know about God. Postmodern Evangelicals think that this is wrongheaded because, as Derrida has shown, we cannot know the world as it is via language. Carl Raschke agrees, arguing that deconstruction "refers to a recognition that reading and interpretation of texts force us to let go of what we regarded as straightforward, obvious and fixed meanings."[44] The foundationalist epistemology and referential semiotics upon which natural theology is built "obscure[s] the fact that meaning and signification are not vertical connections between words and things."[45] This is because we can never escape the contingencies of our language and our place as speakers and listeners. As we receive texts, we deconstruct them as a condition of interpretation. In fact, as Smith contends, the world itself "*is* a kind of text requiring interpretation . . . this interpretation is informed by a number of different things: the context in which I encounter the thing, my own history and background, the set of presuppositions that I bring to the experience, and more."[46] This means that "it is language all the way down."[47] And language does not adequately represent reality. Languages are simply contingent markings and acoustic blasts, the conceptual contents of which do not exist apart from an individual speech act. This is a denial of the metaphysics of signs. Propositions do not exist as extralinguistic mental realities. It is impossible to share a proposition from one mind to another. In referential semiotics, a proposition is that which a declarative statement asserts. It is an abstract object that can be encoded in any number of languages. Postmodernism denies the existence of propositions.

The contingent nature of linguistic signs also confounds foundationalist epistemology which, under the specter of Descartes' evil demon, looks for certainty with respect to knowledge. In this epistemology, there are two kinds of beliefs: beliefs that are justified by other beliefs (or non-basic beliefs) and beliefs that are justified without reference to other beliefs (or basic beliefs). Descartes famously employs methodological doubt of all the items of his knowledge and concludes that through his doubt, he cannot

---

44. Raschke, "Faith and Philosophy in Tension," 63.

45. Raschke, *The Next Reformation*, 53.

46. Smith, *Who's Afraid of Postmodernism?* 39–40.

47. Ibid., 39.

escape the fact that he is doubting and that there is a self who is doing the doubting. The self that is doubting is known because of the cognitive activity (thought) through which doubt comes. Thus, he concludes, "*Cogito, ergo sum*," or, "I think; therefore, I am." This statement becomes a basic belief, justified because of its inescapability or indubitability. According to James K. A. Smith, this search for certainty in knowledge is absurd, leading one to settle for no less than absolute certainty in all of one's beliefs, a quixotic quest for an unattainable goal. Postmodern philosophers and theologians call this Cartesian anxiety, an accusation that foundationalism causes one to restlessly search for the epistemic Sasquatch of certainty. "The modern Cartesian dream of absolute certainty is just that: a dream" because "it rests on a mythical epistemology of immediate access and cognitive certainty."[48] While this is not really an argument against Cartesian epistemology, it embodies the claim of postmodern theologians that Cartesian epistemology requires an objectivity and omniscience that is reserved only for God. Smith, Derrida, and Caputo all argue that we should be skeptical of equating knowledge with certainty and of trying to reconcile faith and reason. "'I don't *know*,' Derrida once said; 'I must *believe*.' In other words, the postmodern theologian says, 'We can't *know* that God was in Christ reconciling the world to himself. The best we can do is believe.'"[49]

This is precisely why Evangelical apologetics is so problematic. "Classical apologetics buys this epistemology," that there is such a thing as objective truth and that knowledge of this objective truth is universally available.[50] This is simply impossible, though, because any account of "objective truth" is really only one possible interpretation. Because the world itself and all of human experience are texts that require interpretation, one cannot connect any single interpretation to reality *an sich*. While the apologist tries to demonstrate that one interpretation is true, she cannot escape the fact that her argument is only one interpretation among many. The apologist and her interlocutor can never be certain that the interpretation under consideration is the true one. Even the relationship between the apologist and her interlocutor is problematic, for apologetics fallaciously attempts to treat one's interlocutor as a potential "lone and atomistic knower capable of independently processing facts against 'reality.'"[51] Because we experience

48. Ibid., 118.

49. Ibid., 118–9.

50. Ibid., 48.

51. Smith, *Who's Afraid of Relativism?* 171.

events subjectively, and our conceptual structures are rooted in communities of understanding, any outside interpretation will be *différance*. We cannot access the pure trace of any text, meaningfully appropriate another's interpretation for ourselves, nor see reality from God's perspective. Apologetics requires seeing the world neutrally and objectively, but "'seeing' is conditioned by the particularities of my horizon of perception."[52] Yet such a kind of sight does not exist. Smith cites John Owen at length to argue that one may give mental assent to some of the truths of the Christian faith, but he will not appropriate these truths in any meaningful way.

> That Jesus Christ is crucified, is a proposition that any natural [i.e., unregenerate] man may understand and assent to, and be said to receive . . . but it is denied that he can receive the things themselves. For there is a wide difference between the mind's receiving doctrines notionally, and receiving the things taught in them really.[53]

In short, one needs the Holy Spirit to make any meaningful reception of the truths of the Christian faith possible. This is because the Holy Spirit provides the correct interpretation directly, not through rational demonstrations. Raschke argues that this is why Reformation theology has always been opposed to the theory of truth required by apologetics. "Without the Spirit, the mind is blinkered. Reformation theology, therefore, refutes the 'correspondence theory' of truth."[54] The "blinkering" is what is referred to by the Derridean critique of referential semiotics, an insight into human inquiry that can be respected by Christian theology. Thus, Penner writes, we need to admit that we have lost "our naïve access to truth and realize that absolute truth only exists for God."[55]

Second, not only does postmodernism criticize the correspondence theory of truth and deny the existence of propositions as truth-bearers, it asserts that truth is relational and existential. Each of our three key authors has a unique take on this. Raschke argues that propositional truth depends on the sufficiency of word-signs as truth-bearers to point to the extra-linguistic realities that are truth-makers. It is "designed to achieve *certainty*" through the "mapping of re-presentational truth functions in terms of sign operations. But whatever certainty is founded in this manner

52. Smith, "Who's Afraid of Postmodernism?" 218.

53. Owen, *The Holy Spirit*, 155; quoted in Smith, *Who's Afraid of Postmodernism?* 49.

54. Raschke, *The Next Reformation*, 127

55. Penner, *The End of Apologetics*, 100.

can finally be no more than subjective certainty, or *self-certainty*."[56] This is because the truthfulness of the signified depends on the sufficiency of the individual's own ability to adequately represent it through language. This is the scandal of the appropriation of Cartesian epistemology by Evangelical apologists. "The true foundation of the truth is the 'I' that authenticates the truth."[57] So the metaphysical view of truth that makes truth a property of propositions dissolves into an epistemology that makes the individual the locus of truth. Christian theology, Raschke contends, holds that truth is personal, but it denies autonomy to the Cartesian epistemology that results from the metaphysics of signs. Instead, Christian theology sees truth as a personal encounter with God. "Propositional, or purely philosophical, truth is conditional truth, even if it claims to be about what is unconditional. It can never be made into the touchstone of Christian truth, which is always personal and relational. Propositional truth statements cannot accommodate paradoxes."[58] Paradoxes like the Incarnation show that truth is revealed personally. The person of Jesus Christ is fully God and fully human. This truth cannot be analyzed according to Cartesian criteria. It can only be revealed personally, as it was in Palestine 2,000 years ago. This is the key truth of Christian theology: God has come to dwell with humanity in Christ. Therefore, "the 'with' of divine relation is contrasted with the 'is' of doctrinal propositions."[59] The truth of Christian faith is known through relation with the divine (knowledge by acquaintance), not through knowledge about the divine (propositional knowledge or knowledge *that*). "God is never what he is 'in himself.' God is always *mit uns* (with us) or *für uns* (for us), as Luther insisted. He is what he is *in relation to us*."[60] This is why faith is vital for Christian truth. Christians are never called to account for certainty of our propositional knowledge, but only for the *"quality of our relationships*. From an evangelical Christian perspective, the supreme criterion of whether we have been 'reborn' as Christ followers is whether we can attest to having an abiding 'personal relationship' with Jesus himself."[61]

Myron B. Penner agrees that truth is personal, and he engages Paul Ricoeur's notion of truth as attestation to that effect. "Attestation is an

---

56. Raschke, *Alchemy of the Word*, 69.

57. Raschke, *The Next Reformation*, 24.

58. Ibid., 209–10.

59. Raschke, *GloboChrist*, 48.

60. Ibid.

61. Raschke, "Faith and Philosophy in Tension," 64–65.

ironic form of truth-telling that happens always in the first person. I am always present in my attestations . . . but never under the illusion that I am objectively justified in what I attest or that it is infallibly true."[62] When Christians proclaim the truth, they are always doing so as a self and to other selves. Christians do not proclaim the truth with certainty, but through offering their selves as witnesses or as evidence of the kind of life entailed by that which they proclaim. One witnesses to the truth that their lives have been edified by the truth, not that they can rationally demonstrate its truthfulness on modernity's terms. This relieves the Christian from Cartesian anxiety of having to prove that Christianity is true through rational means, and it offers the transformed life as evidence of the truth. Further, the concept of truth as attestation shows that "truth-telling is *agonistic*."[63] The Christian struggles to allow the truth to be revealed in her own life. "Christian truth-telling, therefore, is a field of performance and an acting or living out of the truth that is edifying and upbuilding . . . we must win these truths for ourselves."[64] Christians are to be transformed by the truth, living a life that witnesses to the truth of their faith. Therefore, verification of Christian truth claims is not something that is done through rational demonstration or apologetic argumentation, but through examination of the lives of Christians. Truth, then, is not something that one knows, but something that one *is*. "Truth is fundamentally salvific. This existential mode or relation is brought about as the product of a certain kind of self-activity."[65] Through one's relationship with God, one can passionately struggle to become the truth of one's beliefs.

As a replacement for metaphysical theories of truth, James K. A. Smith recommends adopting a pragmatic view of truth, which understands that knowledge cannot be separated from the deeply human conditions of contingency and community through which truth is known. This starts with the key Christian doctrine of creation. Christians believe that God created everything out of nothing; therefore, humanity is wholly dependent on God for everything, including "truth and knowledge, even our epistemology and metaphysics."[66] This gives knowledge a deeply personal aspect because humanity must have a proper relation to God in order to

---

62. Penner, *The End of Apologetics*, 124–25.

63. Ibid., 127.

64. Ibid.

65. Penner, "Kierkegaard's Subjectivity Principle," 75.

66. Smith, *Who's Afraid of Relativism?* 35.

Postmodern Evangelical Rejections of Natural Theology (Part 1)

have knowledge. Human knowledge will always be dependent on the Creator-creation relationship. However, it is not just the relationship between God and humanity that is vital, for knowledge is deeply relational in the communal sense according to Smith. Wittgenstein's theory that "meaning is use" entails that "meaning and knowledge are ineluctably *social* and communal."[67] Our human communities determine for us what counts as truth, and our discursive traditions embody the truth in such a way that confounds any sense of propositional and objective truth. For Christians, it is the church that forms this knowledge-community. (This entails that there are many knowledges, many truths, and many communities.) When one is a part of the church, one can learn how Christians use the truth to make sense of the world. "For human knowers, there is no knowledge outside community. Accordingly, there is no knowledge of God in Christ apart from his body, which is home to his Word."[68] It is not hard to see why this entails that natural theology is absurd. If knowledge can only be attained in the community, then it is no use attempting to demonstrate Christian truth claims to those who are outside the community. One would have to become part of the Christian community first to appropriate the Christian truth claims. Since the meaning of Christian truth claims is determined by the Christian community, outsiders will not understand what Christian truth claims mean.

Raschke, Penner, and Smith reject referential semiotics and the correspondence (or metaphysical) theory of truth and opt instead for pragmatism with respect to knowledge and epistemic accounts of truth. We should not accept their proposals for three key reasons. First, their understanding of foundationalism is unnecessarily conflated with a caricature of Cartesian epistemology. They misrepresent Descartes, conflate all foundationalism with Cartesian foundationalism, and, therefore, misunderstand the relationships of both truth to propositions and certainty to persons. Second, some of their arguments depend on a correspondence theory that they mean to reject, so we should reject their rejection. Third, their rejection of objectivity is wrought with postmodern irony, the kind that makes their undermining of objectivity difficult to sustain.

First, the postmodern rejection of Cartesian epistemology is wrong-headed because it is rooted in a caricature of Descartes' project in the *Meditations*. According to Raschke, Penner, and Smith, Descartes' philosophy

67. Ibid., 60.
68. Ibid., 172.

91

makes two critical errors. It first equates knowledge with certainty by giving into a skeptical methodology for arriving at knowledge. Second, through the *cogito*, it places the self as the autonomous seat of epistemic authority, wrongly displacing God.[69] It is worth saying that the first critique may be correct, but the force of this critique is wrongly wielded against Evangelical natural theologians. For example, Descartes says, "I must avoid believing things which are not entirely certain and indubitable."[70] This is part of his heuristic skepticism, a method provisionally engaged for the purpose of seeking certainty. One may, in fairness, object to this method, noting that this is a bankrupt way to find knowledge, especially because the kind of certainty that Descartes would seem to require would be difficult ever to attain. However, no Evangelical apologist advocates such a criterion for knowledge. In fact, Evangelical apologists often clearly distinguish that premises in a deductive argument may only be probably true, that certainty is a property of persons and not of knowledge, and that varying levels of certainty may accompany our knowledge without fear that lacking full certainty jeopardizes our epistemic and apologetic projects. Indubitability is, indeed, too high a bar for knowledge. It is odd that our authors ever warn of Cartesian anxiety among Evangelical natural theologians when Evangelical apologetics does not require certainty.

Evangelical apologists also distinguish between the kind of foundationalism that Descartes commends and a more modest foundationalism that may be the best way to support natural theology. Cartesian foundationalism holds that properly basic beliefs must be indubitable and that only these kinds of beliefs can serve as the foundation of a proper noetic structure. Even though there may be some indubitable beliefs, most Evangelical apologists reject this version of foundationalism because there are not enough properly basic beliefs that meet this criterion "to ground our entire noetic structure."[71] Modest foundationalism, on the other hand, makes the criterion for proper basicality something more akin to being truth-conducive or truth-indicative. On some forms of modest foundationalism, basicality can be person-relative, and doubts about a properly basic belief do not rule out its place in the foundation. "We need not insist

69. There are other objections to levy against Descartes, for example, his substance dualism; however, a defense of substance dualism is not necessary for the success of this project except to say that mind may be a necessary condition for propositional truth. Moreland, *The Soul.* See also Moreland and Craig, *Philosophical Foundations*, chapter 11.

70. Descartes, *Discourse and the Meditations*, 95.

71. Moreland, "Truth, Contemporary Philosophy, and the Postmodern Turn," 83.

on an infallible or incorrigible belief, let alone an empirically incorrigible one, to be justified in holding that a particular belief is basic for us at this point in time."[72] This lowers the bar for what can serve as a properly basic belief. This epistemology supports natural theology better because items like the existence of God, the knowability of the external world, the existence of other minds, and many other key beliefs can be understood as properly basic (or at least potentially so) without recourse to the criterion of indubitability. Evangelical advocates of natural theology like J. P. Moreland prefer this approach because it is widely accepted "that classical [Cartesian] foundationalism is too ambitious," and because "beliefs grounded in perception, memory, or testimony" can be included in the foundation.[73] These kinds of beliefs are appealed to in arguments like C. S. Lewis argument from desire and in historical cases for the resurrection of Jesus. The larger point, though, is that modest foundationalism is markedly different from its Cartesian counterpart. In short, simply because Evangelical apologists advocate foundationalism (which most do), this should not mean that their philosophies should be subject to the same critique of Cartesian foundationalism levied by Raschke, Penner, and Smith.

Moreover, our authors simply misread Descartes when they charge that Cartesian epistemology entails that "the true foundation of truth is the 'I' that authenticates the truth," unseating the authority of God and the church.[74] If one is concerned on theological grounds that "Descartes sought to replace medieval ecclesiastical authority, based on dogma and tradition, with the primacy of unaided human reason," then it is easy to see why Cartesian epistemology should be rejected by Evangelicals.[75] Descartes' method would entail a rejection of God as the locus of knowledge. However, a broader reading of *The Meditations* shows that this interpretation of Descartes is mistaken. Consider Descartes' ontological argument.

> Because I cannot conceive God without existence, it follows that existence is inseparable from him, and hence that he truly exists; not that my thought can make this be so, or that it imposes any necessity on things, but, on the contrary, because the necessity

---

72. Pojman, *What Can We Know*, 127.

73. Moreland, "Truth, Contemporary Philosophy, and the Postmodern Turn," 83.

74. Raschke, *The Next Reformation*, 24.

75. Ibid.

of the thing itself namely, the necessity of the existence of God, determines my thought to conceive in this way.[76]

The point here is not whether Descartes' ontological argument for the existence of God is successful. Rather, it is to show that Descartes' entire philosophy rests on the premise that God exists. His conceptual paradigms are determined by God. Indeed, if God does not exist, then one "would never have a true and certain knowledge of anything whatever, but only vague and shifting opinions."[77] Raschke, Penner, and Smith seem to focus only on the epistemic methodology of the first and second *Meditations* while missing the (metaphysical) locus of knowledge in the fifth. Their rejection of Descartes ought to merely amount to an objection to Descartes' methodology. His heuristic starting point may be the self in the first two *Meditations*, but that does not entail that the self is the starting point of his philosophy proper. The existence of God looms over Descartes' presuppositions and is indeed the foundation of his epistemology.[78]

Second, in various ways, Raschke, Penner, and Smith reject the correspondence theory of truth, yet their reasons for doing so are undercut as they trade on the language of correspondence in their projects. James K. A. Smith, for example, rejects truth as correspondence as part of his larger agreement with Derrida's principle that "there is nothing outside the text."[79] Smith argues that we do not have knowledge of things in themselves because all we have are our interpretations. Indeed, the world itself is a kind of text that needs interpretation, and our contingency prohibits us from seeing things as they are. Smith argues that Christian theology is consonant with Derrida's principle, "While God's invisible attributes are, on the one hand, 'clearly seen' (Rom 1:20), Paul goes on to emphasize the way in which this is not seen by those whose 'foolish hearts are darkened' (1:21), who thus construe or interpret the world as something other than God's creation."[80] Setting aside for the moment that this is a denial of the epistemic possibility of the accessibility of general revelation, Smith is claiming that people will have different interpretations on whether or not God cre-

---

76. Descartes, *Discourse and the Meditations*, 145.

77. Ibid., 148.

78. For a richer development on how the existence of God is a necessary premise for Descartes' philosophy in general and his ontological argument in particular see Beyssade, "The Idea of God," 174–99.

79. See Smith, *Who's Afraid of Postmodernism?* chapter 2.

80. Ibid., 49.

ated the world. So far, this is commonsensical. When I ask an atheist friend about her view on how everything came to be, she may refer to some kinds of natural causative processes along the lines of Big Bang cosmology and Darwinism. She has a different interpretation than I do because, behind any natural process, I will see supernatural causation. Smith continues, "While I agree that interpreting the world as creation is the true interpretation, this does not negate its status as an interpretation."[81] However, this is where Smith's argument against correspondence loses its force. Of course, there may be rival interpretations of the facts, but true interpretations are set apart by their veridicality. Not all interpretations are created equal. This is precisely what Smith seems to be pointing out. There is one interpretation of the facts here that is different than the others because it true. It does not make sense to say that it is *the* true interpretation according to Smith's pragmatism because the bar for truth is usefulness in a community of interpretation. There could be other communities who would find Smith's belief to be not useful. It would not make sense to refer to *the* true interpretation on a coherence view of truth because truth is merely a matter of a relationship of mutual support and reinforcement between a belief and other beliefs, yet coherence leaves open the possibility of two maximally-developed, yet mutually exclusive belief systems. The only option left for Smith when he refers to *the* true interpretation is correspondence. This is the most natural reading of Smith in this section. Smith believes this because he has knowledge that (i.e. knowledge that it is the case that) God created the world. Yet his denial of correspondence theory and its referential semiotics makes his position all the more confused. Smith must trade in the currency of correspondence to claim that there is such a thing as "the true interpretation," even though he purports to be spending in pragmatism. The whole point of correspondence theory is that if one claims A (in this case, God created the world), A is true if and only if A is the case (if God creating the world is the true interpretation). Should Smith balk at my reading of his view that the belief that God created the world is the true interpretation, it would simply reinforce that there is a true interpretation of Smith on this issue! My interpretation of Smith succeeds or fails only insofar as it corresponds to his actual view.

Correspondence should be accepted not only for the reasons above, but also because of *the descriptive argument* (also called *the phenomenological argument*). This argument attempts to present specific cases where

81. Ibid.

a person experiences truth as truth. J. P. Moreland provides an example where a man named Joe receives a call from the university bookstore telling him that a book that he has ordered has now arrived in the bookstore. Joe then has a new mental state that this particular book is in the bookstore and an accompanying intentional mental state which is about his thought that the book is in the bookstore. While Joe is on the way to the bookstore, his friend Frank joins him. When they arrive, they see the book that has just arrived in stock. They both have a sensory experience of the book,

> But Joe has a second experience not possessed by Frank. Joe experiences that his thought matches and corresponds with an actual state of affairs. He is able to compare his thought with its intentional object and "see," be directly aware of the truth of the thought. In this case, Joe actually experiences the correspondence relation itself and truth itself becomes an object of his awareness.[82]

Of course, this is a commonsense view of truth. Most people would agree that there is a way to ensure whether or not your mechanic is correct when she says that the serpentine belt on your car is broken. One could examine the belt itself and have knowledge both that the statement "your serpentine belt is broken" is true and knowledge about the truth (i.e. the correspondence relation) itself. Penner objects to this argument, however, by arguing that Moreland has failed to demonstrate that Joe has experienced the correspondence relation itself, the relation between his thoughts and the sense-perceptible object. One could easily account for what Moreland calls correspondence on pragmatic or coherentist terms. For example, on a pragmatist understanding of truth, one "could agree in every respect with Moreland's example (minus some of the metaphysical baggage) yet reach the contrary conclusion that Joe experienced the most convenient way to think of and refer to a state of affairs."[83] All Moreland has done is to "conflate this verification process with the truth-relation itself."[84] This argument seems to miss the point. Moreland is arguing that Joe has experienced something unique in that his experience of his intentional object and its verification through sense perception of the actual book has produced a new belief. This belief is also intentional in that it is about the relationship between his

82. Moreland, "Truth, Contemporary Philosophy, and the Postmodern Turn," 79. See also Willard, "Verso una Teoria," 125–47. English translation available at: http://www.dwillard.org/articles/artview.asp?artID=61.

83. Penner, "Cartesian Anxiety, Perspectivalism, and Truth," 88.

84. Ibid.

original belief and the actual book. This has given him knowledge of the correspondence relation itself. Contra Penner, the verification process is a different set of events (walking to the bookstore, having simple sight of the book, etc.) from the belief about the correspondence relation. Moreland has not conflated the two; rather, he has shown them to be two distinct items of inquiry, the latter of which cannot be reduced to the former since the latter is a belief and the former is the procedural application of beliefs.[85]

Third, the postmodern objection to objectivity is wrought with the ironic assertion that humanity can never know something objectively. It is important to clarify that our authors seem to argue that objectivity is possible for God, but impossible for humanity given human contingency and fallenness. Smith says that the fact that there is no objective truth should not discourage Christians, "Our confidence rests not on objectivity but rather on the convictional power of the Holy Spirit . . . the loss of objectivity, then, does not entail a loss of kerygmatic boldness about the truth of the gospel."[86] While Smith's provocative claim here is interesting on its own, it is more important in its assertion that there is no such thing as objectivity for humans.[87] What kind of an assertion is it when one says, "Humans cannot have objective knowledge?" It seems like it is none other than an absolute claim about epistemology. It denies anthropological objectivity *in toto*. However, one could fairly inquire as to whether the assertion applies to itself. Thus, we conclude with Moreland, "Given the self-refuting nature of such claims, and given the fact that we all experience regularly the activity of comparing our conceptions of an entity with the entity itself as a way

85. What Moreland may have added to buttress his case is the argument that substance dualism is the best explanation for the fact that his thought has intentionality or "aboutness." Since mental states have intentionality and physical states do not, dualism is the best account for what kind of thing a thought is. Penner's linguistic account of mental states cannot explain intentionality. It can only be described by referring to the conjunction of semantic expressions with various behaviors.

86. Smith, *Who's Afraid of Postmodernism?* 51.

87. The Christian may joyfully concede that it is not necessary to demonstrate one's objective knowledge to have kerygmatic boldness. After all, Evangelicals are primarily committed to the fact that Christian faith is first a relationship with the person of Jesus Christ. Demonstrating objectivity is not necessary when the goal is to know a person. However, having (not demonstrating) objective knowledge about the person, even if it is knowledge by acquaintance, is vital for the Christian. If the person that I know through Christian faith is not, in fact, Jesus Christ, then I have been somehow duped into the tragic belief that my relationship is not with Jesus himself, but with some other person (or figment of my imagination), the nature and character of whom I am, sadly, ignorant.

of adjusting those conceptions, it is hard to see why anyone, especially a Christian, would adopt the postmodern view."[88]

CONCLUSION

Smith, Penner, and Raschke criticize the possibility of universal reason, the idea that propositions are truth-bearers, and the correspondence theory of truth. They argue that objective reason fails to deliver context-independent truth about the world. I argue that some minimalistic features of universal reason that are expressed in Aristotelean logic are necessarily true. To deny the logical categories used by apologetics is absurd, for one must affirm basic logic in order to deny it. Evangelical apologetics, they say, has bought into the misleading modernist paradigm that we can know objective truth. Truth is not propositional; it is relational. I respond by showing that their ironic rejection of foundationalism is conflated with a caricature of Cartesian epistemology and that their arguments depend on a correspondence theory that they mean to reject. The next chapter will explore some key theological objections to natural theology: the god of natural theology is not the God of Christian faith, true faith makes no appeal to reason, the impossibility of receiving general revelation, the Reformed objection to natural theology, and the ethics of apologetics.

88. Moreland, "Truth, Contemporary Philosophy, and the Postmodern Turn," 87.

4

Postmodern Evangelical Rejections of Natural Theology (Part 2)

To THIS POINT, THE major objections to natural theology posed by the postmodern thinkers Carl A. Raschke, Myron B. Penner, and James K. A. Smith considered here have focused primarily on philosophical issues that have theological implications: the rejection of Universal Reason and the rejection of the correspondence theory of truth along with propositionalism and foundationalism. Now, this work will pivot to address issues more explicitly theological in nature (but not without reference to philosophy). These postmodern Evangelicals reject natural theology because it is incompatible with some biblical principles and theological commitments that they hold dear. In the following sections, we will address the following issues. (1) Natural theology leads to the problem of ontotheology wherein the god of natural theology is incommensurate with the God of Christian faith. (2) Natural theology, they say, is incompatible with the life of faith, which is not accommodating to reason. (3) Revelation is a disclosure of God's self which cannot be received by or known through reason. Through sin, the *imago dei* has suffered a fatal blow so that humanity always suppresses the knowledge of God revealed in nature. (4) Natural theology requires a way of life that the Christian will find abhorrent.

THE GOD (OR GOD) OF NATURAL THEOLOGY

Ontotheology

Penner, Raschke, and Smith reject natural theology because they contend that any philosophical inferences or demonstrations regarding God fall into the category of ontotheology. As shown in the second chapter, this kind of God-talk has been famously disparaged by Heidegger, Caputo, and Westphal. Ontotheology is any attempt to make God a subject of philosophical discourse or to posit God as an explanatory entity with respect to ontology. Speaking of God this way robs the world of mystery, leads to a God who does not inspire awe or worship, and, more dangerously, "opens the way for the unfettered self-assertion of the will to power in the form of modernity, namely the quest of science and technology to have everything at human disposal."[1]

Raschke argues that the critique of ontotheology is actually implicit in the hermeneutical critique of theology proper in Heidegger.[2] Theology attempts to use a finite set of indicators that depends on a logic about God, a *theo-logos*, and is itself dependent on the metaphysics of signs that is undermined by deconstruction.

> The kind of hermeneutics that comes out of the metaphysics of signs regards the text as possessing certain intelligible meaning-contents which have nothing to do with the essential, revealing presence of the words themselves, but which indicate historical, grammatical, or lexigraphical relationships between terms in a web of manipulable re-presentations.[3]

Theology, especially the philosophical theology that speaks of a prime mover or a highest being, intends to capture the reality of the signified even though it is only a set of finite signifiers. Yet language cannot ensure the unity of the "representation and re-presented."[4] Rather, the revelation of God is a gift that is given, not a presence that can be grasped through representations. Language is the mode in which the gift is given, but the mode of language does not guarantee that the recipient can control the gift. This is

---

1. Westphal, "Onto-theology, Metanarrative, Perspectivism," 145.

2. See Heidegger, *Essays in Metaphysics*.

3. Raschke, *Alchemy of the Word,* 64. Raschke is interacting here with Altizer, *Self-Embodiment of God.*

4. Ibid., 65.

precisely what theology does with God as a subject of metaphysical inquiry. It seeks to make God the Ultimately Signified. However, a hermeneutics that overturns the metaphysics of signs shows that this is impossible because God's "'presencing-presence' has been obscured by representative-calculative thought."[5] Ontotheology, as a subspecies of metaphysics, is impossible given the insights of a hermeneutics that overturns the metaphysics of signs.

This insight is presaged, according to Raschke, by Nietzsche's affirmation of the death of God.[6] Nietzsche was responding to Hegel's metaphysics of immanent Being or Spirit in which the idea of God is no longer necessary "apart from our self-awareness."[7] If God is immanently present and can be discovered through philosophical analysis, then this God is merely a reflection of human being rather than the Being of philosophy. Raschke comments on Nietzsche's affirmation of the death of God, "Modern thought can be intimated as Luciferian thought insofar as it launches a kind of angelic rebellion against God as the infinite Other in relation to what at a historical level metaphysical thinking has considered itself incapable of compassing."[8] This means that the God of metaphysics is not a theological response to a general revelation, but a rational pretention that seeks knowledge of God in an improper way. According to Nietzsche, this leads to a nihilism wherein Christian faith is rationalized. Raschke argues that the rationalism of faith that is entailed by ontotheology "empties faith of its content . . . [it] 'kills' God."[9] Postmodern theology, on the other hand, attempts to speak about Being without recourse to metaphysics. "If we are truly to 'let God be God,' as Luther put it, we must not enclose God within even the most elegant architecture of reason, even the kind of thinking that portrays Deity as the highest or supreme Being above all beings."[10] The solution is to assert that there is an ontological difference between Being and all other beings. God is not the highest in a series or the pinnacle of a certain kind of being; rather, God is the Wholly Other, the one of whom philosophical inquiries into metaphysics can say nothing. Since the method cannot comprehend the subject, we have reached the end of ontotheology, and according to Ra-

5. Ibid.

6. See the parable of the madman in Nietzsche, *The Gay Science*, 181–12.

7. Raschke, *The Next Reformation*, 42.

8. Ibid., 43.

9. Ibid., 44.

10. Ibid., 49.

schke, "The End of Theology."[11] The only way to allow God to be God is to abandon talk of the Highest Being and the Unmoved Mover, the God of the philosophers who is no God at all, in favor of the *via negativa*, which "provides a roadmap for overcoming metaphysics and nihilism, since it self-consciously relativizes all pretensions to ontotheological certitude while at the same time permitting a peculiar language of faith that is at once specific and filled with humility."[12] Negative theology allows God to speak through language, but does not permit language to claim that it has discovered or comprehended God. It is a language of devotion rather than a language of rationalized Being.

In his affirmation of the central concerns of the critique against ontotheology, James K. A. Smith is careful to retain a place for a genuinely Christian philosophy. With Christian atheist theologians like John A. T. Robinson, Thomas J. J. Altizer, and Jean-Luc Marion, Smith agrees that there is no comparing the God of philosophical theism with the God of Abraham, Isaac, and Jacob. He quotes Marion approvingly, "'God is, exists, and that is the least of things. At issue here is not the possibility of God's attaining to Being, but, quite the opposite, the possibility of Being's attaining to God.' And in this regard, I too must confess that I am not a theist, that I am a Christian a-theist."[13] The focus of Smith's essay is to retain a place for a Christian philosophy. While Heidegger's Christian atheism "is concerned with excluding faith from philosophy," Smith argues that all philosophy is religious in nature.[14] Yet at the core of his divergence from Heidegger is a central agreement, a presupposition that God is not a subject of philosophical inquiry. He asserts that Christian theism or Christian theistic philosophy is delusory because the God of Christian theology is not the God of philosophical theism.[15] Smith makes his rejection of ontotheology more explicit in *Speech and Theology*. In this book, he argues that the kind of philosophical reflection (particularly that of Hegel) that attempts to conceptualize God through philosophical analysis inevitably does violence to God. "The concept becomes a means of domination, seizure, encompass-

---

11. See Raschke, *Alchemy of the Word*, chapter 5. See also, Raschke, "The End of Theology," 159–79.

12. Raschke, *The Next Reformation*, 57.

13. Smith, "Art of Christian Atheism," 71. Smith is quoting and commenting on Marion, *God Without Being*, xix–xx.

14. Ibid., 72.

15. Ibid., 71.

ing, such that one who has the concept of the thing *has the thing.*"[16] This should never be the case when thinking or speaking of the Infinite, for this attempts to control the concept of God, divorces Christian thought from historic Christian knowledge of God, and marginalizes those who do not share a rationalized or conceptualized picture of God. "What Heidegger decried as 'ontotheology' is a distinctly modern phenomenon. But it is precisely within a theological context that the violence of such concepts is appreciated . . . the concept violates transcendences, reducing and 'cutting down to size' the Infinite."[17] Again, Smith wants philosophy to be able to speak meaningfully about God, but he is concerned that modernity has given license for philosophy to claim to have mastered what is signified by the word *God.* Moreover, he wants to challenge philosophy's ability to have a rationalized knowledge of God.

Myron B. Penner claims that God cannot be a subject of philosophical discourse, especially if that discourse arises from modernity's conception of reason. Nevertheless, Penner argues that premodern philosophy appropriately attempted to make God a subject of philosophical discourse: "In premodernity rational thought begins with an attitude of wonder, and the basic orientation for philosophical reflection is characterized as an attempt to explain the perplexities of the universe (which causes one to wonder)."[18] This makes philosophical reasoning about the Unmoved Mover or the First Cause completely appropriate. God is not the subject of philosophical discourse in the sense that premoderns attempted to capture and contain God via autonomous reason. Rather, the presence of mystery caused the premoderns to posit God as the ground for their wonder. Penner claims that this use of reason to talk about God changes in modernity when the autonomous human knower becomes the paradigm for rationality. "The premodern *logos* entails that human rationality is an external event that comes to one, as it were from the outside . . . Modernity, however, grounds philosophy and philosophical reflection in a rational, self-conscious, and self-possessed human agent."[19] Truth is something that the philosopher owns in modernity, as she reasons about the cosmos and is able to make objective statements using an individualistic rationality. The implication is that if God is a subject of this kind of rationality, then knowledge of God

16. Smith, *Speech and Theology*, 5. Emphasis in the original.

17. Ibid.

18. Penner, "Introduction," 21.

19. Ibid., 23.

loses all of its wonder, and one is able to control the subject at hand through philosophical analysis. However, "Christian truth presumes to *master us*, rather than to be *mastered by us*."[20]

Despite these warnings and insults (Smith: "A number of Christian philosophers continue to delude themselves by thinking that theistic philosophy is Christian."[21]), it is not obvious that Evangelical advocates of natural theology are guilty of the violence or attempted control ascribed to their philosophical theism. First, Heidegger's critique of ontotheology is largely misrepresented by Caputo, Westphal, and—most importantly for our purposes—Raschke. Raschke takes Heidegger's critique of ontotheology as a warning against philosophy requiring God to enter philosophy on philosophy's terms. Instead, Christian theology should resist philosophical theology and embrace apophatics.

> Negative theology provides us with a primitive roadmap for overcoming metaphysics and nihilism, since it self-consciously relativizes all pretensions to ontotheological certitude while at the same time permitting a peculiar language of faith that is at once specific and filled with humility.[22]

Many have taken the Heideggerian critique to entail that God can never be a subject of philosophical inquiry. While this is arguably not the point that Smith and Penner make in their consideration of the critique of ontotheology, it certainly seems to be the strategy appropriated by Raschke. However, Matthew Schunke has convincingly argued that Heidegger's critique does not require a turn to the strategies of apophatic theology. Rather, "it should free philosophy to speak about the divine in a way that does not control or manipulate the divine."[23] While the rest of Schunke's project (a Heideggerian phenomenology of religion) may not be agreeable to most Evangelical philosophers and theologians, his argument attempts to retain religious experience as a topic for philosophical analysis. According to Schunke, Heidegger's method of formal indication, a revisable way of describing a phenomenon of everyday experience without reference to preconceived theoretical frameworks, allows philosophy to describe, albeit subjectively, the phenomena of religious experience.[24] This is far afield from

20. Penner, "Blog 6: Postmodern Apologetics," 139. Emphasis in the original.

21. Smith, "Art of Christian Atheism," 71.

22. Raschke, *The Next Reformation*, 57.

23. Schunke, "Apophatic Abuse," 164.

24. In contrast to what Heidegger calls conceptual indication, formal indication

the demands of apophatics, which would have philosophy be silent in considering the divine so as to avoid the pretensions of control. This is only enough to rebut the claim that the critique of ontotheology requires the remedy of negative theology. Much more is needed to show that the critique of ontotheology is wrongheaded when applied to Evangelical natural theology.

Second, it is not clear that we should apply the insights of Heidegger's critique to Evangelical natural theology, primarily because Heidegger's primary target is Hegel. "For Hegel, thought and being are one and the same . . . The evolution of human consciousness is fundamentally this self-unfolding of God or Spirit, which ultimately thinks all opposites and therefore becomes the thinking of Being as true being of the thinking subject."[25] Now, if Raschke's characterization of Hegel is accurate, then this may entail an attempt by philosophy to exercise control on the divine. As the collective consciousness proceeds in its abstractions about the divine, there is a real metaphysical control over the Being in question. Thinking in this way actualizes Spirit and takes its nature hostage to its philosophizing. However, does this kind of philosophy of religion resemble Evangelical natural theology? Consider William Lane Craig's disclaimers in the final pages of his book *The Kalām Cosmological Argument*. "The *kalām* cosmological argument leads us to a personal Creator of the universe, but as to whether this Creator is omniscient, good, perfect, and so forth, we shall not inquire."[26] He continues by arguing that knowledge of God's existence should lead us to inquire whether or not this God has revealed God's self in such a way that more about God may be learned, namely through special revelation. In his endnotes on this point, Craig says that the argument is not an attempt to give extensive theological knowledge. Rather, he is simply saying that, "If the argument is sound, then it is true that *a personal Creator of the universe exists.*"[27] Rather than controlling God, this leaves us "wide-eyed and open-mouthed" at the idea that this God exists.[28] Natural theology does not necessarily remove one's sense of wonder. Moreover, the argument "does not try to prove *too much*" in terms of conceptual facts about God;

---

is meant to avoid metaphysics. On this topic, Schunke recommends Crowell, *Husserl, Heidegger, and the Space of Meaning*, esp. chapter 7.

25. Raschke, *The Next Reformation*, 41.

26. Craig, *The Kalām Cosmological Argument*, 152.

27. Ibid., 172, note 171. Emphasis in the original.

28. Ibid.

instead it causes us to wonder who this God is and whether God has been revealed in other ways.[29] Perhaps a level of control is entailed by saying that God is personal and that God is Creator, but it is hard to see why any Evangelical would object to thinking about God in these terms. The mere use of the terms "personal" and "Creator" does not imply control of the characteristics tagged by those terms.[30]

Finally, Smith's account of reference and inference seems like it would absolve natural theology of any attempt at control over God. In agreement with Robert Brandom's work on the nature of inferences, Smith argues that epistemic justification is "fundamentally *social*."[31] Reasoned conclusions are rooted in communities of practice, and we know conceptual truth because it is ultimately not a type of knowing-that, but rather a type of know-how.[32] Now many Evangelicals are correspondence theorists, believing that their inferences are valid if they correspond to states of affairs that they purport to describe, but let us assume that Smith (and Brandom) are right. If our references are not a matter of correspondence, but part of an inferential game played in a relevant community (say, Evangelical philosophers of religion), then claiming that an argument in natural theology is a valid inference should not be objectionable. In *Speech and Theology*, Smith argues that ontotheology is objectionable because it entails that the "one who has the concept of the thing *has the thing*."[33] This would mean that philosophizing about God would be an attempt to exert some kind of control over the relevant referential concepts. However, if Smith is right about inferential logic, then one's philosophizing about God cannot correspond to states of affairs in reality. Referential tags like "personal" and "Creator" are defined by the community's practices; therefore, their use does not imply control of the *Ding an sich*.

---

29. Ibid., 173, note 171. Emphasis in the original.

30. At minimum, all that "personal" entails is that God is not non-personal though Craig does argue that "personal" is apt because it implies agency. However, this is not central to the argument itself. "Creator," because it could be used any number of ways, merely implies that God is not a creature. It is difficult to see why the entailment for the first term and the implication for the second are objectionable for Evangelicals. Moreover, the *kalām* cosmological argument does not presume to say what should be understood by these terms.

31. Smith, *Who's Afraid of Relativism?* 130.

32. See Brandom, *Articulating Reasons*, 46–63.

33. Smith, *Speech and Theology*, 5. Emphasis in the original.

This underscores that Evangelical natural theology often assumes that theology (including natural theology) properly practiced is a response to God's revelation. In his *Christian Apologetics*, Douglas Groothuis argues that natural theology is only possible because Scripture speaks of God having revealed God's self in nature. "Because the Bible itself claims that God is revealed in nature and conscience, belief in general revelation is rooted in special revelation."[34] (That is, the definitive authority on our beliefs and practices, the Bible, claims that God has spoken in the natural world.) If God has revealed God's self in the natural world, then it is on no other terms than God's own. The presupposition in Evangelical natural theology is that because God has spoken in nature, it is proper for us to engage God cognitively through analysis of the natural world. However, by employing the ontotheological critique, Raschke, Smith, and Penner seem to be denying God's general revelation. There is no doubt that these authors have much to say on the possibility of natural theology given other issues like human contingency, the noetic effects of sin, etc.[35] Still, their rejection of natural theology in effect challenges God's ability to make God's self known in the natural world. They do not offer a reason why this challenge to God's ability does not amount to an attempt to control the concept (i.e. "God cannot effectively make God's self known in the natural world."), the very thing that the critique of ontotheology warns against. Perhaps, they might object that what is at issue is not God's ability to reveal, but humanity's ability to receive God's revelation. However, this would simply beg the question of God's ability to reveal despite humanity's limits. In either case, one is limiting what God can and cannot do.

The Idolatry Objection

A related issue to the ontotheological objection is that the god that one learns about through natural theology bears scant resemblance to the God of the Christian faith, the God of Abraham, Isaac, and Jacob who is revealed in Jesus Christ. While much of the objection to the god of natural theology is due to a version of the Reformed argument against natural theology, Raschke, Smith, and Penner argue that the god of natural theology is a false god, and one's veneration of the god of natural theology, even if only as a precis to a more robust Trinitarian theology, will amount to idolatry.

---

34. Groothuis, *Christian Apologetics*, 181.

35. See below for a discussion of these issues.

The one who claims *the God of natural theology is God* is an idolater. We will address the Reformed objection below, but for now, we will focus on Raschke's, Smith's, and Penner's argument that the god of natural theology is an idol. They offer two basic arguments for this charge: (1) Any god who is not revealed as the Triune God is an idol; and (2) natural theology turns Reason into a false god.

First, the god of natural theology bears no resemblance to the God revealed in the Scriptures. Carl Raschke argues that the god of natural theology is necessarily minimalistic, reducing God to an idea or a meta-physical best explanation, rather than the God who defies our definitions and speculations. This is because "the God of the philosophers is *logical*. The God of Abraham, Isaac, and Jacob is *relational*. And because God is a Being not in himself, but a Being in relation, we know him through his Word and through the testimony of many who have borne witness to his mighty works."[36] The nature of God as a Being in relation means that logi-cal proofs will distort God's true identity. God relates to humanity, and we know God through God's revelation to God's people, not through a logical proof. Therefore, natural theology "reif[ies] the Supreme Being" by altering his definitively relational action.[37] Logic is one aspect of God's finite world, so using logic to identify God subordinates the Infinite to one finite aspect of creation. (Natural theology, then, confuses the creation [in this case, logic] with the Creator, and this is idolatry.) With Lévinas, Raschke argues that the God of Abraham, Isaac, and Jacob cannot be known through logic because "God's presence as the One who is always for us, as the Other who is in his nature one-for-the-other, is impossible to inscribe within the struc-ture of logic and metaphysics."[38]

James K. A. Smith is concerned that we do not attempt to make God an object of universal language. God as God is in God's self cannot be adequately described or apprehended by language. While his concerns regarding ontotheology do not rule out speaking of God, he claims that us-ing objective rationality about God makes the object of our rationalization an idol. We are actually worshiping the sign rather than the one to whom the sign supposedly points. Any philosophical language that uses reason to produce God as a concept becomes an idol. "The conceptual idol is a kind of semiotic sin, a failure of reference which is a failure to recognize the

36. Raschke, *The Next Reformation*, 81. Emphasis in the original.

37. Ibid., 82.

38. Ibid., 214.

(in)completion of the sign, but rather treats it as an end in itself."[39] If the reference in our rationalizations fails to connect us to the actual God, then we are worshiping a god, an idol, of our own conceptualizations. Silence is not the answer, though; God's incarnation is key for how we are to speak. The Incarnation is a "condescension to the conditions of the finite," but it does not allow us to employ God as a concept.[40] God's appearance in Christ is the condescension of which we may speak, but only insofar as our speech points us toward a proper existential orientation toward the subject. We must offer praise or confession with our speech, for these are the only modes of address that retain God's alterity and transcendence.

> Thus it is possible to speak of God, but in the mode of *praise*, as a non-objectifying, non-positivistic mode of conceptualization which does not reduce God to a concept, but rather employs language in such a way that respects God's transcendence and *refers* the listener to experience the thing itself.[41]

While the thrust behind this development in Smith's thought is not explicitly natural theology, he is clear that this account of speaking of God is superior to "the 'rationalizing tendency of modernity and ontotheology'" that he has elsewhere explicitly identified with natural theology.[42] Because natural theology produces a referent other than the God of the Incarnation and because it fails to produce praise and confession, it leads to idolatry.

Penner is similarly concerned that the God that one encounters in modern apologetics empties Christianity of all of its meaningful content. Modern apologetics is an academic industry valued for its ability to counter the popular appeal of the New Atheism.[43] To do this, it must embrace the secular and rationalistic emphases of the New Atheism as the means to discovering objective truth. Apologists use natural theology to establish the existence of God, which is simply a nonreligious theism, but this God does not have any resemblance to the God that "theists" worship, be they Chris-

---

39. Smith, *Speech and Theology*, 123. He is making a Derridean distinction between the incommensurability between the signified and the sign.

40. Ibid., 126.

41. Ibid., 128.

42. Ibid., 129. Here, Smith is quoting Godzieba, "Ontotheology to Excess," 18. Smith seems to treat this kind of rationalized theology the same way that he treats "correlationist" theology. See esp. Smith, *Who's Afraid of Postmodernism?* 123–27.

43. See Dawkins, *The God Delusion*; Dennett, *Breaking the Spell*; Harris, *The End of Faith*; and Hitchens, *God is Not Great*.

tians, Jews, or Muslims. "When God's existence is established according to modern secular reason, all that really is demonstrated is the dispensability of anything that resembles belief in God."[44] This kind of thinking about God "kills God," leaving in its place the God of theism, an idol that divorces devotees from the richness of the practices of worship that give their faith meaning.[45] Not only is theism an idol, it is not even an accurate tag for the families of religion who believe in the existence of God. The God of theism is not the God revealed in Christ, as any religious person could tell you.

The second argument offered against natural theology related to the idolatry objection is that modern natural theology makes reason into a false god. Carl Raschke bemoans that reason has become the god of modernity in general, but also that the veneration of universal reason has infected the churches who trace their identity to the Reformation. Reformation theology, Raschke argues, commended the faithful to surrender their intellects as they approach God through faith alone. Luther, for example, "regarded the preference for rational examination in coming to conclusions about God as a profound sort of spiritual prostitution. He referred to reason as 'that bitch goddess.'"[46] Sadly, those who embrace natural theology, along with liberal theologians who accept universal reason (albeit with different doctrinal formulations), have turned their backs on their Reformation heritage by blurring "the distinction between the natural and revealed truth about God."[47] This is evidenced among those Evangelicals like R. Scott Smith who reject postmodernism for what they call "'epistemological realism,' a fancy word for 'natural theology,' which evangelicals historically have considered inimical to the Christian revelation itself."[48] In their epistemology and in their witness, these Evangelicals have actually turned their backs on the gospel by requiring "philosophical clarity and coherence," reasonable conditions applied in their natural theology and in their criticism of postmodern Evangelical thought.[49] However, arguing that the conditions of

44. Penner, *The End of Apologetics*, 61–62.

45. Ibid., 62. He continues, "Speaking theologically, we could say that accepting the modern paradigm as I have described it is tantamount to conceptual idolatry and methodological blasphemy."

46. Raschke, *The Next Reformation*, 27.

47. Ibid.

48. Raschke, *GloboChrist*, 156. "Epistemological realism" is R. Scott Smith's term for his alternative to postmodern epistemology, which Smith thinks leads to relativism. See Smith, *Truth and the New Kind of Christian*, 61.

49. Ibid., 157.

clarity and coherence are necessary for Christian theology and practice is "a distinctly unbiblical and even more idolatrous or adulterous contention."[50] These Evangelicals have actually betrayed their relationships to God by subjecting the gospel to the modernist paradigm, and this leads to arrogance, self-deception, and "a swinish and self-congratulatory intellectual faddism," turning the church "into a brothel of philosophical and cultural fashions rather than a genuine house of prayer."[51] If the modernist conception of reason is used in Christian theology and practice, then no trace of Christian devotion remains, and the Church has replaced the worship of God with the worship of an idol.

James K. A. Smith similarly argues that reason can become an object of worship in modernity. "All of humanity is constituted by a religious structure," yet through sin the worship of God is replaced with various idols.[52] These idols can be capitalism, the worship of a god in another religion, "the revelations of reason, or liberal tolerance, or whatever."[53] The revelation of God in Christ is the litmus test for true religion, so any religion that accepts the revelations of reason will be a kind of idolatry.[54] Penner is also concerned that the modernist paradigm of rationalized search for objective reality produces a kind of idolatry. Agreeing with Gabriel Marcel's philosophical anthropology, he argues that the pursuit of truth in modernity is a scientific endeavor "which splits us off from material reality in order to study and know it (empirically, epistemologically). Marcel describes this abstract scientific pursuit of reality as having a hypnotic effect that renders its arbitrary and idolatrous character invisible to us."[55] Natural theology adopts this paradigm which prohibits valuing the truly good. When natural theology is employed in Christian apologetics, this means that reason is the highest court of appeal, impugning God's sovereignty and "disincarnating"

---

50. Ibid.

51. Ibid., 158.

52. Smith, *Introducing Radical Orthodoxy*, 115.

53. Ibid., note 95.

54. Smith does not develop the connection between idolatry and natural theology here, but within his larger critique of reason as a method of discovering truth about God (see below), it is clear that he would apply the charge of idolatry to natural theology because reason is a key method for discovering truth about God revealed apart from special revelation.

55. Penner, *The End of Apologetics*, 89. See also Marcel, *Creative Fidelity*.

human being.[56] Biblical witness makes its appeal only to God; apologetics makes its appeal to its false god.

In the following, I will address these charges that our authors make against Evangelical natural theology by discussing the permissibility of arguing for a minimalistic theism, the nature of God with respect to reason, and whether Evangelical natural theology has accepted the modernist paradigm in an inappropriate way. First, is it the case that the minimalistic theism toward which apologetic arguments point is idolatry? Does Evangelical natural theology turn its advocates into idolaters? It seems like this charge stems from a misunderstanding of what Evangelical apologists are trying to do when they offer arguments for the existence of God. Apologetics does not mean to move the skeptic to worship God through arguments. Rather, arguments may cause skeptics to open their minds to the God revealed in the Scriptures and in the life of the church. The goal is not to have the argument point to the Triune God, but to "move a skeptic or an atheist a bit closer to taking the distinctive claims of the Christian faith more seriously."[57] William Lane Craig argues that a logical argument that results in a minimalistic theism appeals to facts to which all parties may reasonably agree such as the laws of logic or common everyday experiences.[58] This kind of activity can show that Christianity is true by confirming one of its key features, the existence of one God. This is different from knowing that Christianity is true; this knowledge is provided by the Holy Spirit. Since the Holy Spirit attends this knowledge, this would include the personal knowledge of who God is. Someone knows God's triune nature through the Holy Spirit, and it is not obvious why a previous belief in a generic theism is an impediment to the knowledge that the Spirit provides. To the contrary, a generic theism could make the skeptic more open to the Holy Spirit's activity.

This seems to be exactly what Paul does at the Areopagus in Athens in Acts 17:16–34. In this famous passage, Paul, on his secondary missionary journey (ca. 49–52 CE), speaks to the Epicurean and Stoic philosophers in Athens. "For as I walked around and looked carefully at your objects of worship, I even found an altar with this inscription: to an unknown god. So you are ignorant of the very thing you worship—and this is what I am going to proclaim to you" (v. 23, NIV). He finds common ground between an

---

56. Ibid., 88.

57. Groothuis, *Christian Apologetics*, 183.

58. Craig, *Reasonable Faith*, 55–56.

unknown deity and the God that he wishes to proclaim more specifically. Evangelical commentator F. F. Bruce argues, "Since they acknowledged their ignorance of the divine nature, he would tell them the truth about it."[59] This "Unknown God" is similar to the God that one learns of through natural theology. This God does not have a defined nature nor discerned attributes. However, the knowledge of this God's existence is revered. Far from legitimizing the cult that had developed in Athens to this "Unknown God," Paul uses the knowledge of this God's existence to point the hearers toward "the God who made the world and everything in it" (v. 24, NIV). This is the strategy used by natural theologians when establishing a minimal theism. James Barr agrees with this interpretation, saying, "Acts 17 cannot be fully expounded without opening the gate toward some sort of natural theology. If you are as completely against all natural theology as Barth was, the only honest thing to do is to say that Paul, as represented by Luke in this chapter of Acts, was *wrong*."[60] Though he has in mind particularly Barthian arguments against natural theology, Barr's assertion that natural theology is legitimized in Acts 17 applies at a more general level, as well.

Second, the criticisms that Raschke, Smith, and Penner raise against using reason to argue for God's existence are fallacious. Consider Raschke's statement, "The God of the philosophers is *logical*. The God of Abraham, Isaac, and Jacob is *relational*."[61] There are a couple of options of how to interpret Raschke on this score. The first is to say that he is merely arguing that God's essential nature is not logical, but relational. God is not an explanatory principle, but a Being in relation. The second is to say that Raschke is saying that God is irrational and relational. He clearly has the first meaning in mind as he is arguing that God is not the "ultimate *fact* in a metaphysical sense."[62] But I think Raschke has the second meaning in

59. Bruce, *The Book of Acts*, 336.

60. Barr, *Biblical Faith and Natural Theology*, 26. Emphasis in the original. To those who would claim that this kind of apologetic encounter was unsuccessful (see vv. 32–34), Barr replies, "One cannot say, then, that the reception on the Areopagus was an overwhelmingly negative one. To anyone who reads the text as a whole, there can be no doubt that for Luke the incident was not a momentary error or a failure but a high point on the total progress of the gospel from Jerusalem to Rome, through the great cities of the world. Athens, indeed, did not become one of the major centres of early Christianity, as did (say) Antioch and Ephesus, and even Corinth in some measure, and this fact only increases the reader's conviction that for St Luke the Athenian incident was of major symbolic importance." See ibid., 31.

61. Raschke, *The Next Reformation*, 81. Emphasis in the original.

62. Ibid., 82.

mind, as well. This is why he often writes about the "absurdity" of God's actions, particularly the Incarnation, which "remains irrevocably absurd."[63] God's nature cannot be reconciled with reason. But is that the case? It is not clear why the scandals or the paradoxes of God's nature or God's actions (or our limited knowledge thereof) imply that God is not logical. In fact, God invites the people of God, "Come now, and let us reason together" (Isa 1:18, NASB). Carl F. H. Henry argues that "the Logos—not the Irrational or the Paradoxical—became flesh."[64] Douglas Groothuis has shown that Jesus' ministry is characterized by the skillful use of logical argumentation. Jesus escapes the horns of a dilemma (Matt 22:15–22), uses *a fortiori* argumentation (Luke 13:10–17; John 7:21–24), appeals to empirical evidence (Matt 11:4–6; cf. Luke 7:22), and makes a *reductio ad absurdum* argument that he is not casting out demons by the power of Beelzebub (Matt 12:25–27).[65] Raschke simply begs the question when he suggests that God's relationality excludes God's rationality, as if those two attributes cannot together cohere in God. Moreover, knowledge of God as a metaphysical fact that can be known through logic does no more to impugn God's relational nature than does God's relational nature impugn God's identity as the righteous judge. Acknowledging one fact about God does not minimize other facts about God.

Third, Evangelical theologians have not accepted the modernist paradigm with respect to truth and rationality in such a way that makes them guilty of idolatry. Smith is right to note that "all of humanity is constituted by a religious structure," and that apart from the true worship of God in Christ, our religious devotions will be idolatrous.[66] However, it does not follow that if one discovers God's revelation through reason, then that person has become a worshiper of reason. Craig A. Boyd argues that one must use reason to apprehend God's revelation in faith because "there is never any human apprehension or thought that does not employ reason . . . There is no alternative."[67] Nancey Pearcey argues that Enlightenment rationalism does turn reason into an idol because reason is wrongly supposed to be autonomous. However, reason can be used in Christian apologetics because humans are made in the image of God, showing that "human reason has

---

63. Raschke, "Faith and Philosophy in Tension," 52.

64. Henry, *God, Revelation, and Authority*, 3:165.

65. See Groothuis, *On Jesus*, chapter 3.

66. Smith, *Introducing Radical Orthodoxy*, 115. See Romans 1:18–25.

67. Boyd, "Synthesis of Reason," 79.

the high dignity of reflecting the divine reason. Christianity thus affirms the reliability of human cognitive capacities (without becoming rational-istic, turning reason into a god)."[68] Raschke, Smith, and Penner think that, protestations to the contrary, apologists are performatively worshiping reason. However, apologists like Pearcey are aware of this possibility and even make a similar charge against their rationalist interlocutors, yet they root reason's metaphysic in God's nature. It is, therefore, reflected in the *imago dei*, and its proper use simply is a result of proper alignment to the nature of reality under God and not a subversion of, or replacement for, God's authority.

THE NATURE OF FAITH

The conflict over the relationship between faith and reason is no more marked than in the intra-Evangelical debate on natural theology and es-pecially so between advocates of natural theology and their postmodern detractors. Smith, Penner, and Raschke argue that Christian faith is inimi-cal to reason; that is, faith is always a gift received from God against any intellectual power that can be exercised apart from God's gifting. Christian faith is a commitment without reference to and even in spite of evidence. It finds its home not in doctrinal formulations that can be defended accord-ing to scientific reason, but in communities of faith. People have faith that they exercise in embodied contexts. Pauline theology supports this line of argumentation regarding faith. Faith is absurd and only makes sense in the communities that give it meaning. So apologetics with its universal reason and its appeal to the intellect will always be out of place in lived Chris-tian faith. This section will survey these lines of argumentation in Smith's, Penner's, and Raschke's work and then argue that their account of faith is lacking key cognitive elements while taking issue with their misuse of Paul's writings, particularly 1 Corinthians 1–2.

To begin, one of the key issues that must be overcome in attempt-ing to apply the insights of postmodern philosophy to Evangelical faith is that postmodernism is "incredulity toward metanarratives."[69] As a grand story, Christianity may seem to easily qualify as that toward which post-modernism may be suspicious. Insightfully, James K. A. Smith clarifies that Lyotard's principle does not apply to all grand stories, but only to those

68. Pearcey, *Finding Truth*, 49.

69. Lyotard, *The Postmodern Condition*, xxiv.

that would be legitimized by an appeal to Universal Reason. Smith argues that Christianity does not "claim to be legitimated by Reason, but rather trusted in faith."[70] In an apologetic for Jacques Derrida, Smith takes up the Kierkegaardian interpretation of the story of Abraham, whose obedience in faith to the word of God amounted to a transgression against universal ethics and objective knowledge. "According to the register of ethics and reasons, to respond to such a call would be sheer madness—but this madness is reckoned to Abraham as *faith*."[71] The Christian must eschew knowledge and reason in order to receive authentic faith. This faith does not make sense; in fact, it may be seen as madness in terms of modernity's standards for knowledge and respectability.

Raschke argues that "faith always has primacy over philosophy," and this is exactly what the Reformers had in mind with the slogan *sola fide*.[72] Christian belief always stands apart from any kind of rational warrant. The person who has faith that God was in Christ is truly taking a leap of faith against any evidence that could be offered in support. Philosophy cannot "persuade me or encourage me to 'become a Christian,' which in itself is not something I decide once for all but in each decision I make every day."[73] In this way, faith is not truly something that one has but a way of life in which someone chooses to live. Yet this way of life is not grounded in having good reasons or in any philosophical prolegomena like establishing the existence of God or of the historical reliability of the biblical texts. In fact, this way of life will look foolish on philosophical terms. Because we cannot reconcile Christian faith with worldly wisdom, "We must ask ourselves whether we will take the leap of faith in a movement the early church called *sacrificium intellectus*, the surrendering of our deductive and discursive apologetics."[74] In this regard, it seems that Raschke advocates the idea that Christianity is anti-reason, if what we are dealing with is the discourse of rational knowledge in which philosophers trade. Penner similarly argues that apologetics misunderstands the nature of religious commitment in this regard. Faith cannot be analyzed, systematized, and criticized according to philosophical criteria. Apologetics attempts to do this, viewing all religious commitments "as if they were philosophical positions and propositions that are more

70. Smith, "Little Story about Metanarratives," 125.

71. Smith, *Jacques Derrida*, 83. Emphasis in the original.

72. Raschke, "Faith and Philosophy in Tension," 43.

73. Ibid., 49.

74. Raschke, *The Next Reformation*, 131.

or less disembodied and disconnected from the practices and practical concerns of everyday life."[75] But true faith is not like this. Faith is more something that one does rather cognitive positions to which one adheres. These authors closely connect faith to practice, denying any kind of rational support that philosophy might offer to the person of faith.

This way of life enabled by faith is the second way that these authors criticize natural theology with respect to the nature of faith. Penner commends Kierkegaard's subjectivity principle, expressed in the statement "truth is subjectivity," as a model for how Christian faith is not about believing in the truthfulness of objective facts, but about living in such a way that one becomes a unified self.[76] One should avoid "the excesses of modernity with its emphasis on metaphysical-epistemological rationality" by embracing a Christian faith that does not "remove all objective uncertainty" about one's beliefs, but "provides an existential test for propositions and belief policies by exploring them for their conceptual clarity and pragmatic efficacy to actualize a narrative of the self which is fully unified."[77] Natural theology, with its emphasis on objective truth and rational demonstration, is out of place for the person of faith who engages the life of faith for the pragmatic task of self-formation. Therefore, the only way that Christian faith is exclusive is in its ability to save the human person, not in its rational coherence or the correspondence of its faith-statements to objective reality. Raschke agrees with this Kierkegaardian approach, arguing that it is the testimony of one's life of faith that confirms the truth of Christianity. "Faith is irremediably subjective . . . Only *I* can come to terms with the paradox, or contradiction, that Christ died for me, and that I can only do so by living my life for him."[78] The only way to "make sense" of the faith is by this existential test, seeing the truth of Christianity in one's life even if the truth of Christianity includes outright contradictions.

For James K. A. Smith, seeing faith as a way of life rather than a set of beliefs or propositions is key to understanding his postmodern pragmatism. For this, he leans heavily on Wittgenstein's concept of language games. "A language-game is the practical context in which our words and speech make sense—which is why understanding is bound up with, and relative

---

75. Penner, *The End of Apologetics*, 41.

76. Kierkegaard, *Concluding Unscientific Postscript*, 1:189; quoted in Penner, "Kierkegaard's Subjectivity Principle," 74.

77. Penner, "Kierkegaard's Subjectivity Principle," 88.

78. Raschke, "Faith and Philosophy in Tension," 54. Emphasis in the original.

to, the practical *telos* of the language-game, the *end* to which a community of practice is oriented."[79] Drawing upon the work of Ludwig Wittgenstein and George Lindbeck, Smith argues that the church is the community of practice.[80] Faith is not about coherence to objective standards for truth and rationality, but about playing by the rules of which the church is a guiding influence. We cannot use natural theology to know that the Christian story is true. God did not "send us an 'objective' Word; he sends his Son."[81] The Son sends the Spirit who gives birth to the church, and "the church is the language-game in which we learn to read the world aright."[82] This means that the church alone, and not alongside nature, is the locus of revelation. In the church, the Christian learns to live the truth. The practices of the community are the means by which one has knowledge of Christian truth. In fact, "the contingent conditions of a particular community of practice are the *gifts* that enable us to see and understand" that Christianity is true.[83] Thus, faith is not about entrusting oneself to Jesus based on demonstrable truths about Jesus; rather, it is about a community where one learns how to behave in response to the person of Jesus. The community imparts the truths that one believes through practice and not primarily through systematics or apologetics.

Third, Pauline theology provides the biblical roadmap for showing how Christian faith defies rational and apologetic approaches to its legitimation. Carl A. Raschke offers the most developed interpretation of Pauline theology to this effect. Raschke sees in Paul an epistemology of faith, where faith, and not reason, becomes the source of knowledge. 1 Corinthians 1–2 shows that the message of Christian faith is not demonstrable in terms that would be accepted according to the wisdom of the world. The kind of wisdom that can be gained through philosophical argumentation or other worldly discourses "is from God's perspective completely misguided and useless."[84] Theoretical and philosophical knowledge cannot aid in understanding the truth of God revealed in Christ. Paul's use of the

---

79. Smith, *Who's Afraid of Relativism?* 46.

80. See Wittgenstein, *Philosophical Investigations*; and Lindbeck, *The Nature of Doctrine*. Smith notes that one can find similar themes in Hauerwas' work on natural theology, as well. See Hauerwas, *With the Grain of the Universe*, esp. chapters 3 and 4.

81. Smith, *Who's Afraid of Relativism?* 72.

82. Ibid.

83. Ibid., 173. Emphasis in the original.

84. Raschke, "Faith and Philosophy in Tension," 39.

word *skandalon* to refer to the cross is key to Raschke's argument. "The crucifixion becomes a stumbling block to the extent that it would be readily and even indignantly dismissed" by Jews and Romans who had drastically different ideas of how salvation was attained.[85] Jesus' death on the cross as salvific would be absurd according to the wisdom of the age in which Christian faith first emerged. The cross defies rationality "and in the process lays the groundwork for what we may consider an 'alternative rationality' within the Western philosophical tradition, more congenial to Christian faith, that will emerge in the twentieth century."[86] Postmodern philosophy agrees with the notion, first hinted at by Paul, that universal rationality and philosophical argumentation cannot support humanity's most important desires and beliefs. Christian faith especially will balk at the notion that truth can be discovered through philosophical analysis of the world. Natural theology is clearly in view here. "One can never be convinced by another person . . . of the truth of the faith."[87] Any "truth" that one comes to believe in through being convinced by argumentation or rational demonstration will be "the wisdom of this age or of the rulers of this age, who are coming to nothing" (1 Cor 2:6, NIV). This comports well with how most Evangelicals view their faith in Christ. "Most evangelical testimonies about 'faith' have to do with some profession of one's personal experience that led us to realize that we must now rely on guidance from Christ" rather than simply trusting in our own attempts to know.[88] Only through having "the mind of Christ" can one come to know that Christianity is true (1 Cor 2:16, NIV).

Paul's argument in 1 Corinthians 1–2 is precisely why James K. A. Smith rejects apologetics. In this passage, "Paul advocates a method of public engagement that rests not on demonstration, but on proclamation, not on a neutral universal *logos* but on a particular, scandalous *kerygma* (1 Cor 2:1–5)."[89] The fall has made this kind of rational argumentation about God's activity in the world useless. Even things like the existence of God and the existence of objective moral values cannot be demonstrated this way. Christian faith arises through God in Christ saving people out of their sin so that they can see God's revelation. Objective reality cannot be accessed apart from the gift of salvation. In fact, God is constructing reality through

---

85. Ibid., 40.

86. Ibid., 41.

87. Ibid., 42.

88. Ibid., 45. Emphasis in the original.

89. Smith, *Introducing Radical Orthodoxy*, 180.

the redemption of the "are nots" of which Paul speaks in 1 Corinthians 1, those who are not considered wise by worldly standards. Christians are remade through faith, and that is how they are able to participate in true reality. "The real is constructed as much as it is discovered; it is made as much as it is recognized."[90] There is no reality that can be accessed through philosophical argumentation; rather, God makes reality in each person who enters the household of faith.

Myron B. Penner agrees with this interpretation of Paul's approach in 1 Corinthians, noting that Paul could have appealed to these people in ways that would have sought common ground (argumentation, rhetoric, etc.), but he chose not to, opting instead to preach a message of foolishness so that they could be saved. "Though he is adequately trained and equipped to engage them on the basis of his intellectual prowess and persuade them through rational coercion, Paul steadfastly resists any form of persuasion . . . other than the message of the cross and the power of the Holy Spirit."[91] Personal transformation happens through the proclamation of the cross of Christ, not through rational apologetics. Key to Paul's approach was his personal presence, "mak[ing] himself vulnerable to them," so that his weak position with respect to the scandalous message would elevate his hearers as potential recipients of God's gift.[92] Rational argumentation and skill-ful rhetoric objectifies people while the proclamation of the gospel honors them. Faith can then emerge as a genuine existential response to the gift of God rather than to the coercion of apologetics.

These authors all describe faith as a way of life that makes no reference to rationality and may even be a mode of existence that is in opposition to rationality. Faith emerges as a response to the scandal of the cross which is foolishness according to the world's wisdom. But is this understanding of faith in keeping with how Evangelicals understand faith? Does this pic-ture of faith actually comport with the historical and biblical tradition of the Christian church? If this picture of faith is correct, then it entails that natural theology at least plays no proper role in faith formation and at most is a hindrance to faith-development. However, this approach to faith and reason is deeply flawed both in its fideism and in its misunderstanding of the biblical picture of faith. In this section, I will argue against the tradi-tion of fideism in Evangelicalism by pointing to its internal inconsistencies,

90. Smith, *Who's Afraid of Relativism?* 64.

91. Penner, *The End of Apologetics*, 146.

92. Ibid., 147.

defending the tripartite picture of faith as *noticia, assensus,* and *fiducia* championed by the Reformers and many Evangelicals, and present a biblical theology of faith as inseparably linked to reason.

To begin, the authors in this study are committed to the picture of faith as contrary to reason. This is perhaps best summarized by Raschke, "Faith is neither irrational nor *suprarational*. It has nothing to do with 'reason,' per se. Faith, Derrida asserts, is simply a *response* to a divine promise . . . and promissory statements cannot be logically validated."[93] Faith is, then, trust in a person regardless of the evidence, even despite any relevant evidence. Philosophers and theologians have typically referred to this perspective as fideism. Fideism is the position that belief in God is intellectually absurd. Kai Nielsen describes it thusly,

> To be a fideist is to believe that fundamental religious beliefs rest solely and completely on faith. Finite and sinful man cannot by the use of his unaided reason come to know God. Belief and unbelief are intellectually on a par, religious experience is unalterably ambiguous as to the reality of its object, and the existence of God can never be established by empirical investigation or philosophical demonstration.[94]

To the dismay of many Evangelical proponents of natural theology, this picture of the nature of faith is alive and well among many Evangelical thinkers. However, this view of faith is philosophically problematic for two reasons. The first reason is that if proper Christian faith is only belief without evidence or against any relevant evidence, then it is difficult to see how a Christian could ever have knowledge of God. Propositional knowledge always involves good reasons (the justification or warrant criterion) as a necessary condition. The other kinds of knowledge, skill knowledge and knowledge by acquaintance, both require propositional knowledge to be able to get off the ground, as well. For example, my knowledge of how to ride a bike requires propositional knowledge that there is such a thing as an external world with streets, bikes, etc., and knowledge that my physical relationship with the world can be navigated using my sense perceptions and physical capacities. My relationship with Jesus requires the propositional knowledge that Jesus exists. However, if faith is belief without evidence or against any relevant evidence, and thus rejects the justification or warrant criterion, then it would be impossible for Christian faith to serve

93. Raschke, "Faith and Philosophy in Tension," 63. Emphasis in the original.

94. Nielsen, "Can Faith Validate God-Talk?" 158.

as a source of knowledge. "We would have nothing by which to evaluate knowledge-claims and would be subsequently led right back to the insanity of skepticism or the madness of a godless rational explanation."[95]

The second reason that fideism is problematic philosophically is that fideism leads to the inability to evaluate religions from the outside and to choose where to place one's religious commitments. "One would first have to believe in God in order to make any kind of statement, whether true or false, about God."[96] Yet people evaluate other religions from the outside all the time, and historically, "representative intellectuals[97] of religious communities" have thought that their religious truth-claims are capable of being considered by those who are not members of the religious community.[98] For example, one is able, through rational analysis, to argue that any forms of religion that encourage the practice of Female Genital Mutilation do not (in that respect at least) lead to human thriving—due to the suffering inflicted on women—and are, therefore, morally and existentially deficient.[99] People often make rational evaluations of religious beliefs and practices in deciding the content, centrality, and relative strength of their beliefs through reason, experience, appeals to authority, and other activities. For simplicity, we will call these the ubiquity of religious evaluation (URE) activities. Many times, URE activities happen prior to the kind of commitment called faith. To claim that Christian faith requires that one develop belief without making these kinds of rational evaluations is likely to be impossible for many who are considering the Christian gospel message. Moreover, a requirement like this exerts a coercive force on the one who is considering Christian faith, implying that the rational analysis that one is accustomed to employing when considering truth-claims is out of place

---

95. Haddad, *Insanity*, 91.

96. Ibid., 91–92.

97. This is a term Paul Griffiths uses to describe "one who makes pronouncements, either oral or written on matters of doctrine or practice, pronouncements that are taken to be authoritative by nonintellectual members of the community." See Griffiths, *An Apology for Apologetics*, 7.

98. Ibid., 20. "Representative intellectuals of religious communities have typically tended to think of the sentences they construct as being capable of comprehension outside their community; as extending their claims beyond the bounds of their community; as being, simply, both true and important."

99. "Procedures can cause severe bleeding and problems urinating, and later cysts, infections, as well as complications in childbirth and increased risk of newborn deaths." See World Health Organization, "Female genital mutilation," line 4.

when dealing with Christian truth.[100] Even so, it is not clear that fideism is able to avoid giving reasons for belief. For example, consider the position that it is not necessary to provide a reason for one's belief that God exists; one simply believes without evidence or against the evidence without employing URE activities. Jonah Haddad points out that this position has actually provided at least two pieces of evidence.

> First, by sticking to my faith, I have suggested that my cognitive material is functioning well enough for me to unabashedly assert my belief. Second, by giving an object of faith, I have suggested that the existence of God is a believable proposition that can be taken to be true. If I were to claim, as many Christians do, that through my faith I have somehow experienced the object of faith in a real relationship, then I would be adding an experienced-based confirmation of God's existence.[101]

While these are not particularly convincing pieces of evidence to an atheist, one who argues this way is still providing evidence for Christian faith. This means that fideism cannot avoid commending URE activities.

While Protestants have never been univocal about the nature of faith (e.g. Kierkegaard), many key Protestant voices have commended the tripartite picture of faith as *noticia, assensus,* and *fiducia.* On this view, *noticia* is an intellectual component, where one has knowledge of the truth of Christian belief. *Assensus* regards the emotional or convictional element of faith whereby the Christian is convinced that Christian belief is true. *Fiducia* is the volitional side of faith. It includes entrusting oneself to the person of Jesus Christ in a holistic manner.[102] This was explicated by the Reformer Philip Melanchthon. "Faith does not mean merely knowing the story of Christ, for even the devils confess that the Son of God appeared and rose from the dead . . . *True faith* is truly to retain all the words which God has given us, including the promise of grace; it is *a heartfelt reliance*

---

100. Raschke, Penner, and Smith may reply by arguing that this is exactly the point. Rationalism has no role in coming to faith given the nature of human cognition under the conditions of the fall. More will be said on this below, but it is worth saying, for now, that this retort does not obviate the facts that skill knowledge and knowledge by acquaintance require propositional knowledge and that people often use reason to evaluate their religious commitments.

101. Haddad, *Insanity*, 92.

102. For an influential twentieth century version of this tripartite understanding of faith from a Reformed Evangelical, see Berkhof, *Systematic Theology*, 503–6.

on the Savior Christ, a trust."[103] It relies on knowledge that the story of Christ is true, but includes an emotional and volitional aspect. Calvin offers a similar analysis, "[Faith] is certain that God is true in everything . . . Faith also obediently receives his commandments."[104] The Christian has "a steady and certain knowledge of the divine benevolence towards us . . . which is founded upon the truth of the gracious promise of God in Christ, and is both revealed to our minds and sealed in our hearts."[105] Faith has often been understood to be cognitive, emotional, and volitional. Should one remove the cognitive element, it is unclear what remains of the content of Evangelical faith. If one were to have faith in Jesus as the second person of the Trinity incarnate, rejected, slain, and risen without knowledge that Jesus existed in history, the result would be a faith at odds with the high Christology and biblicism commended by Evangelicals.

The significance of the preceding historical argument is minimal because, for Evangelicals, it begs the question of the biblical understanding of faith. Historical theology is relevant for Evangelicals, but given their reverence for the Bible as the definitive source of theology, it is most pertinent to briefly outline the biblical concept of faith.[106] For the purposes of this study on Christian natural theology and faith, we will only briefly focus on the concept of faith in the New Testament, a theological concept which includes belief (trust in a person, and agreement with facts about reality), knowledge, and an obedient way of life.[107] (1) Faith as belief is expressed a couple of ways, both as belief in a person, whether Jesus or God (John 1:12; 3:18; Acts 16:34; Gal 2:16; 1 Thess 1:8; Heb 6:1) and as belief in a message (Mk 1:15; 1 Cor 15:2, 11). This means that belief is both about the character or quality of the person in question and about the conceptual message regarding the character or quality of the person. In particular, "in the debate with Hel[lenistic] enthusiasm and Gnosticism which were based on a speculative understanding of baptism and the gift of the Spirit, Paul stressed historical facts and also his eschatological goal."[108] Faith includes an

103. Melanchthon, "Of the Word 'Faith,'" 158. Emphasis in the original.

104. Calvin, "Faith and the Promises of God," 234.

105. Calvin, "The Nature of Faith," 15.

106. On Evangelicals' reverence for the Bible as a defining trait, see Bebbington, *Evangelicalism in Modern Britain*, 12–14. See also International Council on Biblical Inerrancy, "The Chicago Statement," 41–51.

107. For a good introduction to the concept of faith in the Old Testament, see Erickson, *Christian Theology*, 951–2; Lewis and Demarest, *Integrative Theology*, 84–89.

108. Michel, "Faith," 1:601.

element of factual fidelity. (2) The faith that Jesus preaches about, especially, is characterized by a knowledge of reality. "It stood within the circle of trust . . . and knowledge,"[109] and it "was directed towards reality" (John 6:69; 17:8; 18:37; 1 John 4:6; Titus 1:13; 2:2).[110] (3) Faith also includes a transformational way of life. Paul's triad of faith, hope, and love (1 Cor 13:13; 1 Thess 3:5–8) demonstrates that faith is part of a broader "Christian life, derived from the kerygma, which forms the basis of the life of the church."[111] The result is obedience, wherein the Christian's faith comes to completion in good works (Jas 1:3; 2:22; 1 Pet 1:7). This brief outline demonstrates that the New Testament conception of faith is a multifaceted activity of belief in a person and in facts about reality, knowledge, and obedience. This agrees with the tripartite division of faith as *noticia, assensus,* and *fiducia* described above and contrasts with the postmodern Evangelical notion that faith is merely about a relationship with a person that results in a way of life. One may push back on the grammatical approach represented here through biblical theology, but it would be at the risk of divorcing theological reflection from the semantic world of the New Testament writers.

The idea that Paul's appeal in 1 and 2 Corinthians was a message of foolishness that denies a role for universal reason is a persistent theme among these authors and among other postmodern theologians.[112] An initial reading confirms the suspicion of bringing to theology a philosophy that seeks common ground (via universal reason) with those outside the Christian faith. "Where is the wise person? Where is the teacher of the law? Where is the philosopher of this age? Has not God made foolish the wisdom of the world" (1 Cor 1:20, NIV). However, Anthony Feneuil contends that "any appeal to the foolishness of God in order to disqualify apologetics is somewhat suspicious."[113] The postmodern argument is that reason cannot justify Christian belief because God's foolishness is the true wisdom that shows reason to be the fool that it is. God's foolish wisdom upends the tables of legitimation. This is suspicious, Feneuil argues, because the denial of "reason's ability to grasp the absolute would entail an a priori justification of any belief, *insofar as it does not pretend to be rationally justified.*"[114] A be-

109. Ibid., 1:600

110. Ibid., 1:601.

111. Ibid.

112. For example, see Caputo, "The Weakness of God," 21–58.

113. Feneuil, "The Cross of Wisdom," 173.

114. Ibid., 172. Emphasis in the original.

lief that is believed because it makes no appeal to reason is justified because it makes no appeal to reason. For example, one could be justified in believing one's racism, misogyny, or hatred to be theological truths if one's belief in these things were unreasonable.[115] This is absurd. Therefore, the denial of apologetics by appeal to the foolishness of God entails "the erection of *human* foolishness where *divine* foolishness should be."[116] Divine foolishness, for Feneuil, is of a different kind than human foolishness, and that is the precise point that Paul is making in 1–2 Corinthians. Divine foolishness is a self-disclosure of God on God's terms. If revelation is divine self-disclosure, and God has indeed revealed God's self in the natural world, then knowing God through natural theology is an exercise, not in human wisdom or folly, but in recognizing the self-disclosure of God on God's terms. Because God has revealed God's self, "only God can limit our arguments about God."[117]

An historical-grammatical reading of Paul provides a profitable understanding of these biblical passages. Contextually, the passage does not directly pertain to natural theology. Rather, it is occasioned by Paul's reflection on his call to "preach the gospel" (v. 17) and "the message of the cross" for those "who are being saved" (v. 18). This is a passage about the nature of salvation, not about general revelation or natural theology. The message of and the means to salvation are not something that we can know or proclaim by appeal to the world's cognitive standards. All this shows is that natural theology is insufficient for salvation, which is a point that most Evangelical advocates of natural theology stress.[118] The passage is underscoring that Christ's death on the cross (the means for human salvation) is a scandal to the wisdom of the Second Temple religious establishment and to Greek philosophy of the day. In Second Temple Judaism,

---

115. Feneuil quotes Quentin Meillassoux on this score, "If nothing absolute is thinkable, there is no reason why the worst forms of violence could not claim to have been sanctioned by a transcendence that is only accessible to the elect few." See Meillassoux, *After Finitude*, 47.

116. Feneuil, "The Cross of Wisdom," 177.

117. Ibid., 175.

118. One thinks of Warfield's contention that God has revealed God's self "in diverse manners," including nature (which is explicated by apologetical theology), yet "'the diverse manners' of God's revelation were insufficient for the purposes for which revelation is given." See Warfield, "The Idea of Systematic Theology," 251–2. More recently, see Groothuis, "Proofs, Pride and Incarnation," 75; he argues that theological issues "such as salvation, the pursuit of divine virtues, the afterlife are outside the realm of natural theology proper."

The message of a crucified Messiah was the ultimate scandal. Although in Roman times the Jews did not crucify, they did afterward hang those who had been stoned, especially blasphemers and idolaters. They saw hanging therefore as the ultimate fulfillment of the law ("because anyone who is hung on a tree is under God's curse," Deut. 21:23).[119]

The message that their messianic hope has been fulfilled in this way would have contradicted the conventional view. The same message would have been viewed by Greeks as a foolish superstition.[120] This does nothing to nullify the value of reason in general, but only insofar as one might try to begin with first principles and by the use of reason to arrive at the conclusion that God's salvific plan would include the execution of a Nazarene carpenter on a Roman cross. "No one could start off with the abstract concept of a first mover and deduce that a crucifixion would have happened from this information alone."[121] The cross is counterintuitive, and it shames any attempt to discover the truth about salvation based on human wisdom rather than God's self-revelation. But the cross does not put to shame reason in general. There is no internal contradiction in the idea of the substitutionary atonement, and Paul does not reject reason per se. Moreover, if Paul is arguing against the use of reason and philosophy in evangelism and theology, then this would have contradicted his own practice in Acts 17:16–34 and "his explicit appeal to argument and evidence on behalf of the Resurrection in the very same epistle (1 Cor 15)."[122] Postmodern theology's assertion that Paul denies a role for natural theology in 1 Corinthians 1–2 has no support from the context of the passage in question nor from Paul's broader kerygmatic program. It is far from obvious that Evangelicals should reject natural theology based on this class of arguments that claims that natural theology is at odds with Christian faith. Instead, Evangelicals should reject fideism and develop historical and biblical theologies of faith. Doing so

---

119. Fee, *First Epistle to the Corinthians*, 79.

120. Ibid. See Tacitus, *The Annals*, 15.44; "Christus, from whom the name had its origin, suffered the extreme penalty during the reign of Tiberius at the hands of one of our procurators, Pontius Pilatus, and a most mischievous superstition, thus checked for the moment, again broke out not only in Judaea, the first source of the evil, but even in Rome, where all things hideous and shameful from every part of the world find their centre and become popular."

121. Moreland, *Love Your God*, 68.

122. Ibid., 67.

lessens the cognitive dissonance between the good news that one embraces and professes and the commitment that one makes to Christ.

REVELATION

At the heart of the Evangelical tradition of natural theology is a conviction that God is revealed in both nature and in Scripture. While the Bible is the definitive source of Christian theology, it is not the only source. The Bible itself, along with the persons and works of Jesus Christ and the Holy Spirit, is part of a class of God's self-revelation known as special revelation. However, God has also revealed God's self in the natural world, as well, and this is known as general revelation. John Stott argues that general revelation has four key characteristics. (1) It is made known to everyone. (2) It is disclosed through the created world. (3) It is continually communicated through the natural world. (4) "It is 'creational,' revealing God's glory through creation, as opposed to 'salvific,' revealing God's grace in Christ."[123] Evangelical apologists attempt to rationally reflect on general revelation, and in doing so, they engage in tasks of natural theology. However, a key issue in the postmodern Evangelical rejection of natural theology is whether general revelation can be properly received by humanity given humanity's finitude and fallenness.[124] Penner, Raschke, and Smith all accept the idea of general revelation in the abstract, yet severely restrict its comprehensibility due to their acceptance of what has been called the Reformed objection to natural theology. God's self-revelation is available in nature and in Scripture, but one cannot receive this revelation in any meaningful way until one is made regenerate through the Holy Spirit. This section will explicate each authors' view of general and special revelation and their unique emphases in accepting the Reformed objection. Then, this section will critically engage their understandings of revelation and reason and provide an alternative account of how one may uphold a doctrine of depravity while retaining the efficacy of general revelation for those who have not embraced Christian faith and experienced regeneration.

123. Stott, *The Message of Romans*, 73; quoted in Groothuis, *Christian Apologetics*, 173.

124. The Reformed objection to natural theology has already been discussed with respect to the positions held by Abraham Kuyper, Karl Barth, and Cornelius Van Til. See chapter 2.

Myron B. Penner does not make a strong distinction in his work between general and special revelation, but there is no reason to believe that he does not uphold this distinction. Like many Evangelicals, he seems to focus mainly on special revelation, or "God's words," as definitive for the concept of revelation. What is key for him is not whether he believes that general revelation is a possibility, but whether humanity can receive *any* revelation and whether reason can serve a role in comprehending revelation. He argues that revelation is solely dependent on God's action. God's revelation is given to the "apostle," the speaker who receives God's words and delivers them to others. The words of the apostle are not authoritative because of the apostle's intellect or facility with reason, but only "because the source is God."[125] God's revelation is not something that can be discovered through reason or human reflection on the natural world. God's words "are not realities humans will discover through their research projects."[126] However, the impossibility of using reason to discover divine revelation does not mean that reason can play no role for the Christian in knowing the truth. Reason can be employed as one reflects on revelation, yet it will never be able to adjudicate truth from error. This is because sin limits reason's efficacy. Sin is an "open wound" in one's rational capacities "that must constantly be acknowledged and must continually give way to a word from God."[127] Sin entails that reason can never serve as a grounding or legitimating authority for revelation. Should reason be a legitimating authority, it would place the grounds for legitimation outside of God, which would be an offense against God's independence, and it would make legitimation a matter of anthropology. Humanity cannot serve as a legitimating ground for God's authority because humanity's sin is "irrational, alienating, and caused by the individual."[128] God's revelation is legitimized only by virtue of the fact that it comes from God.

Carl A. Raschke's larger project of marrying the insights of the Reformation with postmodern philosophy and theology upholds the distinction between general and special revelation. "Reformation thought had drawn an unmitigated distinction between 'natural' and 'supernatural' knowledge of God."[129] God has revealed God's self in nature and in the Bible; how-

125. Penner, *The End of Apologetics*, 51.

126. Ibid.

127. Ibid., 67.

128. Ibid., 52.

129. Raschke, *The Next Reformation*, 27.

ever, the Bible is the definitive authority in Reformation thought "because it mediates God's magnificent reality to each one of us."[130] If one wants to hear what God would say, one must read the Bible in the interpretive community of the church, and in so doing, one hears the Holy Spirit. The process for how this is so begins with the Holy Spirit delivering God's original revelation to "the apostolic witness," whose words comprise various "faith-statement[s]" that become part of the *Lebensform* of the community of faith.[131] In this sense, the meaning of special revelation is bounded up with the faith-tradition of the community which is traceable back to the original apostolic witness. The key, then, for receiving special revelation is joining the community of faith. This requires, however, "approaching God through faith and surrendering the intellect."[132] One must receive the wisdom of God as distinct from the "wisdom" of the world, and this is precisely what revelation provides. Revelation secures faith through a rejection of worldly reason, allowing the Christian to "grasp the difference between human understanding and the 'wisdom' that Christ was crucified."[133] One then takes the leap of faith to receive God's revelation. Reason is incapable of serving as an avenue for accepting revelation because sin confounds one's ability to understand that the crucified Christ is the true wisdom of God. Even though God has made God's self known in the natural world "to all humanity (Rom 1:19, NRSV), Paul writes, original sin and the corruption of the mind and the will" has led humanity into futile thinking.[134] "Luther made the repeated argument that only the Holy Spirit" can reveal truth about God because "without the Spirit, the mind is blinkered."[135] So any appeal to reason as an avenue to receive the truth about God in nature (and thereby, to engage in the task of natural theology) ignores how sin has definitively marred humanity's ability to know the truth about God. Only the Holy Spirit reveals the truth about God to the individual through the community of faith.

James K. A. Smith also affirms a distinction between God's revelation in creation and God's special revelation. The Augustinian and

---

130. Ibid., 117.

131. Raschke, *Alchemy of the Word*, 58–59. *Lebensform* is a Wittgensteinian term for the form of life in which the meaning of a community's beliefs are embedded.

132. Raschke, *The Next Reformation*, 27.

133. Raschke, "Faith and Philosophy in Tension," 47.

134. Raschke, *The Next Reformation*, 27.

135. Ibid., 127.

Reformed tradition in which Smith's Evangelicalism is rooted affirms that "God's nature and attributes are available to be perceived in the structure of creation."[136] General revelation is a legitimate theological category for Smith. However, like Raschke and Penner, he focuses his analysis of the concept of revelation primarily in the special revelation of the Bible and the Holy Spirit, particularly the Spirit's work in the church. The primary theological category for understanding revelation in Smith's work is the Incarnation. In the Incarnation, God engages humanity and speaks in such a way that God's self may be known. "In giving itself, the Transcendent does not give up its transcendence, but rather reveals itself; in fact, if the Wholly Other did not give itself in terms of the conditions of the finite perceiver, there would be no revelation, only silence or ignorance."[137] God paradoxically lowers God's self and relates with humanity, yet retains his otherness and transcendence. Smith describes this as a kenotic condescension, where God does not pull humanity up into transcendence, but empties God's self and enters into a relation with humanity on God's terms.[138] How God has done this "is a paradox which cannot be comprehended," and one which reason cannot elucidate.[139] Rather, it is a gift given freely by God and received by the people of God in their varied historical situations "in the incarnation, in the Word, in the people of God" (the church).[140] God is compelled only by God's will to offer revelation in the contingent communities of the people of God.

Smith argues that though the gift is given freely, it carries conditions that must be met in order to receive the gift.[141] Even though God has spoken in nature, "sin has marred the perceptive capacities of humanity such that these aspects of creation are not and cannot be recognized."[142] Smith aligns his project with a larger Reformed project (embodied in people like

136. Smith, *Introducing Radical Orthodoxy*, 164.

137. Smith, *Speech and Theology*, 160.

138. Smith, *Who's Afraid of Relativism?* 110.

139. Smith, *Speech and Theology*, 163.

140. Smith, *Who's Afraid of Relativism?* 111.

141. Though he rejects natural theology, Smith agrees with Emil Brunner "that even if we want a theology that begins from revelation, that revelation must first be *received*, and there are conditions for that reception: all reception is according to the mode of the perceiver. Thus any revelation must be given in terms that are in some sense commensurate with the conditions for its reception by the receiver—in this case, finite human beings." See Smith, *Speech and Theology*, 167. Emphasis in the original.

142. Smith, *Introducing Radical Orthodoxy*, 164.

Abraham Kuyper, Herman Dooyeweerd, Cornelius Van Til, Francis Schaeffer, and Alvin Plantinga) that rejects natural theology because of the noetic effects of sin.[143] One simply cannot see the revelation of God (natural or special) because, prior to regeneration, one's mind and heart are "'futile' and 'darkened' (Rom 1:18–31). It is clear from the Gospel narratives, for instance, that not everyone sees what the centurion sees when on Golgotha he proclaims, 'Truly this was the Son of God' (Matt 27:54 NASB)."[144] People can be taught the objective meaning of God's revelation, but they cannot receive it subjectively apart from the Holy Spirit's work of regeneration.[145] Smith argues that the Reformed tradition of rejecting natural theology "would affirm a certain 'givenness' or 'objectivity' of God's revelation in creation, [but] the effectiveness of this natural revelation is mitigated by the epistemic effects of sin on the perceptual capacities of sinful perceivers."[146] God's revelation will remain objective to God, yet its subjective reception is affected by sin and also by the historical and cultural contingencies of the linguistic communities by which it is received. It is the work of the Holy Spirit in those communities that ensures the "correct" interpretation, not any reflection that is made successful by reference to reason. Moreover, only the Holy Spirit's work of regeneration can make an individual a member of the community. Therefore, any attempt to help the unregenerate person to "see" God's revelation in nature (through natural theology) or in the Bible will fail until the person is born again through the work of the Holy Spirit.

There is much to agree with in our authors' analysis of revelation. God's self-revelation in nature and in Scripture is indeed given freely. God's actions and the meaning of God's words are not constrained by an external force or legitimizing authority. God certainly could have done otherwise than to reveal God's self, and any revelation that humanity may receive is categorically a gift of God's grace. Even though I uphold a more robust place for reason in receiving revelation, the human exercise of reason is not the proper legitimizing authority for God. Indeed, God's self-revelation is legitimized by God alone. Any place for reason in the legitimation of revelation only obtains insofar as it is God who is employing reason as an

143. He specifically cites Kuyper, *Calvinism*; Dooyeweerd, *Twilight of Western Thought*; Schaeffer, "The Question of Apologetics," 175–87; Plantinga, "The Reformed Objection," 49–62.

144. Smith, "Who's Afraid of Postmodernism?" 217.

145. Smith borrows this distinction from Owen, *The Holy Spirit*, 148.

146. Smith, "Questions About the Perception," 592.

aspect of God's nature. When God invites the listener, "Come now, and let us reason together" (Isa 1:18, NASB), the invitation is on God's terms, and the propriety of such activity is due to God's legitimizing authority. Further, sin is humanity's most basic and catastrophic problem. Its effects touch every aspect of the human person, including one's ability to reason and to receive revelation. However, the extent to which reason is affected by sin is a key issue in the broader debate over natural theology (see chapter 2), and our authors ignore how the doctrine of the *imago dei* informs this debate. I will argue that Penner's, Raschke's, and Smith's failure to engage this key biblical doctrine about humanity hampers their analysis of reason, truth, and the extent of the effects of sin.

First, these authors ignore that the key issue in theological reflection on the noetic effects of sin is how sin affects the image of God in humanity. The closest that our authors get to applying the concept of the *imago dei* to the debate over natural theology comes in Smith's *Speech and Theology*, where he briefly examines the debate between Barth and Brunner.[147] However, Smith explains the debate primarily in terms of the "point of contact" (*Anknüpfungspunkt*) for humanity to receive the revelation of God, yet he omits the fact that the Brunner/Barth debate was primarily about how sin had affected the formal and material *imago dei*. "Materially the *imago* is not in the least touched—whether sinful or not, man is a subject and is responsible. Materially the *imago* is completely lost, man is a sinner through and through and there is nothing in him which is not defiled by sin."[148] Our authors' failure to examine the issue of natural theology in light of the doctrine of the image of God is a major omission. Evangelicals have often argued that the image of God is the key to receiving general revelation. Carl F. H. Henry, for example, argues that if sinful humanity cannot know the truth about God, then this leads to skepticism about the nature of the divine.

> But skepticism is self-refuting, since it claims to know that we cannot know. Moreover, Scripture refutes the view that men have no knowledge of God . . . Had man's rational competence not survived the fall, he could neither know nor communicate intelligible

---

147. Smith, *Speech and Theology*, 166–8. Raschke writes about the image of God primarily in terms of the human capacity for relationship with God. See *The Next Reformation*, 153–4.

148. Brunner, "Nature and Grace," 24.

truth, nor could intelligible revelation be appropriated by him or meaningfully addressed to him.[149]

This is because Henry believes that the ability to receive God's revelation persists in humanity after the fall via the image of God, in which all humanity is made. The image enables humanity to have the capacity to reason, and it grounds humanity's moral responsibility. Even though humanity has suffered a "catastrophic personality shock" in the fall, humanity retains the divine image.[150] "Although sullied by the fall, the divine image in man was not totally shattered."[151] He argues that, despite sin, Calvin insisted that humanity still has the knowledge of God's existence through general revelation. This position has been advocated by other Evangelical proponents of natural theology like Douglas Groothuis, who argues that the knowledge of God is available through creation (general revelation), and human reason can be used to analyze that revelation apart from salvation (natural theology). "Reason itself—the logical structure of being and argument—is based on the eternal character of God as the Word (the *Logos* [John 1:1]), and on his bestowal of reason to creatures made in his image and likeness. In that sense, reason is not fallen."[152] Moreover, sinful humanity does not cease to be made in God's image. This would be a kind of unmaking of humanity, one that would remove their differentiation from other creatures.[153] Therefore, the capacities to receive revelation and to use reason remain. While humanity may use reason in sinful ways, reason itself remains a reflection of the divine image in humanity that is not lost through the fall. Penner, Raschke, and Smith do not engage this line of argumentation in their work; rather, they repeatedly make reference to the noetic effects of sin as if to play the trump card, forestalling any effort to find a point of contact for general revelation in fallen humanity. Since they overlook the doctrine of the *imago dei* in this regard, Evangelicals considering their appeal to the

---

149. Henry, *God, Revelation, and Authority*, 2:136. While Henry's presuppositionalist apologetics are not the approach recommended in this work, his perspective seems to imply that positive knowledge of God is possible for the one who does not profess Christian faith.

150. Ibid., 2:134.

151. Ibid., 2:136.

152. Groothuis, *Christian Apologetics*, 177. See also Moreland, *The Recalcitrant Imago Dei*, esp. chapter 4.

153. See Henry, *God, Revelation, and Authority*, 2:136.

noetic effects of sin to reject natural theology lack vital theological analysis that may further clarify their positions.

Second, the postmodern Evangelical rejection of natural theology confuses how reason properly functions in response to revelation. For example, as part of his chapter, "Apologetics, Suspicion, and Faith," Myron B. Penner makes the assertion that "human reason is less than adequate to ground the full truth, or the truth as it would appear to God."[154] His broader argument in this chapter is that apologetics undermines the gospel that it attempts to defend. The assertion that human reason is inadequate is made in the context of claiming that, by using human reason, apologetics "experts" or "geniuses" usurp the proper role of the apostle in the proclamation of revelation from God.[155] However, apologists do not claim to be delivering God's revelation on the basis of *human* reason. Rather, they are attempting to apply reason *proper* (that is, reason grounded in the *Logos* [John 1:1]) to the revelation of God that already exists in nature. The goal of natural theology is not to reason one's way to God, but to employ reason in reflection upon God's revelation delivered by God. Therefore, the use of reason is not an exercise in attempting to legitimize God's revelation through human reason (and thereby to usurp God's revelatory prerogative), but to employ reason as a tool of corroboration. Conceptual corroboration of the truth of God's revelation is commended in Scripture. Consider the Bereans who are commended for "examin[ing] the Scriptures every day to see if what Paul said was true" (Acts 17:11, NIV). Also, Jesus' *a fortiori* argument in Matthew 6:26 commands examining the natural world to determine that if the birds are provided for by God's hand, then humanity will be cared for even more. Reason is not the truth-maker, but it can help humanity to see the truth of revelation. Penner is correct to warn that reason's deliverances are "provisional and potentially reversible," and therefore, reason cannot function as any kind of final authority on a matter.[156] God is the ultimate authority. Yet if God is the locus of reason (through the *Logos* [John 1:1]), then human reason can be rightly employed to allow one to see the truth. Any provisional status of the deliverances of reason is only due to a possible poor use of reason, not to reason's inherent impotence. Natural theology may fail to provide truth if its arguments misuse reason, but natural theol-

---

154. Penner, *The End of Apologetics*, 52. He clarifies that by "truth," he is simply referring to a kind of *seeing that* a proposition is true.

155. Ibid., 49–52.

156. Ibid., 53.

ogy does not fail if it uses reason properly. Of course, God alone is the final arbiter of whether or not reason is used properly, but that should not dissuade us from attempting to faithfully use reason in reflection upon God's revelation; rather, it should motivate us to think that much more diligently, humbly, and prayerfully in doing natural theology.

THE ETHICS OF APOLOGETICS

Myron B. Penner relates a tragic and true story in *The End of Apologetics* about an atheist friend of his named John who was once engaged by two young Evangelical seminarians who had recently completed a course in Christian apologetics. Shortly after meeting John, the two apologists quickly took to the task of attempting to poke holes in John's atheistic worldview and to argue that Christianity is true. Even though John expressed his displeasure with the young men's actions, they persisted in arguing with John about his beliefs. Penner's lament is worth quoting at length:

> What bothered him, he said, was the impersonal way both he and his beliefs were being treated—as if they were abstract entities (like propositions) instead of reflections of spiritual realities with which he personally struggled. John told the apologists he found what they were doing offensive. Undaunted, our defenders of the faith assumed the apologetic right-of-way and continued with their inquisition in the name of unloading their responsibility for John's errors into God's hands—informing John at one point that it was necessary so that his "blood would not be on their heads" (actually citing Ezek. 3:18). Needless to say, this did not make a positive impression and did nothing to *show* John the truth of Christianity.[157]

This story illustrates the sad truth that sometimes Christians attempt to do God's will, but fail to employ God's ways. How one obeys the call to defend the faith matters greatly. This story represents a minor, but important, objection that Penner, Raschke, and Smith make regarding the ethics of apologetics. These postmodern Evangelicals argue that apologetics betrays the Christian way of life by reinforcing values like consumerism and coercive power and by neglecting values like embodiment and listening. Because this betrayal of Christian ethics is an essential component of apologetics, they conclude that the church should not do apologetics in the mode of employing arguments of natural theology in their evangelism.

157. Ibid., 78. Emphasis in the original.

"The church does not *have* an apologetic; it *is* an apologetic," a way of life that out-narrates the culture of modernity and nihilism.[158] This section will explore the ethical critique of apologetics levied by these authors, and it will conclude by arguing that these valid ethical concerns apply only to apologists, and not to apologetics. That is, apologists should be warned against certain behaviors and reminded to hold fast to others, but the values of consumerism and coercive power are not essential elements of the task of apologetics. Finally, I will argue that the church may both be and have an apologetic; these are not mutually exclusive.

First, these authors argue that apologetics affirms values that are alien to authentic Christian faith such as consumerism and coercive power. This is illustrated by the story of the two young apologists who attempt to use apologetics to bully John out of his atheism and into the Christian religion. Penner argues that William Lane Craig is particularly guilty of these sins. Craig views his apologetics debates with leading atheist philosophers as a kind of "power encounter," hoping "to shape the minds and attitudes of young people and counteract the power of prevailing ideologies of our culture."[159] Penner thinks that this reinforces a culture of modernity with its consumer-driven belief selection model that undermines genuine faith in God. It vilifies one's ideological opponents and makes Christianity a commodity to be consumed. Smith argues that this power encounter "feeds into the colonizing of the political by the religious that also tends to cut the other way—namely, the church becomes allied with the interest of the state."[160] If the goal is to shape young minds, then one is really attempting to create a Christian culture among the polity at large. The university-centered strategy reinforces a politics of belief, that attempts to coerce the country's future leaders into Christian belief. Moreover, this approach necessarily creates a consumerist gospel where one can choose which God one worships, either "a rational god who can be known apart from Jesus Christ or a therapeutic god who seems to exist to meet my needs and make me happy."[161] Since apologetics focuses on natural theology arguments, it ends up commending a generic theism that allows the consumer to fill in the theological gaps to create a god in the consumer's own image.

158. Smith, *Introducing Radical Orthodoxy*, 181.

159. Ibid., 60. The language of the "power encounter" is Craig's and makes reference to missiology. See Craig, *Reasonable Faith*, 21.

160. Smith, *Introducing Radical Orthodoxy*, 51.

161. Smith, *Who's Afraid of Relativism?* 172.

Second, these authors argue that apologetics is opposed to the kinds of values required by Christian evangelism such as embodied listening and the commendation of a transformative way of life that can be experienced and that is deeply tied to one's identity. Penner argues that the professional model of apologetics leads one to adopt the strategy of the disembodied monologue, where the apologetic expert speaks and the other becomes the listener. This one-directional mode of evangelism betrays kerygmatic proclamation, which "involves *listening* to others, as well as speaking, and it involves *being with* others."[162] Since apologetics sets up the expert-listener monologue instead of the equal-exchange dialogues, it should be rejected. This is because coming to embrace Jesus Christ in faith is a matter of engaging in the community of the church where one is invited "to 'try on' Christian faith as a way to make sense of the cosmos and [one's] place in it."[163] Apologetics merely focuses on the propositions that one believes and not on the way of life that Christianity engenders. Smith argues that the church is vital to this experiential process of conversion because the church is called to be "the body of Christ, in a way that is hospitable and inviting— in a way that invites others to find their identity and vocation in Christ, to become 'new creations' and thus become the humans they were called to be."[164] Raschke agrees, arguing that the experience of worship in the church "has a lot more to do with prompting conversion than the forcefulness of apologetics."[165] Apologetics does not need the church since apologetics is done by individual experts in a non-communal and not necessarily ecclesial fashion. Since apologetics fails to embody these values, Evangelicals should opt instead to embody a more faithful and relational Christianity in the church, inviting others to experience a new way of life in the practices of regular worship and community. This is why "the church does not *have* an apologetic; it *is* an apologetic."[166]

These authors are right to warn against ethical infidelity to God in our attempts to proclaim the gospel and to defend the faith. While I disagree that apologetics is necessarily a betrayal of Christian ethics, there is much to gain from the warnings that Penner, Raschke, and Smith provide. First,

162. Penner, *The End of Apologetics*, 83.

163. Smith, *Who's Afraid of Relativism?* 174.

164. Smith, *Desiring the Kingdom*, 206.

165. Raschke, *The Next Reformation*, 175.

166. Smith, *Introducing Radical Orthodoxy*, 181. Note how this is similar to Stanley Hauerwas' paradigm in *With the Grain of the Universe*, esp. chapter 8.

the life of the church is central to Christian faith, and apologetics should do more to emphasize this. Christian faith must include a new way of living that is rooted in the family of God and not just assent to the arguments of natural theology. While most apologetics projects do not focus on the life of the church, the conceptual resources for reflection on this topic are available in the cumulative case method of Christian apologetics. This method examines evidence that supports "the hypothesis that Christian theism is the best-attested worldview."[167] All aspects of Christian belief and practice can be called on as potential witnesses, as in a court case, to confirm the hypothesis against any competing claims of other worldviews. "Each witness in isolation gives only part of the story, but when multiple witnesses, all speaking from different areas of knowledge, agree on their judgment, the overall case is strengthened considerably."[168] On this topic, the hypothesis is that participation in the church is central to one's *telos*. "The body of Christ . . . invites others to find their identity and vocation in Christ, to become 'new creations' and thus become the humans they were called to be."[169] This hypothesis can be compared to other visions of human teleology including the nihilistic *a*teleology implied by the philosophical naturalism of the New Atheism. If the Christian vision for human teleology is more likely to be true than false (or is at least preferable to any alternatives), then this provides one point of corroboration with the greater hypothesis of the truth of the Christian worldview.[170] Though Evangelical apologetics may be weak in this area, it has the conceptual resources to fruitfully engage this topic in the future.

Second, a subtext of the story of John and the seminarians is that these young apologists were arrogant in their treatment of John. Penner is right to warn Christians concerned with the proclamation of the gospel that their proclamation must be attended by humility and genuine respect for the other. Indeed, Christians (perhaps especially apologists) need to learn to communicate the truth of the gospel in a humble way in the current postmodern milieu.[171] However, as D. A. Carson points out, humility does not

167. Groothuis, *Christian Apologetics*, 59.

168. Ibid.

169. Smith, *Desiring the Kingdom*, 206.

170. Worldview confirmation is a difficult task, not least in attempting to fairly survey and evaluate all alternative perspectives. However, the task is not impossible. See Sire, *The Universe Next Door*.

171. For an exemplar in this regard, one may look to mathematician and philosopher of science John Lennox. About him Os Guinness writes, "The church has been grateful

preclude valuing truth and rationality. Christians need to learn to empha-size both "feelings and affections" and "linear thought and rationality," sub-mitting experience to the test of truth, emphasizing "inclusion over against exclusion," and emphasizing "participation over against individualism."[172] These emphases can be fruitfully wedded together. One can be a humble apologist, "speaking the truth in love" (Eph 4:15, NIV), having confidence in the rationality of the Christian faith while being open-hearted toward others with whom one disagrees about what matters most.

Third, our authors are correct to warn against any potential wedding of Christian faith with the consumerism of late modernity. Evangelicals are particularly susceptible to celebrity culture, becoming devotees of apolo-gists, artists, preachers, and bloggers. Though apologists rightly care about exposure to their ideas (What other godly reason could one have for going through the trouble of publishing a book?), the dangers of vanity and pride can attend influence. However, Penner, Raschke, and Smith do nothing to show that celebrity culture is a central element of the task of apologetics. Though consumerism may attend apologetics, it is not an essential element of apologetics. Most apologists do not headline at large conferences, nor do most earn lavish salaries or honoraria. Philosophy of religion is not usually a lucrative field.[173] However, Christian theology is opposed to greed, vanity, and pride, but not to lucrative work. "The elders who direct the affairs of the church well are worthy of double honor, especially those whose work is preaching and teaching. For Scripture says, 'Do not muzzle an ox while it is treading out the grain,' and 'The worker deserves his wages'" (1 Tim 5:17–18, NIV). Apologists who truly serve the church should be financially rewarded for their efforts. Yet Christian apologists, like all of those who follow Christ, must constantly examine their motivations in light of Scrip-ture and in the context of the church. Those interested in natural theology

---

. . . for the humility and humor of Professor John Lennox of Oxford University in his recent debates with the new atheists. Yet not all Christian debaters have displayed the same blend of love, truth and grace." Guinness, *Fool's Talk*, 171.

172. Carson, *Becoming Conversant*, 29.

173. Surely there are counterexamples to this general truth. In his history of the Gifford lectures, Stanley L. Jaki reports on the honoraria given to various lectures. Originally, "the sum was almost twice the yearly salary of a professor and the minimum income needed through late Victorian times to maintain middle-class life standard. No wonder that Pfleiderer, the third Gifford lecturer in Edinburgh, made the comment still remembered there: 'Die Ehre ist nicht gross, ader der Gehalt ist kolossal' ('The honor is not great but the honorarium colossal'). Soon the honor was a great as the honorarium." Jaki, *Lord Gifford and His Lectures*, 10.

and apologetics must constantly examine their hearts to ensure that their devotion is to Christ alone and not to apologetics as a discipline or to any particular apologist.

Further, the values of consumerism in late modernity can encourage individualism with respect to belief selection, and our authors are right to warn about this. Apologetics could lead someone to merely discard atheism or to embrace a minimalistic and generic theism.[174] People do not simply switch religious commitments in a holistic fashion. While the warning against consumerism with respect to belief selection is helpful, it is far from obvious that merely discarding atheism or embracing a minimalistic theism is altogether a bad thing. In fact, a committed philosophical naturalist is unlikely to seriously entertain the notion that membership in the body of Christ is central to human teleology without a previous openness to plausibility of the existence of God. Apologetics is important because it can alter one's plausibility structure to see that certain Christian beliefs are possibly true. Should one discard atheism to embrace a minimalistic theism, one would be that much more likely to consider the Christian worldview. According to J. Gresham Machen, "God usually exerts that power in connection with certain prior conditions of the human mind, and it should be ours to create, so far as we can, with the help of God, those favourable conditions for the reception of the gospel."[175] Further, despite the danger of reinforcing consumerism with respect to belief formation and the politics of religious preference, it is not inappropriate to view apologetic debates as "power encounters" in the way that Craig does. He claims that debates help to inspire Christians in their evangelism by giving them confidence in the truth of Christian faith. "Many Christians do not share their faith with unbelievers simply out of fear. They're afraid that the non-Christian will ask them a question or raise an objection that they can't answer."[176] He claims that training in apologetics gives people confidence to be able to answer the questions that those outside the faith may ask them. Why is that a bad thing? Most importantly, Craig argues that the reason for these kinds of apologetic activities is genuine love and concern for the other. "Every person is precious to God, a person for whom Christ died. Like a missionary called to reach some obscure people group, the Christian apologist is burdened to

---

174. See Flew, *There Is a God*; and Nagel, *Mind and Cosmos*.

175. Machen, address delivered on September 20, 1912; quoted in Moreland, *Love Your God*, 89.

176. Craig, *Reasonable Faith*, 21.

reach . . . persons who will respond to rational argument and evidence."[177] Many have attempted to use religion to control and manipulate others. By his words, it is difficult to accuse Craig of this sin. It remains for our authors to show this by Craig's actions, something they do not attempt to do.

Fourth, our authors are right to warn that it is possible for apologists to disrespect their interlocutors, valuing gamesmanship above relationship and preachiness above reciprocity. Again, though, these negative values and the behaviors that come with them are not central to the task of apologetics. There is nothing inherent in the task of apologetics that requires one to be disrespectful. In fact, one may simply look to the examples of successful apologists to see the actual strategies that they encourage. For example, when William Lane Craig famously debated Sam Harris in The God Debate II at the University of Notre Dame in 2011, Craig models a serious concern to fairly and accurately represent Harris' views.[178] Francis A. Schaeffer, in recommending that the Christian ought to push one's interlocutor toward the unfavorable logical conclusions of that person's non-Christian worldview, says,

> As I seek to do this, I need to remind myself constantly that this is not a game I am playing. If I begin to enjoy it as a kind of intellectual exercise, then I am cruel and can expect no real spiritual results . . . He must feel that I care for him. Otherwise I will only end up destroying him, and the cruelty and ugliness of it all will destroy me as well.[179]

Christian apologetics should be done with humble care for the other, not with a win in mind, but with the motivation of genuine love for the other. Indeed, apologists should "Always be prepared to give an answer to everyone who asks you to give the reason for the hope that you have. But do this with gentleness and respect" (1 Pet 3:15, NIV). Christian apologists would do well to remember that their interlocutors are always deserving of love and respect.

These authors provide some timely warnings, even if they may overstate their case, painting apologetics as arrogant, disrespectful, consumer-driven, and unconcerned with the life of the church. However, the broader accusation levied against apologetics is that it is a betrayal of Christian ethics. I have attempted to show how this is not necessarily the case. Our

177. Ibid., 22.
178. Harris and Craig, "The God Debate II."
179. Schaeffer, The God Who is There, 156.

authors have not shown that the ethical offenses that they describe are inherent in the task of apologetics. Moreover, the ethical offenses they describe may arise in other intellectual and religious activities. There is no shortage of arrogance, shameless consumerism, or disrespect in the academy and in the church. What they describe are behaviors that result from sinful human hearts, not behaviors that are necessarily tied to apologetics. In fact, both Jesus and Paul provide model examples of how to do apologetics without transgressing into the vices listed here.[180] As I argue above, Jesus' ministry is characterized by the skillful use of logical argumentation in service of defending religious truth. Jesus appeals to empirical evidence to defend his identity as the Messiah (Matt 11:4–6; cf. Luke 7:22), and he makes a *reductio ad absurdum* argument that he is not casting out demons by the power of Beelzebub (Matt 12:25–27).[181] Jesus refutes falsehood and commends the truth. Paul argues that the resurrection of Christ is good reason to believe in the general resurrection of the church in 1 Cor 15. Using Greek philosophy, he argues for common ground between an unknown deity and "the God who made the world and everything in it" at the Areopagus in Athens (Acts 17:24). Jesus and Paul are moral exemplars in the proper use of apologetics, people whose ability to speak the truth in love should be emulated.

CONCLUSION

I have outlined the various objections to natural theology presented by Carl A. Raschke, Myron B. Penner, and James K. A. Smith. They argue that objective reason fails to deliver context-independent truth about the world. I argue that some minimalistic features of universal reason that are expressed in Aristotelean logic are necessarily true. To deny the logical categories used by apologetics is absurd, for one must affirm basic logic in order to deny it. Evangelical apologetics, they say, has bought into the misleading modernist paradigm that we can know objective truth. Truth is not propositional; it is relational. I respond by showing that their ironic rejection of

---

180. I argue this fully aware that to refer to Jesus or Paul as apologists flirts with anachronism, especially if by the term we mean something like a classical or evidential apologist in the style of William Paley, B. B. Warfield, or Gary Habermas. However, I am using the term loosely here to refer to someone who criticizes non-Christian worldviews and defends the truth of Christian faith via reason and evidence.

181. See Groothuis, *On Jesus*, chapter 3. See also Sire, *Habits of the Mind*, 184–97.

foundationalism is conflated with a caricature of Cartesian epistemology and that their arguments depend on a correspondence theory that they mean to reject. They think that any philosophical inferences or demonstrations regarding God fall into the category of ontotheology. I argue that this is a misappropriation of Heidegger's critique of natural theology and results in a denial that God is able to reveal God's self in nature. They argue that the god of natural theology is a false god, and one's veneration of the god of natural theology will lead to idolatry. I contend that arguing for a minimalistic theism is permissible because it may cause the skeptic to open his/her mind to the God revealed in the Scriptures and in the life of the church. Evangelical apologists do not worship reason; rather, they worship the *Logos*. They maintain that Christian faith is a commitment without reference to and even in spite of evidence. I argue against the tradition of fideism in Evangelicalism by pointing to its internal inconsistencies, commending the tripartite picture of faith as *noticia*, *assensus*, and *fiducia*, and presenting a biblical theology of faith as linked to reason. These authors severely restrict the comprehensibility of general revelation due to their acceptance of the Reformed objection to natural theology, and I respond by arguing that they do not properly engage the doctrine of the *imago dei* and that they fail to see how reason is an expression of God's nature that helps humanity to receive revelation. Finally, Penner, Raschke, and Smith argue that apologetics ethically compromises the Christian, and while their warnings should be seriously considered by those who do apologetics, they do not show how the ethical offenses of arrogance, disrespect, consumerism, and a lack of concern for the life of the church are inherent in apologetics. Rather, these sins are really just characteristics of a fallen world and a fallen humanity which Christians should overcome with God's help. This and the previous chapter amount to a rebuttal of the project of rejecting natural theology championed by these postmodern Evangelicals. What remains is to chart a course for the future of natural theology and apologetics given the critiques of postmodernism and the postmodern milieu in which Christians seek to live and minister.

5

Natural Theology After
the Postmodern Critique

A Proposal

IN THE PREVIOUS CHAPTERS, I attempted to faithfully represent Carl A. Raschke's, James K. A. Smith's, and Myron B. Penner's philosophical and theological reasons for rejecting natural theology and apologetics. These critiques were carefully considered and rejected by appealing to systematic and biblical theology and by applying an analytic philosophical method to assess their claims. Though the rejection of natural theology posed by these authors fails in various ways, North American Evangelicals still live and minister in a world characterized by postmodern ways of thinking. On a cultural level, people diminish the importance of objective truth (except with respect to the sciences), doubt humanity's ability to use reason in the search for knowledge, and have difficulty employing concepts of truth and rationality to religious commitments. Evangelicals care about crafting a thoughtful witness to the truth of Christian faith in this postmodern milieu. How can Evangelical natural theology thrive after the rejection of natural theology? How can Evangelicals engage in natural theology in their current postmodern cultural context? To answer these questions, I make four suggestions for natural theology after the postmodern critique. First, Evangelicals need to become apologists for truth, defending truth as correspondence and the centrality of truth for Evangelical witness. Second, in how Evangelicals do natural theology and apologetics, the postmodern critique ought to encourage humility, and the failure of the critique of natural theology ought to engender a healthy confidence. Third, Evangelicals should become advocates for scientific research, engaging the sciences as an authoritative source of knowledge that can point to general revelation. Fourth, Evangelical colleges and seminaries ought to invest anew in requiring training in apologetics and promoting research in natural theology among its faculty.

APOLOGISTS FOR TRUTH

The nature of truth is a contentious philosophical issue, notwithstanding the complexities introduced by a discussion on the nature of religious truth. I have defended a correspondence theory of truth against the postmodern accounts offered by Raschke, Smith, and Penner (see chapter 3). The lack of consensus on this issue among philosophers, along with the postmodern philosophical deflation of truth, contribute to a broader cultural context in which objective truth seems to matter less and less. This is illustrated by an American president who, during his time in office, equivocated on the meaning of the word *is*. It is further illustrated by others in politics who seem to think that reference to states of affairs can admit of appeals to facts on the one hand and to "alternative facts" on the other.[1] The nature of truth is even more problematic when considering the nature of religious truth, yet Evangelicals care about proclaiming the message of God in Christ in a way that makes reference to God's work in history. That is, Evangelicals believe that their religious truth-claims refer to states of affairs in reality. When doing natural theology, Evangelicals believe that their arguments stake a claim on reality, as well. But in a postmodern milieu, it is necessary to first make a case for truth. Arguments may be sound and even persuasive, but if one's interlocutor does not view truth as a representation of reality, then Christian faith will be merely one interesting interpretation of life among many. In that respect, I maintain that, alongside their explorations in natural theology and their evangelistic endeavors, Evangelicals must become apologists for truth. Evangelicals must be able to defend truth as correspondence and understand the pertinence of the correspondence theory for natural theology and apologetics with respect to evangelism.

First, Evangelicals must defend a correspondence theory of truth. One reason for this is that rejections of correspondence theory fail the test of

1. Jaffe, "Kellyanne Conway."

coherence. Consider the proposition, *there is no such thing as objective truth*. This statement, particularly when employed by postmodern philosophers and theologians, supposedly means that it is impossible to know whether our beliefs and statements correspond to reality. Human finitude, sin, and cultural and chronological limitations set up an absolute limit against any human's ability to know things as they are. However, Evangelicals ought not to accept this proposition because it fails a basic test of internal coherence. One needs only to pose the interrogative, seeking affirmation of the proposition's veracity, "Is it the case that there is no such thing as objective truth?" The postmodernist must respond in the affirmative. But if the postmodernist does this, then she is affirming that the proposition corresponds to states of affairs in reality. Therefore, the proposition, *there is no such thing as objective truth*, is self-refuting and false.[2] Now if by affirming this proposition the postmodernist merely means that in her language-game community, call it "North American postmodern philosophy," one is playing by the rules to affirm that there is no objective truth, then we are under no compulsion to reject the proposition, but neither are we under obligation to accept it as meaningful in any broader sense. Postmodernism cannot escape this basic incoherence. To claim that there is no objective truth is to affirm that there is objective truth. To state that truth claims cannot correspond to reality is to make a claim about reality.[3]

The correspondence theory is the most defensible view philosophically. The correspondence theory states that "a proposition is true just in case it corresponds to reality, when what it asserts to be the case is the case."[4] A proposition, or that which a declarative statement asserts, is the truth-bearer. Propositions may be stated in any number of languages or signs, but the proposition is what is of interest to correspondence theorists. The prop-

2. Douglas Groothuis says something similar when he argues, "Postmodernist pronouncements on rejecting objective truth tend to contradict themselves in that they claim to be applicable to reality itself, not merely to their own language game or constructed map," in *Christian Apologetics*, 129. One could add that this postmodern statement conflates knowledge with truth. The nature of truth is a different issue from one's knowledge that a proposition is true.

3. There is an option here that the postmodernist can take. She can simply say, "What we mean by the term *truth* should not be conflated with that which corresponds to reality." That is a separate issue that I think she can raise. However, this is merely a dispute about the agreed meaning of the term, not an argument for the postmodern view per se. Moreover, it raises the issue of whether my interpretation of the postmodern view corresponds to the understanding of that view affirmed by its proponents.

4. Moreland, "Truth, Contemporary Philosophy, and the Postmodern Turn," 77.

osition is true if it corresponds to states of affairs in reality, or simply, facts. "A fact is some real, that is obtaining, state of affairs in the world."[5] Facts are the truth-makers in the correspondence view. As I argued in chapter 3, a strong argument in favor of the correspondence view is the descriptive argument (or phenomenological argument). In J. P. Moreland's thought experiment of the descriptive argument, he tells of how Joe has a belief that a book is in the university bookstore. Frank, who does not have this prior belief, goes to the bookstore with Joe where they both see the book. They both have the sensory experience of the existence of the book, but Joe has an additional experience that his previous thought about the existence of the book corresponds to reality. "He is able to compare his thought with its intentional object and 'see,' be directly aware of, the truth of the thought. In this case, Joe actually experiences the correspondence relation itself and truth itself becomes an object of his awareness."[6] Direct awareness of the correspondence relation affirms the correspondence theory.

The correspondence view comports well with Aristotelean logic, as well. The law of the excluded middle states "either A or non-A." This means that it is either the case that A, or it is the case that non-A. There is not a third option. Consider a belief (C) that there is a coyote near the pond behind the library. Either there is a coyote there now (C), or there is not (not-C). One may add to this consideration the law of noncontradiction which states, "A is not non-A in the same time and in the same respect." If there was a coyote there yesterday, and there is not a coyote there now, then not-C. If there is a wolf that looks like a coyote there now, but there is not a coyote there now, then not-C. The belief that there is a coyote near the pond behind the library either is the case, or it is not the case. The terms of the correspondence view (a true proposition is one that corresponds to reality) match what is at stake in Aristotelean logic (Either A or non-A. A≠non-A.). We have previously argued that denying Aristotelean logic must assume its truthfulness. One is under no constraint to accept the *terms* of a denial of noncontradiction if noncontradiction itself is denied. If one denies the law of noncontradiction, one is, without being aware of it, presuming it to be true. Since the correspondence view comports so well with Aristotelean logic, this suggests that the correspondence theory is true, as well. The comportment between the two is best explained by the correspondence theory being true.

5. Ibid., 78.

6. Ibid., 79. See also Willard, "Verso una Teoria," 125–47.

Bertrand Russell argues that only the correspondence theory can make sense of falsehoods. A theory of truth must make sense of falsehoods because "on many subjects different people hold different and incompatible opinions: hence some beliefs must be erroneous."[7] He offers the example of Othello believing that Desdemona loves Cassio (DLC). There are three objects of belief: Desdemona, loving, and Cassio. If this belief is true, then the objects Desdemona, loving, and Cassio are a complex unity which is itself an additional (a fourth) object of Othello's belief. It is the true belief that holds the objects together, and the belief is true if it corresponds to reality. If this belief is false, then there is no complex unity of the objects of belief. The unity simply does not exist. Only in the true belief can the three objects be unified into a complex unity (indeed, a fourth object which can only obtain if factual). In a false belief, the objects are related by virtue of being believed, but not united by virtue of being true. Only the correspondence theory can account for the fact that there are three objects of belief for Othello if the belief DLC is false and four objects of belief for Othello if the belief DLC is true. An error in belief prohibits the terms from being a single complex object of belief if DLC is false. This argument will not be persuasive for one who thinks that accounting for error is not an important component of a theory of truth. However, if accounting for the fact that people hold different and, at times, mutually exclusive beliefs, is an essential aspect of a theory of truth, then Russell's view commends the correspondence theory.[8]

Second, of even greater interest to Evangelicals is that the correspondence theory is assumed in the key elements of their biblical confession of faith. The Christian confession that Jesus is Lord is toothless unless it corresponds to reality. Believing that it is a fact that Jesus is the Lord of the universe is what motivates repentance, clarifies the meaning of life, inspires missionary work, and secures one's eternal destiny. Evangelicals hold that "Jesus is Lord" is either a true or false proposition, and that there is no *tertium quid*. People have differing beliefs about whether the statement is true, but the statement is either true or false regardless of one's opinion. Evangelicals' beliefs about historical events (e.g. the existence of the people of Israel, the life of Jesus, the death and resurrection, etc.) make sense only

---

7. Russell, "Truth and Falsehood," 17.

8. He argues that the coherence theory, with its hypothetical allowance for two coherent, but mutually exclusive systems, cannot account for falsehoods "because there is no proof that there can be only one coherent system," in ibid., 19.

within a correspondence framework. Jesus' exclusive statement in John's Gospel is illustrative, "I am the way and the truth and the life. No one comes to the Father except through me" (John 14:6, NIV). If Evangelicals' interpretation of this passage is correct, then "there is no exception or exemption from this claim: there is but one way to the Father—Jesus himself."[9] Of course, many Evangelicals recognize that it is possible that the exclusivist interpretation of this passage may be incorrect. In this case, Evangelicals committed to a high view of Scripture will still maintain that *whatever Jesus meant* by this claim is what corresponds to reality. Nowhere is an assumed correspondence view of truth clearer than in Paul's writing on the resurrection of Jesus in 1 Corinthians 15. Paul presents the gospel that he had originally presented to them, that Jesus died, was buried, and was raised from the dead, and that Jesus appeared to many people including Paul. Yet some people denied that Jesus had, in fact, been raised from the dead. In response, Paul says, "If there is no resurrection of the dead, then not even Christ has been raised. And if Christ has not been raised, our preaching is useless and so is your faith" (1 Cor 15:13–14, NIV). Paul views the truth of the Christian message as wholly dependent on whether a particular historical event actually took place. Further, he thinks that the Christian faith is useless or empty or vain (*kenos*) if Jesus did not, in fact, rise from the dead. Evangelicals ought to recognize that only the correspondence theory can make sense of the biblical witness about Christian faith.

Being apologists for truth is a necessary aspect of fidelity to the Christian message. Evangelicals ought to view a defense of the nature of truth as vital for the success of the Christian mission, especially in a North American culture that is suspicious of objective religious truth claims. At the heart of this mission is a desire to see others confess faith in Jesus. This impulse is what historian David Bebbington calls "*conversionism*, the belief that lives need to be changed."[10] This is commanded by Jesus in Matthew 28, "Go and make disciples of all nations, baptizing them in the name of the Father and of the Son and of the Holy Spirit, and teaching them to obey everything I have commanded you" (Matt 28:19–20, NIV). However sincere one's attempt to explain the Christian message will be to those who are not yet disciples of Christ, the postmodern milieu of twenty-first century North America will weaken its reception. This is because an Evangelical approach to the correspondence theory when applied to religious truth does not

9. Groothuis, *Truth Decay*, 69.

10. Bebbington, *Evangelicalism in Modern Britain*, 2.

comport well with this culture. Should one explain one's belief that Jesus is Lord and that Jesus rose from the dead, representative responses might be something like, "I am so happy that you found your truth." Or, "That is great that you have discovered meaning in your faith." The Barna Group, which conducts surveys on religious attitudes and behaviors in the United States, in 2013 found that "nearly half of Americans agree with [the] statement (31% of Americans agree somewhat, while 16% agree strongly)" that "the Bible, the Koran and the Book of Mormon are all different expressions of the same spiritual truths."[11] When applied only to the identity of Jesus, such a belief will yield incredible contradictions. While Evangelicals believe that Jesus is the eternally existing second person of the Trinity, Mormons believe that Jesus is a finite son of God, and Muslims believe that Jesus is a merely a key prophet.

Before the work of evangelism proper (via the proclamation of the death, resurrection, and lordship of Jesus), Evangelicals need to defend the basic categories of truth as correspondence, including some basic logic that makes possible the Evangelical confession of faith. This is because Evangelical beliefs about the divinity of Jesus, the historicity of the resurrection of Jesus, and a high view of Scripture are outside the plausibility structure of many twenty-first century North Americans.[12] Defending the correspondence theory of truth can make the conversation into these central beliefs more fruitful for those with whom Evangelicals wish to share the good news. This will clarify that one's beliefs about the identity of Jesus are either true or false and hopefully show that one's beliefs may be supported or undermined by the marshalling of various kinds of historical, philosophical, and existential evidence, and not necessarily by the degree to which the belief is sincere.

Natural theology, in particular, can benefit from Evangelicals being apologists for truth. Consider William Lane Craig's version of the *kalām* cosmological argument.

1. Everything that begins to exist has a cause of its existence.

2. The universe began to exist.

---

11. The Barna Group, "What Do Americans Really Think?" lines 85–87.

12. "Plausibility structure" is a sociological term coined by Peter Berger for the kinds of beliefs that someone is willing to entertain as plausible. See Berger, *A Rumor of Angels*, 38–42.

3. Therefore the universe has a cause of its existence.[13]

The argument depends on a correspondence relationship between its propositions and reality. Craig argues that the premises are true by appealing to philosophical truths and to "empirical confirmations" to support the premises.[14] The argument's subjective cogency, however, depends to a high degree on whether one's interlocutor has a plausibility structure such that belief in God can correspond to reality and be confirmed by philosophy and science. If one's interlocutor does not hold that religious beliefs can correspond to reality, then Craig's argument is more or less worthless in helping that person to entertain the notion of God's existence. Natural theology needs defenders of truth in its corner to make its deliverances plausible in a postmodern milieu.

HUMILITY, CONFIDENCE, AND NATURAL THEOLOGY

The current cultural context not only requires able defenders of truth, it requires a delicate blend of humility and confidence in the practice of natural theology.[15] It should not need to be said that Christian virtues ought to be at the heart of doing natural theology. However, stories like those of the atheist John, as told in Penner's *The End of Apologetics* remind advocates of natural theology after the failure of the postmodern critique that a certain way of life is required of those who do natural theology. "John told the apologists he found what they were doing offensive. Undaunted, our defenders of the faith assumed the apologetic right-of-way . . . informing John at one point that it was necessary so that his 'blood would not be on their heads' (actually citing Ezek. 3:18)."[16] Clearly, these young apologists lacked good listening skills and the ability to show John both love and pastoral concern for his life. Most importantly, the story illustrates that the young apologists seemed to be arrogant in their discussion with John. In chapter four, I agree with D. A. Carson that Christians who do natural theology and apologetics can be both rational and emotional and both inclusive of others

---

13. Craig, *The Kalām Cosmological Argument*, 63.

14. See ibid., 65–140.

15. Others have addressed well the importance of virtues in apologetics. See Stackhouse, Jr., *Humble Apologetics*, esp. chapter 8; Guinness, *Fool's Talk,* esp. chapter 9; and Koukl, *Tactics.*

16. Penner, *The End of Apologetics*, 78.

and unflinching in their commitment to the truth.[17] Christians can be both humble and confident in their apologetic endeavors. In this section, I will outline why both humility and confidence are necessary for natural theology after the failure of the postmodern critique. I will use two of James K. A. Smith's "slogans of postmodernism" as examples of why humility and confidence are central virtues.[18] First, Derrida writes, "There is nothing outside the text."[19] Second, as Lyotard says, postmodernity is "incredulity toward metanarratives."[20] These "slogans" provide unique cases for why Christians need to cultivate both humility and confidence in their apologetic endeavors.

First, consider Derrida's slogan, "there is nothing outside the text." Postmodern philosophers and theologians employ this idea to argue that we do not have knowledge of things in themselves because all we have are our interpretations. The world itself is a kind of text that needs interpretation, and our contingency prohibits us from seeing things as they are. This threatens the kind of natural theology commended by Evangelicals like J. P. Moreland, William Lane Craig, and Douglas Groothuis because it rules out the possibility of a single correct interpretation of the natural world (and of general revelation) such that one could employ philosophical argumentation to demonstrate that God exists. No demonstration will be convincing because all claims are subject to any number of valid interpretations. Christians ought to respond to this challenge with confidence, showing that this postmodern principle is problematic. For example, most people in North America do not think that data regarding the Holocaust is up for interpretation, nor do they think that interpretive communities can legitimately determine that certain behaviors like rape or torturing the innocent are morally acceptable. Moreover, postmodern writers object when their texts are misinterpreted.[21] Evangelicals who have a firm commitment to the

---

17. See Carson, *Becoming Conversant*, 29.

18. Smith, *Who's Afraid of Postmodernism?* 21.

19. Derrida, *Of Grammatology*, 158.

20. Lyotard, *The Postmodern Condition*, xxiv. The third "slogan" that Smith cites is *power is knowledge* from Michel Foucault. "It is not the activity of the subject of knowledge that produces a corpus of knowledge, useful or resistant to power, but power-knowledge, the processes and struggles that traverse it and of which it is made up, that determines the forms and possible domains of knowledge," in Foucault, *Discipline and Punish*, 28.

21. For example, Michel Foucault says, "when I read—and I know it has been attributed to me—the thesis, 'Knowledge is power,' or 'Power is knowledge,' I begin to laugh, since studying their *relation* is precisely my problem. If they were identical, I would not

truth need to be confident in how they do natural theology and apologetics, taking the opportunity to expose the cracks in the postmodern façade and to commend the truth of the Christian faith. In equal measure, though, Evangelicals ought to exhibit humility, acknowledging that the plurality of interpretations about religious truth around the world may pose an obstacle for the reception of natural theology. Because one's interlocutor may not immediately consent to a philosophical demonstration of God's existence, one must be humble, taking time to listen and respond to objections. One may be humble enough to recognize a lack in one's philosophical or theological abilities, and one may be humble enough to work at developing these skills for the purpose of being a better apologist.

Second, Jean-François Lyotard provides helpful insight into the postmodern condition when he says that postmodernism is "incredulity toward metanarratives." This is helpful because Evangelical advocates of natural theology need to understand the suspicion that many in the West have toward all-encompassing explanations of reality, and particularly of what matters most. Though I disagree with James K. A. Smith's application of Lyotard's principle to Christian life and ministry, I agree with his interpretation of Lyotard, the claim that the attitude of incredulity is not aimed at all big stories, but particularly those that "claim to be able to legitimate or prove the story's claim by an appeal to universal reason."[22] However, I argue in chapter three that Smith's method for commending Lyotard's principle used a conjunction of a disjunctive syllogism and a *modus ponens*. No one, including Smith, is able to escape basic logical categories in any discourse. Meaningful debate and discussion requires basic logical categories, and one must affirm the law of noncontradiction in order to deny it. Regarding religious truth claims, Paul Griffiths argues that, for example, both Vishishtadvaitavedanta Hinduism and Anglican Christianity hold in common a commitment to basic logic, including "the principles of identity, noncontradiction, and excluded middle; the argument forms at least to material implication and contraposition."[23] Evangelicals doing natural theology and apologetics ought to confidently employ reason as an element of common ground between themselves and those who do not have

---

have to study them and I would be spared a lot of fatigue as a result," in *Politics, Philosophy, Culture*, 43.

22. Smith, *Who's Afraid of Postmodernism?* 65.

23. Griffiths, *An Apology for Apologetics*, 28–29.

Christian religious commitments.[24] This confidence should be tempered by humility, as well, for reasons similar to those stated above with respect to the issue of a plurality of interpretations. Many people do not understand basic logic and will, therefore, have an incredulous attitude toward truth-claims legitimized by reference to logic. Evangelicals often lack the ability to employ reasoning well in their theology and evangelism. An Evangelical doing natural theology should take a humble self-assessment, recognizing that one may have an opportunity to grow in employing reason and in helping others to understand claims that require reasoning skills. In addition, sometimes one's interlocutor may identify a flaw in one's reasoning. Evangelicals doing natural theology should respond to such a challenge with gratitude, humbly receiving the intellectual correction and working to revise, restate, or reject bad arguments and to do the hard work of crafting good arguments. Never should an Evangelical receive such a challenge with defensiveness, table-turning arrogance, or flippancy. Doing so is a repudiation of the Christian way of life. The postmodern milieu in which Evangelicals live and minister requires both humility and confidence. These virtues make natural theology more in keeping with the way of life that Christians seek to live as they follow the example of Jesus.

ADVOCATES FOR SCIENCE

Evangelicals who want to see natural theology thrive after the failure of the postmodern critique will care deeply about developing strategies for defending the Christian faith. One strategy, already engaged in by Evangelical advocates of natural theology, is appealing to the sciences for evidence of God's general revelation in the natural world. In a Western context, this approach may be especially effective among many young adults who, according to a Barna Group survey, "feel disconnected from church or from faith" because of perceived tension between Christian faith and science.[25] This feeling is part of the postmodern *zeitgeist*, especially because science is still seen by many to be the paradigm for discovering truth in the West.[26] Despite the fact that science cannot answer some of life's most important

24. See Studebaker, "Common Ground," 161–65.

25. The Barna Group, "Six Reasons Young Christians Leave Church," line 39.

26. This is despite the fact that many postmodern philosophers, including some described in this work, are critical of the place that science seems to hold in Western culture.

questions, Alvin Plantinga says, "Some treat science as if it were a sort of infallible oracle, like a divine revelation—or if not infallible . . . at any rate such that when it comes to fixing belief, science is the court of last appeal."[27] Since Christianity in general, and Evangelical Christianity in particular, tend to see God or the Bible as the last court of appeal, many feel there is tension between Christianity and science. This feeling is avoidable and can actually be reversed so that Christianity can benefit from and contribute to the success of the sciences in the twenty-first century. Evangelicals ought to become advocates for the sciences, showing how Christianity has what Plantinga calls "deep concord" with science.[28] This section will outline Plantinga's defense of Christianity's beneficial relationship with science and briefly examine how the recent suggestion that the fine-tuning of the universe illustrates how science can benefit natural theology.

Plantinga concedes that there is a perceived conflict between Christianity and science, but he claims that this conflict is often mistakenly alleged or superficial in nature. According to Plantinga, the concord between Christianity and science is deep.[29] First, Plantinga points to fine-tuning data in cosmology that shows that "several of the basic physical constants—the velocity of light, the strength of the gravitational force, and of the strong and weak nuclear forces—must fall within very narrow limits if intelligent life of our kind is to develop."[30] I will briefly examine these data and their significance below, but they are significant for Plantinga because the fine-tuning of the universe would be what we would expect to discover if theism were true. "Given theism; fine-tuning is not at all improbable; given atheism, it is; therefore theism is to be preferred to atheism."[31] Second, he recognizes the significance of the "irreducible complexity" of some mo-

---

27. Plantinga, *Where the Conflict Really Lies*, xii.

28. Ibid., see esp. Part III. Part IV of this work, though beyond the scope of this study, fascinatingly outlines the ways in which there is deep conflict between naturalism and science. This section is crowned by Plantinga's Evolutionary Argument Against Naturalism. See ibid., 311–50.

29. See ibid., 129, where Plantinga argues, "There is no conflict between theistic belief and evolutionary theory, including the thought that all of life has come to be by way of natural selection operating on random genetic mutation. According to theistic religion, God has created the world and created human beings in his image. It is perfectly possible, however, that he did so by employing, guiding, and directing the process of genetic variation and natural selection. He may not in fact have done it in that fashion; perhaps you think it rather unlikely that he did it that way. Still, he certainly could have."

30. Ibid., 194.

31. Ibid., 199. It is beyond the scope of this work to fully assess this claim.

lecular structures in biology such that these systems could not have evolved "from simpler systems, by way of the small, incremental steps required by a Darwinian explanation."[32] These kinds of systems and structures offer serious support for the existence of an intelligent designer. While not offering "irrefragable arguments for theism," both fine-tuning and irreducible complexity do "present us with epistemic situations in which the rational response is design belief."[33] Finally, he argues that scientific values and prerequisites like simplicity, the match between our cognitive faculties and physical world, the regularity and predictability of the world, the laws of nature, the efficacy of mathematics when applied to sciences, and the ability for humans to learn from experience are all most plausible if God exists. These things make scientific advancement possible, but cannot be grounded in science itself. A theistic worldview, however, makes sense of them. There is deep concord between Christianity and science, and if Evangelicals receive information like this as general revelation, then this can energize and enrich the discipline of natural theology and make its arguments that much more convincing.

To illustrate the possibilities for Evangelicals engaging the sciences, it is helpful to examine the kinds of fine-tuning data that Plantinga commends. Starting in the late twentieth century, a fascinating string of discoveries in physics and cosmology were published, which suggested to some that the universe is finely-tuned for the emergence of intelligent life.[34] These discoveries, also called anthropic data, show that the universe meets "many special requirements" that allow for the "delicate and complex phenomenon" of the emergence of intelligent observers.[35] Martin Rees famously outlined six constants in the universe that are necessary for life. (1) "The strength of the electrical forces that hold atoms together divided by the force of gravity between them;"[36] (2) the strong nuclear force; (3) the amount of matter in the universe, including galaxies, gases, and dark matter; (4) the force of antigravity, which keeps the universe from expanding too quickly; (5) "the ratio of gravitational binding force to rest-mass energy;"[37] and (6) the three

---

32. Ibid., 226.

33. Ibid., 264.

34. See Rees, *Just Six Numbers*; Davies, *Cosmic Jackpot*; Barrow and Tipler, *The Anthropic Cosmological Principle*.

35. Davis, *Cosmic Jackpot*, 131.

36. Rees, *Just Six Numbers*, 2.

37. McGrath, *A Fine-Tuned Universe*, 119.

spatial dimensions. Among Evangelicals, there are differing interpretations of the significance of the data of fine-tuning. Alister McGrath argues that fine-tuning provides "conceptual resonance with, not deductive proof of, the Christian vision of God."[38] McGrath does not do much to substantiate this interpretation.[39] He argues that fine-tuning data are merely the kinds of data that we should expect to see if the universe were created by a benevolent God who is interested in relationships with other intelligent beings. J. P. Moreland and William Lane Craig, on the other hand, see fine-tuning as part of a teleological argument for the existence of God that can profitably be stated in deductive terms:

1. The fine-tuning of the universe is due to either physical necessity, chance or design.

2. It is not due to physical necessity or chance.

3. Therefore, it is due to design.[40]

They attempt to argue that physical necessity, chance, or design are indeed the only options for interpreting fine-tuning data and that physical chance or design are highly unlikely. Though I agree with Moreland and Craig over McGrath, both of these approaches to interpreting anthropic data illustrate how Evangelicals can embrace the discoveries of science for natural theology. To that end, Christians ought to commend scientific pursuits to those in their churches and make room for programs of study in the sciences in their colleges and universities. Christians ought to be champions for science, showing how the philosophical presuppositions and values necessary

38. Ibid., 121. Plantinga would agree with this basic interpretation. See Plantinga, *Where the Conflict Really Lies*, 199, 224.

39. His work shows a more programmatic rejection of deduction as an argument form in natural theology. This seems to be more pragmatic, for he notes that deductive arguments simply do not command the kind of assent that many philosophers think they should. However, he also seems to argue that William Lane Craig's argument for the existence of God from the beginning of the universe is subject to the same objections levied by J. L. Mackie on Leibniz's cosmological argument, namely, that "it is based on the assumption that 'things should be intelligible through and through.'" See McGrath, *A Fine-Tuned Universe*, 40. It is worth noting that McGrath does not provide an argument that supports the conclusion that deduction of the variety offered by Craig does, in fact, show the same weakness as Leibniz's deduction. This seems to be a textbook case of the bad company fallacy. The argument that he is considering is from Craig, "Existence of God and the Beginning," 85–96; and Craig, "Timelessness and Creation," 646–56.

40. Moreland and Craig, *Philosophical Foundations*, 484. It is beyond the scope of this work to assess whether this argument is successful.

for science are best supported by the Christian picture of reality and by embracing scientific discoveries for the purpose of showing Christianity to be true.

A PROPOSAL FOR EVANGELICAL COLLEGES AND SEMINARIES

In the previous section, I maintained that Evangelicals need to champion scientific pursuits in their churches, colleges, and universities. This contention applies all the more with respect to natural theology. A major hurdle to Evangelicals embracing natural theology after the failure of the postmodern critique is that the disciplines of philosophy and theology have been minimized or forgotten in many courses of study across North America. High school graduates seldom have exposure to philosophy, and many state and private colleges include only minimal training in philosophy and religion. In a Wabash Center for Teaching Theology and Religion colloquy in 2005, religion scholars noted "the growing gaps in the curriculum on Christianity . . . the loss of many courses that resemble theology (including topics like Philosophy of Religion), and a decreased emphasis on biblical studies."[41] How can Evangelicals engage natural theology if colleges and universities are reducing courses in philosophy of religion? The obvious answer might be to look to Evangelical leaders (pastors, teachers, and missionaries) as potential sources of training in apologetics. People can go to church to learn about these things. Yet Evangelical leaders often have no training in apologetics and philosophy, and often only a little training in theology.[42] As Mark Noll famously states, "The scandal of the evangelical mind is that there is not much of an evangelical mind."[43] How can Evangelicals embrace natural theology when their intellectual leaders often lack training in these disciplines?

Apart from broader reforms in public school and university curricula (which I will not address here), I maintain that Evangelical colleges and seminaries need to invest in training in philosophy, theology, and apologetics as part of their missional mandate as centers for training Christian leaders. Gavin D'Costa argues that "Christian culture and civilization are

41. Gravett, Hulsether, and Medine, "Conversation," 164.

42. This is, of course, excluding the many Evangelicals trained in philosophy and apologetics working in the academy and in apologetics-specific ministries.

43. Noll, *Scandal of the Evangelical Mind*, 3.

at stake if we do not attend to the nature of the university, a major institution that fosters the cultural and intellectual life of nations and trains the intelligentsia of the ecclesia."[44] Consider an excerpt from the "Statement of Mission and Purpose" from Liberty University, the largest Christian university in the United States: "The University educates men and women who will make important contributions to their workplaces and communities, follow their chosen vocations as callings to glorify God, and fulfill the Great Commission."[45] A commitment to educating men and women with the Great Commission in mind—a commitment shared by many Christian colleges, universities, and seminaries—is precisely why these institutions need to include training in philosophy, theology, and apologetics.

To support this, one only needs to consider the challenge of fulfilling the Great Commission in twenty-first century North America. Prior to his ascension, Jesus says,

> All authority in heaven and on earth has been given to me. Therefore go and make disciples of all nations, baptizing them in the name of the Father and of the Son and of the Holy Spirit, and teaching them to obey everything I have commanded you. And surely I am with you always, to the very end of the age (Matt 28:18–20, NIV).

This famous passage entails some important prerequisites. It assumes a belief in God, which is steadily decreasing, especially among young people in the United States.[46] It also requires some basic understanding regarding the nature of the Triune God and the message of Jesus. Yet Stephen Prothero recounts that "only half of Americans can name even one of the four Gospels," "only one-third know that Jesus (no, not Billy Graham) delivered the Sermon on the Mount," and "a majority of Americans wrongly believe that the Bible says that Jesus was born in Jerusalem."[47] The Great

---

44. D'Costa, *Theology in the Public Square*, 215. D'Costa's broader point is not about natural theology and apologetics, but about Christian culture and civilization.

45. Liberty University, "Mission Statement," lines 15–17. Liberty University includes classes in philosophy, theology, and the Christian worldview as part of its core competency requirements for many majors.

46. It is not as if belief in God is rare. 83% of Americans are still either "absolutely certain" or "fairly certain" that God exists. However, this number drops to 73% when considering those aged 18–29. In some urban areas, belief in God among adults drops even more: Seattle (68%) and San Francisco (62%). See Pew Research Center, "Religious Landscape Study."

47. Prothero, *Religious Literacy*, 30.

Commission importantly assumes that people can commune with ("I will be with you"), understand and obey God, and that relationship with God is possible. While not disparaging the efficacy of minimalistic preaching of the message of Jesus, Christians need to be able to help people who are interested in Christian faith, who are not theists, who do not understand Christian theology, and who have not read the Bible. Natural theology is a vital avenue to reflection on the two former issues.[48] Those who graduate from Christian colleges and seminaries should be able to have meaningful discussions about the existence of God with those who do not believe. Pastors and missionaries should be able to train those under their care to present arguments for the existence of God. Christian educators should have the ability to point students to resources that can enrich their discussions about natural theology for the purpose of helping others to see that God exists. As Douglas Groothuis argues, "Christians need a confident, courageous, and compelling conviction that Christianity is the flaming truth the world needs to hear, that it can withstand rational testing and that the God of truth sponsors our humble apologetic efforts."[49] This cannot be done without required courses in philosophy, apologetics, and theology, and it is this contention I leave with my readers on the significance of this project.

CONCLUSION

A final word on this project should be brief. I have argued that natural theology is vital for Evangelicals for a proper understanding of the nature of the revelation of God, in biblical faithfulness, and in Christian witness. The project of Myron B. Penner, James K. A. Smith, and Carl A. Raschke of rejecting natural theology and apologetics on postmodern grounds (though coming from a place of genuine Christian concern) is wrongheaded. It suffers from major logical and theological flaws. I have identified these flaws in detail in chapters 3 and 4. Though their work should be read and considered by Evangelicals, their rejection of natural theology ultimately fails. Instead, the rich tradition of natural theology inherited by Evangelicals from prior generations of Christians should be engaged and mastered. Moreover, Evangelical Christians need to become apologists for the truth. Renewed confidence and humility should be marshalled in engaging the

48. Prothero recommends that all Americans be trained in basic biblical literacy simply for the purpose of responsible civic engagement. See ibid., 132–5.

49. Groothuis, *Christian Apologetics*, 650.

postmodern milieu in which we live and minister. Christian colleges and seminaries should train future leaders in natural theology. Arguments for the existence of God and scientific discoveries like the fine-tuning of the universe should be offered to the world as evidence of the one whom Francis Schaeffer calls "the God who is there," whom Carl F. H. Henry calls the "God who speaks and shows," and whom the Scriptures call the "God and Father of all, who is over all and through all and in all" (Eph 4:6, NIV). To God alone be the praise.

Bibliography

Alston, William. "Religious Diversity and Perceptual Knowledge of God." In *Faith and Philosophy* 5, no. 4 (1988) 433–48.

Altizer, Thomas J. J. *The Self-Embodiment of God*. New York: Harper & Row, 1977.

Aquinas, Thomas. *Summa Theologiae: A Concise Translation*. Edited by Timothy McDermott. Westminster, MD: Christian Classics, 1989.

Aristotle. "Posterior Analytics—Book I." In *The Philosophy of Aristotle*, edited by Renford Bambrough, translated by J. L. Creed and A. E. Wardman, 161–214. New York: Signet Classic, 1963.

Arnaud, M. E. *Manual de Dogmatique: ou exposition méthodique et raisonnée de doctrines chrétiennes*. Paris: Fischbacher, 1891.

Bahnsen, Greg. *Van Til's Apologetic: Readings and Analysis*. Phillipsburg, NJ: Presbyterian and Reformed Publishing Company, 1998.

The Barna Group. "Six Reasons Young Christians Leave Church." Barna. Last modified September 27, 2011. Accessed July 19, 2017. https://www.barna.com/research/six-reasons-young-christians-leave-church.

———. What Do Americans Really Think About the Bible?" Barna. Last modified April 10, 2013. Accessed July 18, 2017. https://www.barna.com/research/what-do-americans-really-think-about-the-bible.

Barnes, Hunter and Myron Bradley Penner, eds. *A New Kind of Conversation: Blogging Toward a Postmodern Faith*. Colorado Springs, CO: Paternoster, 2006.

Barr, James. *Biblical Faith and Natural Theology: The Gifford Lectures for 1991: Delivered in the University of Edinburgh*. Oxford: Oxford University Press, 1994.

Barrow, John D., and Frank J. Tipler. *The Anthropic Cosmological Principle*. Oxford: Oxford University Press, 1986.

Barth, Karl. *Church Dogmatics: I.1 The Doctrine of the Word of God: § 1–7 The Word of God as the Criterion of Dogmatics*. Edited by G. W. Bromiley and T. F. Torrance. Translated by G. W. Bromiley, G. T. Thomson, and Harold Knight. London: T&T Clark, 2009.

Bebbington, David. *Evangelicalism in Modern Britain: A History From the 1730s to the 1980s*. London: Routledge, 1989.

Berger, Peter. *A Rumor of Angels: Modern Society and the Rediscovery of the Supernatural*. New York: Doubleday, 1990.

Bergson, Henri. *Creative Evolution*. Translated by Arthur Mitchell. New York: Henry Holt Company, 1911.

Berkhof, Louis. *Systematic Theology*. 4th Edition. Grand Rapids, MI: Eerdmans, 1941.

Beyssade, Jean-Marie. "The Idea of God and the Proofs of His Existence." In *The Cambridge Companion to Descartes*, ed. John Cottingham, 174–99. Cambridge: Cambridge University Press, 1992.

Boyd, Craig A. "The Synthesis of Reason and Faith Response." In *Faith and Reason: Three Views*, edited by Steve Wilkens, 76–84. Downers Grove, IL: IVP Academic, 2014.

Brandom, Robert. *Articulating Reasons: An Introduction to Inferentialism*. Cambridge, MA: Harvard University Press, 2000.

Bruce, F. F. *The Book of Acts*. Revised Edition. The New International Commentary on the New Testament. Grand Rapids, MI: Eerdmans, 1988.

Brunner, Emil and Karl Barth. *Natural Theology Comprising "Nature and Grace" by Professor Dr. Emil Brunner and the reply No! by Dr. Karl Barth*. Translated by Peter Fraenkel. London: Centenary, 1946.

Calvin, John. "John Calvin on Faith and the Promises of God." In *The Christian Theology Reader*, edited by Alister E. McGrath, 233–34. Cambridge, MA: Blackwell, 1995.

———. "John Calvin on the Nature of Faith." In *The Christian Theology Reader*, edited by Alister E. McGrath, 15. Cambridge, MA: Blackwell, 1995.

Caputo, John D. *Heidegger and Aquinas: An Essay on Overcoming Metaphysics*. New York: Fordham University Press, 1982.

———. "How to Avoid Speaking of God: The Violence of Natural Theology." In *Prospects for Natural Theology*, edited by Eugene Long. Studies in Philosophy and the History of Philosophy, vol. 25, 128–50. Washington, DC: The Catholic University of America Press, 1992.

———. *The Prayers and Tears of Jacques Derrida: Religion without Religion*. Bloomington, IN: Indiana University Press, 1997.

———. "The Weakness of God: A Radical Theology of the Cross." In *The Wisdom and Foolishness of God: First Corinthians 1–2 in Theological Exploration*, edited by Christophe Chalamet and Hans-Christoph Askani, 21–87. Minneapolis, MN: Fortress, 2015.

Carson, D.A. *Becoming Conversant with the Emerging Church: Understanding a Movement and Its Implications*. Grand Rapids, MI: Zondervan, 2005.

Craig, William Lane. "The Existence of God and the Beginning of the Universe." In *Thought: A Journal of Modern Thought* 3 (1991) 85–96.

———. *The Kalām Cosmological Argument*. Eugene, OR: Wipf & Stock, 2000.

———. *Reasonable Faith: Christian Truth and Apologetics*. 3rd Edition. Wheaton, IL: Crossway Books, 2008.

———. "Timelessness and Creation." In *Australasian Journal of Philosophy* 74 (1996) 646–56.

Craig, William Lane and J. P. Moreland, "Introduction," in *The Blackwell Companion to Natural Theology*, edited by William Lane Craig and J. P. Moreland, iv–xiii. Malden, MA: Wiley-Blackwell, 2009.

Copleston, S. J., Frederick. *A History of Philosophy: Volume I: Greece and Rome*. New York: Image Books, 1993.

Crowell, Steven. *Husserl, Heidegger, and the Space of Meaning: Paths Toward Transcendental Phenomenology*. Evanston, IL: Northwestern University Press, 2001.

Davies, Paul. *Cosmic Jackpot: Why Our Universe Is Just Right For Life*. New York: Houghton Mifflin Company, 2007.

Davis, Richard B. and Paul Franks. "Against a Postmodern Pentecostal Epistemology." In *Philosophia Christi* 15, no. 2 (2013) 129–45.

Dawkins, Richard. *The God Delusion*. Boston: Houghton Mifflin, 2006.

D'Costa, Gavin. *Theology in the Public Square: Church, Academy and Nation*. Malden, MA: Blackwell, 2005.

Dennett, Daniel. *Breaking the Spell: Religion as a Natural Phenomenon*. New York: Penguin, 2006.

Derrida, Jacques. *Acts of Religion*. New York: Routledge, 2002.

———. "Afterword: Toward An Ethic of Discussion." In *Limited Inc.*, 111–60. Evanston, IL: Northwestern University Press, 1988.

———. *Of Grammatology*. Translated by Gayatri Chakravorty Spivak. Baltimore and London: The Johns Hopkins University Press, 1967.

———. "Signature Event Context." In *Margins of Philosophy*, trans. Alan Bass, 307–30. Chicago: The University of Chicago Press, 1982.

Descartes, René. *Discourse on Method and the Meditations*. Translated by F. E. Sutcliffe. Middlesex, UK: Penguin Books Ltd., 1968.

DeWeese Garrett J., and J. P. Moreland. *Philosophy Made Slightly Less Difficult: A Beginner's Guide to Life's Big Questions*. Downers Grove, IL: IVP Academic, 2005.

Dooyeweerd, Herman. *In the Twilight of Western Thought: Studies in the Pretended Autonomy of Philosophical Thought*. Edited by James K. A. Smith, Collected Works, B/4. Lewiston, NY: Edwin Mellen, 1999.

Doyle, G. Wright. *Carl Henry—Theologian for All Seasons: An Introduction and Guide to God, Revelation, and Authority*. Eugene, OR: Pickwick, 2010.

Edgar, William, and K. Scott Oliphint. "Abraham Kuyper." In *Christian Apologetics Past & Present: A Primary Source Reader*, edited by William Edgar and K. Scott Oliphint, vol. 2, 331–60. Wheaton, IL: Crossway, 2011.

Erickson, Millard. *Christian Theology*. 2nd Edition. Grand Rapids, MI: Baker Academic, 1998.

Fee, Gordon D. *The First Epistle to the Corinthians*. Revised Edition. The New International Commentary on the New Testament. Grand Rapids, MI: Eerdmans, 2014.

Feneuil, Anthony. "The Cross of Wisdom: Ambiguities in Turning Down Apologetics (Paul, Anselm, Barth)." In *The Wisdom and Foolishness of God: First Corinthians 1–2 in Theological Exploration*, edited by Christophe Chalamet and Hans-Christoph Askani, 167–81. Minneapolis, MN: Fortress, 2015.

Flew, Antony. *There Is a God: How the World's Most Notorious Atheist Changed His Mind*. With Roy Abraham Varghese. New York: HarperOne, 2007.

Foucault, Michel. *Discipline and Punish: The Birth of the Prison*. Translated by Alan Sheridan. New York: Pantheon, 1977.

———. "Nietzsche, Genealogy, History." In *Language, Counter-Memory, Practice: Selected Essays and Interviews*, edited by D. F. Bouchard, 138–64. Ithaca, NY: Cornell University Press, 1977.

———. *Politics, Philosophy, Culture: Interviews and Other Writings of Michel Foucault*. Edited by Lawrence D. Kritzman. New York: Routledge, Chapman & Hall, 1988.

———. *Power/Knowledge: Selected Interviews and Other Writings 1972–1977*. Edited by Colin Gordon. Translated by Colin Gordon, Leo Marshall, John Mepham, and Kate Soper. New York: Pantheon, 1980.

Frame, John M. *Cornelius Van Til: An Analysis of His Thought*. Phillipsburg, NJ: Presbyterian and Reformed, 1995.

Gamow, George. *One, Two, Three, . . . Infinity*. London: Macmillan & Co., 1946.

Gilson, Etienne. *Reason and Revelation in the Middle Ages*. New York: Charles Scribner's Sons, 1939.

Godzieba, Anthony J. "Ontotheology to Excess: Imagining God Without Being." In *Theological Studies* 56 (1995) 3–20.

Gravett, Sandie, Mark Hulsether, and Carolyn Medine. "Conversation: Rethinking the Christian Studies Classroom: Reflections on the Dynamics of Teaching Religion in Southern Public Universities." In *Teaching Theology and Religion* 14, no. 2 (April 2011) 158–66.

Griffiths, Paul J. *An Apology for Apologetics: A Study in the Logic of Interreligious Dialogue*. Eugene, OR: Wipf & Stock, 1991.

Groothuis, Douglas. *Christian Apologetics: A Comprehensive Case for Biblical Faith*. Downers Grove, IL: InterVarsity, 2011.

———. *On Jesus*. Wadsworth Philosophers Series. Belmont, CA: Wadsworth/Thomson Learning, 2003.

———. "Postmodern fallacies: A response to Merold Westphal." In *Christian Century* 120, no. 15 (July 26, 2003) 41–42.

———. "Proofs, Pride and Incarnation: Is Natural Theology Theologically Taboo?" In *Journal of the Evangelical Theological Society* 38, no. 1 (March 1995) 67–76.

———. *Truth Decay: Defending Christianity Against the Challenges of Postmodernism*. Downers Grove, IL: InterVarsity, 2000.

Grudem, Wayne. *Systematic Theology: An Introduction to Biblical Doctrine*. Grand Rapids, MI: Zondervan, 2000.

Guinness, Os. *Fool's Talk: Recovering the Art of Christian Persuasion*. Downers Grove, IL: InterVarsity, 2015.

Haddad, Jonah. *Insanity: God and the Theory of Knowledge*. Eugene, OR: Wipf & Stock, 2013.

Harmon, Gilbert H. "The Inference to the Best Explanation." In *The Philosophical Review* 74, no. 1 (January 1965) 88–95.

Harris, Sam. *The End of Faith: Religion, Terror, and the Future of Reason*. New York: Norton, 2004.

Harris, Sam, and William Lane Craig. "The God Debate II: Harris vs. Craig (video)." YouTube, posted by University of Notre Dame," April 12, 2011. Accessed August 11, 2017. https://www.youtube.com/watch?v=yqaHXKLRKzg.

Hauerwas, Stanley. *With the Grain of the Universe: The Church's Witness and Natural Theology*. Grand Rapids, MI: Baker Academic, 2001.

Heidegger, Martin. *Essays in Metaphysics: Identity and Difference*. Translated by Kurt Leidecker. New York: Philosophical Library, 1960.

Henry, Carl F. H. *God, Revelation, and Authority*. 6 vols. Waco, TX: Word, 1976.

Hitchens, Christopher. *God is Not Great: How Religion Poisons Everything*. New York: Twelve, 2007.

International Council on Biblical Inerrancy. "Appendix: The Chicago Statement on Biblical Inerrancy." In R. C. Sproul, *Explaining Inerrancy: A Commentary*. ICBI Foundation Series 2, 41–51. Oakland, CA: International Council on Biblical Inerrancy, 1980.

Jaffe, Alexandra. "Kellyanne Conway: WH Spokesman Gave 'Alternative Facts' on Inauguration Crowd." NBC News. Last modified January 22, 2017. Accessed July 13, 2017. http://www.nbcnews.com/storyline/meet-the-press-70-years/wh-spokesman-gave-alternative-facts-inauguration-crowd-n710466.

Jaki, Stanley L. *Lord Gifford and His Lectures: A Centenary Retrospect*. Edinburgh: Scottish Academic, 1986.

Jenkins, Philip. *The Next Christendom: The Coming Age of Global Christianity*. Oxford: Oxford University Press, 2011.

Kierkegaard, Søren. *Concluding Unscientific Postscript to Philosophical Fragments*. Vol. 1. Translated by Howard V. Hong and Edna H. Hong. Princeton, NJ: Princeton University Press, 1992.

King, Alex, and Martin Ketley. *The Control of Language: A Critical Approach to Reading and Writing*. London: Longmans Green, 1939.

Kreeft, Peter. "C. S. Lewis's Argument from Desire." In *G. K. Chesterton and C. S. Lewis: The Riddle of Joy*, ed. Michael H. MacDonald and Andrew A. Tadie, 249–72. Grand Rapids, Eerdmans, 1989.

Koukl, Gregory. *Tactics: A Game Plan for Discussing Your Christian Convictions*. Grand Rapids, MI: Zondervan, 2009.

Kuyper, Abraham. *Calvinism: Six Stone Foundation Lectures*. Grand Rapids, MI: Eerdmans, 1943.

———. *Encyclopedia of Sacred Theology: Its Principles*. Translated by J. Hendrik De Vries. New York: Charles Scribner's Sons, 1898.

———. *Lectures on Calvinism*. Grand Rapids, MI: Eerdmans, 1953.

———. "Use and Abuse of Apologetics." In *Bibliotheca Sacra* 65 (1908) 374–9.

Labron, Tim. *Wittgenstein and Theology*. London: T&T Clark, 2009.

Lewis, C. S. *The Abolition of Man (or Reflections on education with special reference to the teaching of English in the upper forms of schools)*. New York: HarperOne, 1944.

———. *Mere Christianity*. San Francisco: HarperSanFrancisco, 1952.

Lewis, Gordon R., and Bruce A. Demarest. *Integrative Theology. Vol 3: Spirit-Given Life: God's People Present and Future*. Grand Rapids, MI: Zondervan, 1994.

Liberty University. "Mission Statement." Liberty University. Last modified March 7, 2014. Accessed July 19, 2017. http://www.liberty.edu/aboutliberty/index.cfm?PID=6899.

Lindbeck, George A. *The Nature of Doctrine: Religion and Theology in a Postliberal Age*. Louisville, KY: Westminster John Knox, 1984.

Locke, John. *The Reasonableness of Christianity with A Discourse of Miracles and Part of A Third Letter Concerning Toleration*. Edited by I. T. Ramsey. Stanford, CA: Stanford University Press, 1958.

Lyotard, Jean-François. *The Postmodern Condition: A Report on Knowledge*. Translated by Geoff Bennington and Brian Massumi. Manchester: Manchester University Press, 1984.

Machen, J. Gresham. Address, the opening of the 101st session of Princeton Theological Seminary, Princeton, NJ, September 20, 1912.

Mackey, James P. *The Critique of Theological Reason*. Cambridge: Cambridge University Press, 2000.

Marcel, Gabriel. *Creative Fidelity*. Translated by Robert Rosthal. New York: Noonday, 1964.

Marion, Jean-Luc. *God Without Being*. Translated by Thomas A. Carlson. Chicago: University of Chicago Press, 1991.

Marsden, George M. "Introduction" In *Evangelicalism and Modern America*, edited by George M. Marsden, vii–xix. Grand Rapids: Eerdmans, 1984.

McGlasson, Paul C. *Church Doctrine: Volume 2: God*. Eugene, OR: Cascade, 2014.

McGrath, Alister E. *A Fine-Tuned Universe: The Quest for God in Science and Theology.* Louisville, KY: Westminster John Knox, 2009.

————. *The Intellectual World of C. S. Lewis.* West Sussex, UK: Wiley-Blackwell, 2014.

————. *Surprised By Meaning: Science, Faith, and How We Make Sense of Things.* Louisville, KY: Westminster John Knox, 2011.

Medawar, P. B. *The Art of the Soluble.* 6th ed. London: Metheun, 1967.

Meillassoux, Quentin. *After Finitude: An Essay on the Necessity of Contingency.* Translated by R. Brassier. London: Continuum, 2008.

Melanchthon, Philip. "Of the Word 'Faith.'" In *Melanchthon on Christian Doctrine: Loci Communes 1555,* trans. and ed. Clyde L. Manschreck, 158–9. New York: Oxford University Press, 1965.

Michel, Otto. "Faith." In *The New International Dictionary of New Testament Theology,* ed. Colin Brown, vol. 1, 587–606. Grand Rapids, MI: Zondervan, 1975.

Minnemeier, Gerhard. "The Logic of Abduction, Deduction and Induction." In *Ideas in Action: Proceedings of the Applying Pierce Conference,* ed. Mats Bergman et al., 239–51. Helsinki: Nordic Pragmatism Network, 2010.

Moreland, J. P. *Love Your God with All Your Mind: The Role of Reason in the Life of the Soul.* 2nd Edition. Colorado Springs, CO: NavPress, 2012.

————. *The Recalcitrant Imago Dei: Human Persons and the Failure of Naturalism.* Veritas. London: SCM, 2009.

————. *Scaling the Secular City: A Defense of Christianity.* Grand Rapids, MI: Baker, 1987.

————. *The Soul: How We Know Its Real and Why It Matters.* Chicago, IL: Moody, 2014.

————. "Truth, Contemporary Philosophy, and the Postmodern Turn." *In Journal of the Evangelical Theological Society* 48, no. 1 (March 2005) 77–88.

Moreland, J. P., and William Lane Craig. *Philosophical Foundations for a Christian Worldview.* Downers Grove, IL: InterVarsity, 2003.

Nagel, Thomas. *Mind and Cosmos: Why the Materialist Neo-Darwinian Conception of Nature is Almost Certainly False.* Oxford: Oxford University Press, 2012.

Nash, Ronald. *Faith and Reason: Searching for a Rational Faith.* Grand Rapids, MI: Academie, 1988.

National Association of Evangelicals. "What is an Evangelical?" National Association of Evangelicals. Accessed July 30, 2017. https://www.nae.net/what-is-an-evangelical.

Nielsen, Kai. "Can Faith Validate God-Talk?" In *Theology Today* 20, no. 2 (July 1963) 158–73.

Nietzsche, Friedrich. *The Gay Science.* Translated by Walter Kaufmann. New York: Random House, 1947.

Noll, Mark A. *The Rise of Evangelicalism: The Age of Edwards, Whitefield and the Wesleys.* Downers Grove, Ill.: InterVarsity, 2003.

————. *The Scandal of the Evangelical Mind.* Grand Rapids, MI: Eerdmans, 1994.

————. "What is 'Evangelical'?" In *The Oxford Handbook Evangelical Theology,* edited by Gerald R. McDermott, 19–32. Oxford: Oxford University Press, 2010.

Owen, John. *The Holy Spirit.* Reprinted, Grand Rapids, MI: Kregel, 1954.

Pascal, Blaise. *Pensées.* Translated by A. J. Krailsheimer. London: Penguin, 1995.

Pearcey, Nancey. *Finding Truth: 5 Principles for Unmasking Atheism, Secularism, and Other God Substitutes.* Colorado Springs, CO: David C. Cook, 2015.

Penner, Myron B. "Cartesian Anxiety, Perspectivalism, and Truth: A Response to J. P. Moreland." In *Philosophia Christi* 8, no. 1 (2006) 85–98.

————. "Introduction: Christianity and the Postmodern Turn: Some Preliminary Considerations." In *Christianity and the Postmodern Turn: Six Views*, ed. Myron B. Penner, 13–34. Grand Rapids, MI: Brazos, 2005.

————. "The Normative Resources of Kierkegaard's Subjectivity Principle." In *International Journal of Systematic Theology* 1, no. 1 (March 1999) 73–88.

Penner, Myron Bradley. "Blog 6: Postmodern Apologetics." In *A New Kind of Conversation: Blogging Toward a Postmodern Faith*, edited by Myron Bradley Penner and Hunter Barnes, 137–42. Colorado Springs, CO: Authentic, 2006.

————. *The End of Apologetics: Christian Witness in a Postmodern Context*. Grand Rapids, MI: Baker Academic, 2013.

Pew Research Center, "Religious Landscape Study," Pew Research Center: Religion & Public Life, accessed July 20, 2017, http://www.pewforum.org/religious-landscape-study.

Pierce, Charles S. *Collected Papers*. 5 vols. Edited by Charles Hartshorne and Paul Weiss. Cambridge, MA: Harvard University Press, 1960.

Plantinga, Alvin. "The Reformed Objection to Natural Theology." In *Proceedings of the American Catholic Philosophical Association* 54 (1980) 49–62.

————. *Where the Conflict Really Lies: Science, Religion, & Naturalism*. Oxford: Oxford University Press, 2011.

Pojman, Louis J. *What Can We Know?: An Introduction to the Theory of Knowledge*. 2nd Edition. Belmont, CA: Wadsworth/Thomson Learning, 2001.

Polanyi, Michael. *Science, Faith and Society*. University of Durham Riddell Memorial Lectures: Eighteenth Series. London: Oxford University Press, 1946.

Prothero, Stephen. *Religious Literacy: What Every American Needs to Know—and Doesn't*. San Francisco: HarperSanFrancisco, 2007.

Raschke, Carl A. *The Alchemy of the Word: Language and the End of Theology*. Vol. 20. AAR Studies in Religion. Missoula, MT: Scholars, 1979.

————. "The End of Theology." In *Journal of the American Academy of Religion* 46, no. 2 (June 1978) 159–79.

————. "Faith and Philosophy in Tension." In *Faith and Reason: Three Views*, edited by Steve Wilkens, 35–67, 116–24, and 160–8. Downers Grove, IL: InterVarsity, 2014.

————. *GloboChrist: The Great Commission Takes a Postmodern Turn*. The Church and Postmodern Culture. Grand Rapids, MI: Baker Academic, 2008.

————. *The Next Reformation: Why Evangelicals Must Embrace Postmodernity*. Grand Rapids, MI: Baker Academic, 2004.

Re Manning, Russell, ed. *The Oxford Handbook of Natural Theology*. Oxford: Oxford University Press, 2013.

Rees, Martin. *Just Six Numbers: The Deep Forces That Shape the Universe*. New York: Basic, 2000.

Ricoeur, Paul. "From Metaphysics to Moral Philosophy." In *Philosophy Today* 40, no. 4 (Winter 1996) 443–58.

————. *History and Truth*. Translated by Charles A. Kelbley. Evanston, IL: Northwestern University Press, 1965.

————. *Living Up to Death*. Translated by David Pellauer. Chicago: The University of Chicago Press, 2009.

————. *Oneself as Another*. Translated by Kathleen Blamey. Chicago: The University of Chicago Press, 1992.

———. "Philosophy and Religious Language." In *The Journal of Religion* 15, no. 1 (January 1974) 71–85.

———. *The Philosophy of Paul Ricoeur: An Anthology of His Work.* Edited by Charles E. Regan and David Stewart. Boston, MA: Beacon, 1997.

Russell, Bertrand. "Truth and Falsehood." In *The Nature of Truth: Classic and Contemporary Perspectives*, ed. Michael P. Lynch, 17–24. Cambridge, MA: The MIT Press, 2001.

Schaeffer, Francis A. *The God Who is There.* 30th Anniversary Edition. Downers Grove, IL: InterVarsity, 1998.

———. "The Question of Apologetics." In *Trilogy*, 175–87. Wheaton, IL: Crossway, 1990.

Schunke, Matthew. "Apophatic Abuse: Misreading Heidegger's Critique of Ontotheology." In *Philosophy Today* 53 (2009) 164–72.

Sire, James W. *Habits of the Mind: Intellectual Life as a Christian Calling.* Downers Grove, IL: InterVarsity, 2000.

———. *The Universe Next Door: A Basic Worldview Catalog.* 5th Edition. Downers Grove, IL: IVP Academic, 2009.

Smith, James K. A. "The Art of Christian Atheism: Faith and Philosophy in Early Heidegger." In *Faith and Philosophy* 14, no. 1 (Jan. 1997) 71–81.

———. *Desiring the Kingdom: Worship, Worldview, and Cultural Formation.* Cultural Liturgies Vol. 1. Grand Rapids, MI: Baker Academic, 2009.

———. *The Fall of Interpretation: Philosophical Foundations for a Creational Hermeneutic.* Grand Rapids, MI: Baker Academic, 2012.

———. *Introducing Radical Orthodoxy: Mapping a Post-Secular Theology.* Grand Rapids, MI: Baker Academic, 2004.

———. *Jacques Derrida: Live Theory.* New York: Continuum, 2005.

———. "A Little Story About Metanarratives." In *Christianity and the Postmodern Turn: Six Views*, ed. Myron B. Penner, 123–40. Grand Rapids, MI: Brazos, 2005.

———. "Questions About the Perception of 'Christian Truth': On the Affective Effect of Sin." In *New Blackfriars* 88, no. 1017 (2007) 585–93.

———. *Speech and Theology: Language and the Logic of Incarnation.* New York: Routledge, 2002.

———. "Who's Afraid of Postmodernism? A Response to the 'Biola School.'" In *Christianity and the Postmodern Turn: Six Views*, ed. Myron B. Penner, 215–28. Grand Rapids, MI: Brazos, 2005.

———. *Who's Afraid of Postmodernism?: Taking Derrida, Lyotard, and Foucault to Church.* The Church and Postmodern Culture. Grand Rapids, MI: Baker Academic, 2006.

———. *Who's Afraid of Relativism?: Community, Contingency, and Creaturehood.* The Church and Postmodern Culture. Grand Rapids, MI: Baker Academic, 2014.

Smith, James K. A. and Shane R. Cudney. "Postmodern freedom and the growth of fundamentalism: Was the Grand Inquisitor right." In *Studies in Religion/Sciences Religieuses* 25, no. 1 (1996) 35–49.

Smith, R. Scott. *Truth and the New Kind of Christian: The Emerging Effects of Postmodernism in the Church.* Wheaton, IL: Crossway, 2005.

Stackhouse, Jr., John G. *Humble Apologetics: Defending the Faith Today.* Oxford: Oxford University Press, 2002.

Stott, John. *The Message of Romans: God's Good News for the World.* The Bible Speaks Today. Downers Grove, IL: InterVarsity, 1994.

Studebaker, Jr., J. A. "Common Ground." In *New Dictionary of Christian Apologetics*, eds. Campbell Campbell-Jack and Gavin J. McGrath, 161–5. Leicester, UK: Inter-Varsity, 2006.

Tacitus, *The Annals*. Translated by Alfred John Church and William Jackson Brodribb. The Internet Classics Archive. Edited by Daniel C. Stevenson, 15.44. Accessed June 15, 2017. http://classics.mit.edu/Tacitus/annals.mb.txt.

Taylor, A. E. *Does God Exist?* London: Macmillan, 1947.

Thiel, John E. *Nonfoundationalism*. Guides to Theological Inquiry Series. Minneapolis, MN: Augsburg Fortress, 1994.

Van Til, Cornelius. *A Christian Theory of Knowledge*. Philadelphia: Presbyterian and Reformed, 1969.

———. *Common Grace and the Gospel*. Philadelphia: Presbyterian and Reformed, 1977.

———. *The Defense of the Faith*. Phillipsburg, NJ: Presbyterian and Reformed, 1955.

———. *An Introduction to Systematic Theology*. Volume V of the Series In Defense of Biblical Christianity. Phillipsburg, NJ: Presbyterian and Reformed, 1974.

———. *The Reformed Pastor and Modern Thought*. Philadelphia: Presbyterian and Reformed, 1971.

———. *A Survey of Christian Epistemology*. Volume II of the Series In Defense of Biblical Christianity. Philadelphia: den Dulk Christian Foundation, 1969.

Walton, Douglas. "Objections, Rebuttals and Refutations." In *Argument Cultures: Proceedings of the OSSA 09*, ed. J. Ritolla, 1–10. Windsor, ON: OSSA, 2009.

Warfield, Benjamin B. "Christian Evidences: How Affected by Recent Criticisms." In *Selected Shorter Writings of Benjamin B. Warfield*, vol. 2, ed. John E. Meeter, 124–31. Nutley, NJ: Presbyterian and Reformed, 1973.

———. "The Idea of Systematic Theology." In *The Presbyterian and Reformed Review* (1896) 243–71.

———. "Introduction to Francis R. Beattie's Apologetics." In *Selected Shorter Writings of Benjamin B. Warfield*, vol. 2, ed. John E. Meeter, 93–105. Nutley, NJ: Presbyterian and Reformed, 1973.

———. "A Review of De Zekerheid des Geloofs." In *Selected Shorter Writings of Benjamin B. Warfield*, vol. 2, ed. John E. Meeter, 106–23. Nutley, NJ: Presbyterian and Reformed, 1973.

———. *Studies in Theology*. Vol. 9 of The Works of Benjamin B. Warfield. Grand Rapids, MI: Baker, 2000.

Warfield, Benjamin B., William Adams Brown, and Gerald B. Smith. "The Task and Method of Systematic Theology." In *The American Journal of Theology* 14, no. 2 (April 1910) 192–233.

Westphal, Merold. "Blind spots: Christianity and postmodern philosophy." In *Christian Century* 120, no. 12 (June 14, 2003) 32–35.

———. *Kierkegaard's Critique of Reason and Society*. Macon, GA: Mercer University Press, 1987.

———. "Of Stories and Languages." In *Christianity and the Postmodern Turn: Six Views*, ed. Myron B. Penner, 229–40. Grand Rapids, MI: Brazos, 2005.

———. "Onto-theology, Metanarrative, Perspectivism, and the Gospel." In *Christianity and the Postmodern Turn: Six Views*, ed. Myron B. Penner, 141–3. Grand Rapids, MI: Brazos, 2005.

———. *Overcoming Onto-Theology: Toward a Postmodern Christian Faith*. New York: Fordham University Press, 2001.

————. *Suspicion and Faith: The Religious Uses of Modern Atheism*. New York: Fordham Press, 1998.

Willard, Dallas. "Verso una teoria fenomenologica della verita come corrispondenza." In *Discipline Filosofiche* 1 (1991) 125–47.

Wittgenstein, Ludwig. *Philosophical Investigations*. Translated by G. E. M. Anscombe. Oxford: Blackwell, 1974.

World Health Organization. "Female genital mutilation," World Health Organization. Last modified February 2017. Accessed June 6, 2017. http://www.who.int/mediacentre/factsheets/fs241/en/.

Worthen, Molly. *Apostles of Reason*. Oxford: Oxford University Press, 2014.

————. "A Match Made in Heaven: Why conservative evangelicals have lined up behind Trump." *The Atlantic*, May 2017. Accessed July 30, 2017. https://www.theatlantic.com/magazine/archive/2017/05/a-match-made-in-heaven/521409.